YOU GOTTA HAVE HEART

You Gotta Have Heart

DALLAS GREEN'S REBUILDING OF THE CUBS

Ned Colletti

DIAMOND COMMUNICATIONS, INC.
SOUTH BEND, INDIANA

1985

YOU GOTTA HAVE HEART
Copyright © 1985 by Diamond Communications, Inc.

Manufactured in the United States of America

Views expressed in this book reflect those of the
author and do not necessarily reflect those of
the Chicago Cubs organization, players, staff, or
parent company.

Diamond Communications, Inc.
Post Office Box 88
South Bend, Indiana 46624
(219) 287-5008

Library of Congress in Publication Data

Colletti, Ned.
    You gotta have heart.

    1. Chicago Cubs (Baseball team)—History. 2. Green,
Dallas. 3. Baseball—United States—Team owners.
I. Title.
GV875.C6C64 1985   796.357'64'0977311   85-4405
ISBN 0-912083-11-5

To Dad

Contents

Foreword

On April 15, 1961 the Chicago Cubs rallied from a deficit to defeat the Milwaukee Braves 9–5 at Wrigley Field.

It was a true beginning if ever there was one for a young Cub fan.

The sky was gray. The temperature was falling through the 30s. There were snow flurries in the air.

The Cubs had trailed the Braves and slowly they came back until the score was tied in the bottom of the ninth. The weather being what it was, not many of the 6,207 paying customers remained. With two outs in the ninth and the bases loaded the Cubs centerfielder, Al Heist, hit the first grand slam of his career.

Everybody in the place had to have heart.

There is no debating the warmness and the intrinsic feelings those words portray. For every Cub fan has had to have heart in order to follow a team through a 39-year wilderness.

Time and again, Ernie Banks would be the one beacon in the night shedding light and good cheer on anyone who ever had the pleasure and the honor to meet him. The man spoke eloquently—and always from the heart.

And then there was Dallas Green. If Dallas has one drawback it is that his voice box has acoustics that belong in Carnegie Hall. But one of his many, many plusses is his heart. There have been numerous times when he said he felt in his heart he could help turn the Cubs into winners. There were also many instances where the man showed extreme compassion.

Yes, you gotta have heart. There is no other way to survive in life. To Cub fans it's more than a phrase—it is a set of words to live by.

The 1984 Cubs obviously were full of heart as were the 2.1 million fans who paid their way into Wrigley Field.

As beautiful as the 1984 season was, there is no concealing the hurt and frustrations of not advancing into the World Series. But just another notch or two below losing Game 5 to the San Diego Padres was another reason for feeling blue—the season was over.

It was the grandest summer in many years for many people. It was certainly the best for myself. For 15 years, I thought nothing compared to the summer of 1969—I was wrong. That year will always have a place in every Cub fan's heart but 1984 was, oh, so much better. And yes, when it was over, it was so very empty, so reminiscent of any kid who has ever been out on a baseball field as darkness fell and through the dusk, heard a mother's voice calling a halt thought nothing compared to the summer of 1969—I was answer was always "just one more inning," or "just one more at-bat." Cub fans will never have squeezed enough out of 1984.

I consider myself tremendously fortunate to have been a Cub fan since at least April 15, 1961 and also to have the opportunity to earn a living watching the team I have loved for as long as I knew the game of baseball existed.

I am not attempting to project the maudlin. Rather, I wish to accent the universality of what the Cubs mean to Chicago in specific and to society in general. And what the Cubs mean to solitary people whose lives revolve around the game.

I have been told that my father's father was an avid Cub

fan dating back to the days when Frank Chance managed World Champion Cubs. It is little wonder that his love for the Cubs was passed on to his children.

My father took the time to put a part of his life into mine when he took me to that first Cubs game. He also put a part of his life into my heart when in the autumn of his life he told me never to forget that giving of yourself to people is a much more fulfilling feeling than receiving. He proved it every day of his life.

With that in mind, I have taken the opportunity through this project to give very ill children the chance to come with their families to Wrigley Field and watch the Cubs. A portion of all author royalties will be donated to this cause.

In closing, the writing of this work was truly a labor of love. It was all Jim Finks said it would be when he put his blessing on the project in September of 1984.

With deep respect, I thank Jim and Dallas for all they have meant to my family, myself and to Chicago. I thank them for allowing me a forum for my feelings.

A special thank you to Dave Callahan, my brother Doug and Jon Saraceno for their cutting and wizardry as they touched up the original manuscript with their thoughts and expertise.

For all their support through great rallies and long losing streaks, I thank Jill and Jim Langford and, of course, Jim Frey, Mary Beth Hughes, Stephen Green and John Swart. And the greatest rally builder of all, my mother Dolores.

I would remiss in not offering a hand and a pat on the back to Vedie Himsl and E.R. (Salty) Saltwell for their long dedication to the Chicago Cub franchise. In the same vain, it is appropriate to thank the Wrigley Family for building an aura around a franchise and a ballpark that millions have grown to love and support.

A very special debt of gratitude is due Tribune Company

and Stanton Cook, John Madigan and Andrew McKenna for assembling a front office team that helped put together the 1984 team. And, of course, there would be fewer fond memories if not for all of the 1984 Cubs.

Lastly, and certainly most importantly, I thank and cherish Gayle and our two children, Lou and Jenna—another generation of Cub fans are already in place. They will know very soon that you gotta have heart.

Ned Colletti
December 1984

1 In the Beginning

Sweet home Chicago.

The city sparkled in the distance while the moon and the earth cradled United Airlines flight #5002 as it cruised home.

It was closing in on midnight, September 26, 1984. Off to one side of O'Hare Field, the world's busiest airport, waited 5,000 of the world's greatest fans hoping to catch a glimpse of and pay a tribute to Chicago's happiest sports team.

It had been little more than 72 hours since Rick Sutcliffe threw strike three past Pittsburgh's Joe Orsulak for the final out in the game that clinched the Cubs' first championship in 39 years. It was the final out that sprung open the door slammed shut in October of 1945 when the Detroit Tigers stopped the Cubs in the seventh game of the World Series.

For just short of four decades the weight of the world, the wisecracks of the cynics and the curse of defeat had covered the Cubs like a cheap suit.

It was all over now. The 1984 Cubs had made history.

The jubilation that spilled into the streets three nights earlier was still boiling in the souls of Chicago. The crowd that greeted the Cubs in a special 10-minute ceremony was but a microcosm of those whose heart and feelings were with a baseball team.

Cub fans have always given their team the gift that keeps on giving: their love. The people were bursting with pride.

As the players boarded buses that carried them to the apron where the fans waited, Dennis Eckersley summed up his feelings. "I've waited my entire career for something like this to happen. I am glad to be a part of it. I think it's great."

The city was on a high. It had been building into a slow crescendo since June. It finally exploded in the final week of September and continued on through the first week of October.

It may be presumptuous to suggest that Chicago has never been more thrilled and excited about a sports team than it was about the 1984 Cubs. Consider, however, the way America's concept of sports has changed since Chicago last toasted a major sports champion. The interest has never been greater. Television brings sports into the home daily. There was never this madness when the Bears won the NFL championship in 1963 or when the Black Hawks won the Stanley Cup in 1961 or when the White Sox last represented Chicago in a World Series in 1959. The magnitude is greater, the scope broader, the exposure non-stop. Sports has taken on added significance in the daily routine. It is no longer a pastime as much as it is an obsession for some people.

Obsessed? Is there any other way to describe the Cub fans of 1984? When the Cubs beat the Pirates 4-1 on September 24, it fulfilled every boy's dream, every Cub follower's vision that it could be done.

Fathers hugged their sons for maybe the first time in years. Families rejoiced. No doubt there were people who had watched the game with a bottle of champagne chilling in the refrigerator. Whether they watched alone, or with family and friends, it was a moment worth committing to memory. What Cub fan didn't make at least one phone call that evening to someone special? What Cub fan didn't hold a glass high and face in the direction of Pittsburgh or Wrigley Field and offer a toast to success?

Every Cub fan's world lit up.

George Orwell was right on the money; 1984 would be something special.

By the time 1984 turned to 1985, the Cubs had been graced with a record-attendance year both at Wrigley Field and on the road. More than four million fans paid to watch the Cubs play in 1984, nearly one million more than the franchise's previous record.

The hardware filled the Cubs trophy cases. Ryne Sandberg won the Most Valuable Player Award, the first Cub to win the award since Ernie Banks won his second straight in 1959. Ryno had one of the greatest seasons on record. He batted .314 with 200 hits, 36 doubles, 19 triples, 19 homers, 84 RBI and 32 stolen bases along with a league-high 114 runs. He came within one triple and one homer of becoming the first player in the history of the game to have 200 hits plus 20 or more doubles, triples, homers and stolen bases. No one had done it before. Not Ruth, nor DiMaggio, Williams, Hornsby, Mays or Musial. No one came as close as Sandberg. By no means was he one-dimensional. He also won his second straight Gold Glove at second base.

"You could see it early in the season," Hall of Famer and one-time MVP Lou Boudreau said. "Sandberg was having one of those incredible seasons when everything he does works like magic."

He was a marvel.

Joining Sandberg with his first career Gold Glove was Ryne's longtime friend, center fielder Bobby Dernier.

Next to the Most Valuable Player Award, there is no personal award as prestigious as the Cy Young Award. Sutcliffe won that easily to become the first pitcher in the history of the award to win it after being traded in mid-season from one league to another. Rick also became only the fourth pitcher in major league history to record 20 wins in a season split between leagues. He was a masterful 16-1 through the regular season with the Cubs.

While Sandberg won the MVP, Sutcliffe finished fourth, Gary Matthews fifth and Jody Davis 10th. Dernier, Ron Cey and Leon Durham also received votes. The balloting speaks volumes for the type of season the Cubs had. There are teams that didn't have one player pull in one vote. And here were the Cubs, pre-season picks to finish fifth, or maybe fourth, claiming four of the top 10 and seven in the top 20.

Post-season awards didn't stop there. Jim Frey was selected as the Manager of the Year and Dallas Green, the man with the plan, the architect, earned Executive of the Year honors. The awards went around and round.

While there was joy and laughter, there was also sorrow. As Dallas said when he learned he had won the Executive of the Year Award, "I would trade this award and all the hardware in it for one more win in San Diego."

The Cubs were one win from the World Series. More specifically, the Cubs could have been one clutch hit in Game 4 away or just eight outs away in Game 5.

To the pure-breed baseball man there is no solace in coming close. There is little peace to be gained from a team that came from nowhere and arrived on the brink of a pennant only to be stopped short of the classic ending.

Granted, there are more than mere remnants remaining of a very good team and a season of multiple success stories. But winning the pennant and the World Series are the only two true bottom lines in baseball.

"We still have something more to accomplish," Dallas said as the fall of 1984 turned to winter. "We've left the job undone at the end. I think we all know that."

It was so close for four days after the Cubs opened the

National League Championship Series with a pair of solid victories over San Diego at Wrigley Field.

When it was over there were those who claimed the 1984 NLCS ranked second only to the 1980 series between Philadelphia and Houston as far as classic confrontations are concerned. How history views the 1984 NLCS is one thing. How the Cubs, coaches, Jim Frey and Dallas view those final days in San Diego will always be different.

The Cubs were one win away.

The Cubs were eight outs away.

"When do you get over it?" someone asked Cubs pitching coach Billy Connors a week after the season ended.

"When?" Connors reasked. "You never get over not winning it and not going to the World Series. Never.

"No matter how many times you get to the World Series, being a part of it is what playing baseball means. Being that close and not winning is something that will dissipate in time. But you never totally forget it or totally get over it."

No season is longer, no sport more demanding day-to-day for any team, any great team. It was, for six months, a perfect season.

Check the magic of a winning season and there are always reasons beyond great talent. The weather, the injuries, the schedule, the chemistry all play a role along with a team's accepted hot and cold streaks.

The weather for the most part was exceptional. The summer went without any of the typical three-week periods of 90-degree temperatures and 90-percent humidities.

There was rain early. It cost the Cubs perhaps 100,000 in home paid attendance and added five doubleheaders to the Cubs schedule.

Fortunately, when the Cubs were rained out it was either against Eastern Division teams or the rain continued east forcing cancellation of the Cubs' counterparts. All teams were equal. The Cubs proved more than equal to the task of playing in doubleheaders. They won five and split two of the seven they played.

While the Cubs placed players on the disabled list eleven times, the only everyday player the Cubs lost was first baseman Leon Durham. Leon missed 15 days. In 1983, he missed 62 games.

Cey was hurt most of the season but played on. Dernier missed a few games here and there and Ryne missed a set of games after a collision in Houston, but all in all the Cub regulars stayed clear of the disabled list.

Certainly, the pitching staff took the majority of the space on the injured list in the first couple of months. The biggest losses were starters Scott Sanderson and Dick Ruthven. Both missed considerable time, but the team was able to stay afloat while Dallas went out and acquired Eckersley, Sutcliffe and George Frazier.

The schedule was also a definite advantage. The Cubs opened the season on the West Coast in much the same weather as they were accustomed to during spring training. There is no telling what a psychological edge that is. It certainly compares favorably to playing for six weeks in 75-degree weather only to start the season 30-degrees colder.

The Cubs also finished their West Coast regular-season trips before the All-Star break. On the other hand, both the Phillies and the Mets had to go to the West Coast during the second half.

The chemistry was also as close to perfect as any Cub team in the last 39 years. The blend between veterans and kids profited both. Matthews' leadership coupled with Larry Bowa's and Cey's experience provided the anchor while the pitching staff rode the talents and alignments of five proven starters and the perfect mix of long, short and closing relievers.

It was a team that stayed together and grew stronger

through any adversity. It was a team that tried very hard and succeeded.

The coaching staff from Frey on down fit all the needs. There was Ruben Amaro, Frey's right hand man in the dugout. There was John Vukovich, a first base coach in 1984 and the one responsible for the pre-series scouting meetings. Don Zimmer coached third, giving Frey a great counterpart. Having Zimmer and Frey together was like having two managers. Johnny Oates was hired after 1983 to work as the bullpen coach and to help Davis rediscover his defensive skills. Davis' passed ball total dropped from a league-leading 21 in 1983 to 10 while he threw out nearly 15% more runners attempting to steal. There was also pitching coach Billy Connors.

Only Vukovich and Connors had coached on the first three Cub teams under Dallas. They had been through it all. Through the teaching, cajoling, pleading and praying that a pair of lowly fifth-place finishes put coaches through. Of all the jobs on the coaching staff none was tougher than Connors', especially early.

Connors' first two staffs were put together with string and bailing wire. They literally tried to get by on a wing and a prayer—until 1984 when Dallas went out and practically revamped the entire group in the space of one season.

What Connors accomplished was amazing. In all, Connors had 22 different pitchers for at least a majority of one season through his first three years. Of the 22, nine or 43% had their best seasons either in wins, earned run average or saves. Eight or 38% had what could easily be considered as typical seasons, two were first-year players in the majors and four (Bill Campbell, Fergie Jenkins, Willie Hernandez and Mike Proly) were either rescued from the minor leagues or were on the verge of being handed their outright release, with the possible exception being Campbell. All four pitched well for at least a season under Connors.

He had a knack for getting the most from his pitchers. The man genuinely cared for each one, at times more than they seemed to care for themselves.

His own major league pitching career had been short. He was 0-2 lifetime with the Cubs and the Mets and had pitched 43 innings in the majors.

Originally signed by the Cubs, Connors left the organization in 1967. Soon after, he sat down and wrote a letter to Philip K. Wrigley, the Cubs owner. Connors thanked Mr. Wrigley for the opportunity to pitch professionally. He also wrote that one day he would like to be able to come back to the organization and repay the Wrigley family for the opportunity they gave him.

Suffice it to say, the bill is paid in full.

At every juncture, everything was in the Cubs' favor in 1984.

The sights and the sounds of the 1984 season will last many years. Who will ever forget the WGN Television cameras panning the Wrigley Field grandstand, the bleachers and the upper deck? There were people everywhere. They were cheering, standing, hugging, applauding and adding the support the club thrived on. Winning brought acclaim to the Cub fans, people already famous for persistence and doggedness but never for pouring champagne over each other.

Who will ever forget the many scenes?

Picture: Gary Matthews forever tipping his batting helmet off whenever he put the ball in play. Or the tap he gave the helmet when he homered.

Picture: The Sarge barrelling into third base, arms swinging, fists clinched. The Sarge saluting the left-field bleacher fans.

Picture: Ryno with those smooth strides and that flowing swing.

Picture: Jody digging into a fat fastball and driving it to dead center field, high into the vacated bleacher section.

Picture: Leon scooping a low throw out of the dirt or diving for the play to stop a sure double down the line.

Picture: Cey with his head tucked, bat cocked, swaying ever so slightly as he waited for a pitch he could drive.

Picture: Bobby Dernier starting at one end of center field as the ball met the bat. Seconds later, he outruns the ball on the other side of center field. How many times did that happen? Ten? Twenty? Forty?

Picture: Moreland ripping hit after hit against the Mets in early August on the way to Player-of-the-Month honors. Yes, August, the month that was to cost the Cubs. The month where the heat of the summer and race would shrink their lead and challenge their mettle. Besides Moreland, Sutcliffe won the Pitcher-of-the-Month Award giving the Cubs four monthly award winners for the season (Durham in May and Sandberg in June).

Picture: Sut with his unorthodox wind-up, the hesitation as he lowers his right arm and cups the ball ever so slightly at the low point of his delivery. Who will ever forget the night in Pittsburgh and the look of relief and satisfaction that filled his face after the last strike had been rung up?

Picture: Lee Smith with that slow, easy walk from the bullpen. He gripped the ball as a teenager would grip a golf ball.

Picture: The fans, literally millions of them singing the Cubs' praises from all parts of the country. Cub fans were beyond mere description. They came to Wrigley Field early and stayed late. The Cubs were the city's pride and its passion.

The Cubs' 1984 season brought media from across the country. There was no escaping the Cubs' story.

Many members of the media marvelled at the love affair the fans shared with the ballclub.

Bob Ryan of the *Boston Globe* wrote in mid-September: "Believe this: Wrigley Field has become a baseball Fantasyland. A baseball game is an excuse for one big party, and things are happening here that don't happen anywhere else. . .

"Many (of the crowd) sat wrapped in blankets to ward off the effects of a stiff Chicago breeze, but what they're actually doing here in Wrigley Field is wrapping their troubles in the dream of the Cubs' first world championship in 76 years."

The Cubs brought reaction from all stations of life. From Ronald Reagan and political columnist George Will on Capitol Hill to Johnny Carson and Frank Sinatra in Beverly Hills.

Cub fans sprouted across the nation and beyond. On September 25, half a world away, the *Pacific Daily News* in Guam trumpeted the biggest sports story in decades across the top of its front sports page: "CUBS FINALLY NAIL DOWN A TITLE."

From June through September, the Cubs were featured in every major newspaper, in the sports journals like *Sports Illustrated* and *The Sporting News* and also in the news magazines, *Time*, *Newsweek* and *People*.

Cub players appeared on every Chicago morning television show as well as *CBS Morning News*, *Good Morning America* and the *Today* show. For a while it seemed that America began each day with news of the Cubs.

It reached a peak during the playoffs, but just prior to the playoffs came one of the greatest outpourings of emotion the city has ever witnessed from the fans and the players.

In their last regular season game the Cubs had nothing more to gain and their opposition, the Cardinals, had nothing more to lose. Just two years earlier, the Cubs and Cards also closed out the regular season at Wrigley Field. In 1982, it was the Cardinals who were heading into post-season play and the Cubs who were going home.

The paid crowd of 33,100 was watching a pitchers' duel that left the Cubs trailing the Cardinals 1-0 in the ninth. St. Louis manager Whitey Herzog brought in Bruce Sutter. Sutter was three outs away from a record 46th save. But he couldn't hold the lead.

First, Thad Bosley came through with a pinch hit to tie the game. Moreland followed with a slow roller in front of the plate. Catcher Glenn Brummer pounced on the loose ball and overthrew first base. Bosley never stopped running. He came around to score and beat Sutter 2-1.

By then most of the Cub regulars had long since been removed from the game. Matthews, Dernier, Durham, Sandberg, Cey and Davis had all returned to the clubhouse.

But when the Cubs beat Sutter the crowd opened its heart. For a solid 10 minutes they stood and cheered and called for the Cubs to return to the field. In the clubhouse, word spread that no one was leaving the park. It was curtain-call time.

Led by Frey, the players came out on the field. There were tears in the stands and tears on the field. The team walked toward second base acknowledging the tribute. The Cubs went to left center and then to right center before moving back to the seclusion of the clubhouse.

It was a love affair nurtured at Clark and Addison Streets, hard by the El tracks. In a neighborhood of corner taps and three-flat apartments, the bond grew air-tight even though this club had been assembled quickly. The magic was still there.

"I have never seen anything like that in all my life," Frey said. "It was quite a tribute. It was out-and-out love. Aren't these fans the greatest?"

"It was a moment I'll never forget," Durham said.

"If there are any better fans in the country I want to know where they've been hiding," Chicagoan Scott Sanderson said. "A lot of them probably won't be here for the playoffs but they should be. I'm glad they made it here today."

"It was a high," Bosley said. "Fans like that make you never want to leave. Hopefully the best is yet to come."

There was still more to come. For the first two days of the National League Championship Series, there was nothing better.

Sweet, sweet home Chicago.

On the day before the playoffs, the media assembled to laud the Cubs' rise and salute Dallas and Jim Frey. The assembling of this team through trades was considered a masterful feat. With contract restrictions being what they are, baseball people told all who would listen that trading was practically impossible.

Yet, Dallas had gone out and scraped and traded and bartered and bickered until he had a renovated club in three years and a solid pitching staff, the lifeblood of any club, in less than a full season.

"For the first two years I didn't think I could make a mistake trading," he said. "Whoever I got rid of and received in return had to be a plus. If nothing else it would flush out some of the losing that permeated the organization."

"Dallas made some moves that took a lot of guts," Frey said. "He traded Bill Buckner and Carmelo Martinez and some others and took heat from the fans. But deals like that are what made this team a winner."

From October 15, 1981 to October 7, 1984 was more than just a journey through practically three calendar years. It was a trek through a tremendous rebuilding program, through second-guessing among fans and media, through a tedious program that put the Cubs a win away from the Fall Classic.

The task facing Dallas Green in October of 1981 was staggering. There was no other way to describe it. It wasn't that Dallas was fighting the simple observation that the players who made up the Cubs were not as talented a unit as other clubs. It was much more. He was going against a stigma as well. A stigma that was engrained in the minds of many people involved in the game and outside of the game. The stigma was that the Cubs couldn't win.

There was a mystique that hung over the entire picture. People would talk about the Cubs of the 1950s and they'd remember that Roy Smalley, Sr. made 51 errors one season. People would talk about the Cubs of the early 1960s and point to the chaos of the College of Coaches. Who can name them all? Who knew them all? Not even the players could figure that system out at times. There were trades that simply couldn't be rationalized either on the day they were made nor today.

While baseball teams tried to win pennants, the Cubs seemed to be devising ways to add a new twist to losing.

In 1962, the Cubs' pitching staff consisted of Bob Buhl, Dick Ellsworth, Don Cardwell, Cal Koonce, Glenn Hobbie, Bob Anderson, Barney Schultz and Don Elston. That club finished with a 59-103 record. Not one of the pitchers won more games than he lost. The Houston Colt 45s, in that franchise's first year of operation, won five more games.

It was two years later that the Cubs traded Lou Brock for Ernie Broglio. Broglio had won 21 games in 1960. Brock cried when he was traded. Cub fans have been crying ever since. Brock ran himself into Hall-of-Fame induction and played on three World Series teams.

While the rest of the baseball world seemed to be taking the game seriously (excepting the early Met teams), the Cubs seemed content to provide a great outlet for the family. The prices were always right, the park comfortable and quaint and there was never a problem getting a ticket. It was as far from a serious business as could be. From a fan's point of view it was all very much the game it had always been. The Cub fan learned to appreciate a different view from other fans. There is no other way to explain the great following the club has had. Cub fans proved winning wasn't everything.

From the mid-1950s through the early 1960s, Cub fans could always cling to Ernie Banks and Hank Sauer. They could always count on Ernie for a smile and a good word. He was truly a great baseball player, his fingers playing the bat handle like a flute, the line drives soaring into the bleachers, onto the catwalk in left. It is incredible to consider that Ernie won back-to-back Most Valuable Player Awards for a team that finished fifth both seasons. It was quite a testimonial.

It wasn't until Leo Durocher was hired in 1966 as manager that the organization showed signs of a more serious approach. In 1966, the Cubs had one manager and three coaches. There was nothing unusual about that except that it was the first time in four seasons that there were fewer coaches than position players.

In the three previous years while the Cubs were finishing seventh, eighth and eighth, the College of Coaches staff had accumulated a total of 41 coaches, including the club high of 15 in 1965.

Leo, of course, made an infamous quote upon being hired. He said the Cubs were not an eighth-place club, their 1965 standing. Leo was right, although not in the sense he intended. The Cubs finished 10th his first season with a 59-103 record. It marked the first year that the five-year-old Mets had escaped the cellar. It was quotes like Leo's that the nation believed stood for the Cubs.

By the time Leo came to Chicago, the Cubs did have a little more offensive punch besides Ernie. By 1966, Ron Santo and Billy Williams had joined the star list. The trio could play, but who could pitch?

It wasn't long before Leo and general manager John Holland assembled a competitive club for the first time since the war years. That club grew into the 1969 team that captured the hearts of Chicago like no team had in decades. That club led the division from Opening Day until September 10 when the Mets blew by them and went on to win the World Series. The Cubs fielded competitive clubs the next four seasons.

But after the 1973 season, the Cubs again dropped back into the pack. For every Cubs star there were three or four players who would have struggled to play for another club. Ernie retired. Santo, Williams, Fergie Jenkins, Randy Hundley, Ken Holtzman and Glenn Beckert, the heart of Leo's stellar teams, were traded. In their place were younger, but less qualified players. There was no changing of the guard, no smooth transition.

In 1978, the Cubs made their first free-agent acquisition when they signed Dave Kingman.

But for every Kingman homer that busted a window on Waveland Avenue, there was someone else who made an error or took a called third strike.

The stigma returned. The cynics once again had fun with the Cubs.

Still, Cub fans enjoyed the game, enjoyed the peace and tranquility Wrigley Field offered. These were faithful people, nice people, going to a nice ballpark to watch nice players get pounded year-after-year by players playing for teams that were committed and dedicated to challenging for championships. Through the years, there must have been players who were overjoyed to be traded to the Cubs. Why not? The expectations were less. A trade to the Cubs was the equivalent of a career-prolonging move.

The Cubs won their last National League pennant in 1945. Since then the Cubs have used World War II, the atom bomb and 3¢ newspapers to mark time with.

Since then teams have sprung up across the Mississippi, air travel has replaced trains, natural grass has been replaced by manufactured turf in some arenas, Babe Ruth's two most treasured home run records fell, players became bigger and stronger, baseball moved indoors, television became popular, dynasties were built and crumbled and rebuilt, the world's population skyrocketed. Man even walked on the moon. Everything in the world changed, but the Cubs remained the same.

From 1946 through 1981, the year before Dallas came to Chicago, the Cubs finished in the first division 11 times and finished out of the first division 25 times.

From 1946 through 1961 the league consisted of eight teams. Here are the Cub finishes in a 16-year period:

1st	2nd	3rd	4th	5th	6th	7th	8th
0	0	1	0	3	2	6	4

From 1962 through 1968, the league consisted of 10 teams. Here are the Cub finishes in those seven years:

1st	2nd	3rd	4th	5th	6th	7th	8th	9th	10th
0	0	2	0	0	0	1	2	1	1

From 1969 through 1981, the league consisted of two six-team divisions. Here are the Cub finishes for those 13 years:

1st	2nd	3rd	4th	5th	6th
0	3	2	2	3	3

The Cubs finished above .500 just eight times from 1946 through 1981, a 36-year stretch.

From 1946 through 1961 when the league consisted of eight teams the Cubs finished with 1,072 victories and 1,389 defeats, 317 games below .500.

From 1962 through 1968 when the National League consisted of 10 teams the Cubs won 519 and lost 614, 95 games below the break-even point.

From the advent of six-team divisional play in 1969

through 1981 the Cubs won 979 games and lost 1,060 falling another 81 games into the red.

Overall, from the year after the Cubs last won a pennant to the year before Dallas' arrival, the Cubs were 2,570 and 3,063, 493 games below .500.

In the final five years before Dallas' arrival, the Cubs combined for a 342-409 record. It was no wonder that when Tribune Company purchased the club in June of 1981, its first move was to find someone who could begin anew.

The poor souls who tried to accomplish the rebuilding process in the previous five years were probably shell-shocked. The vast majority were well-respected and accomplished baseball men. But money was as tight as a lumberjack's grip. Once again, while baseball shifted gears and entered the multi-million dollar salary era and conglomerate ownership, the Cubs stayed behind and tried to make castles from sand. Those who came before Dallas were at a great financial disadvantage from the outset.

In September of 1981, the Phillies and manager Dallas Green came to Chicago for a series. Tribune Company had received permission to talk with Dallas. Stanton Cook and Andrew McKenna met with him while their wives also got together. The selling of Chicago to Dallas had begun.

It wasn't easy. Dallas was being asked to leave a comfortable situation. He had managed the Phillies to the first World Championship in the franchise's 97-year history just a season before. He was toasted through the Delaware Valley as a success, a man who grew up in the Philadelphia-Delaware area and who had played most of his career in the Phillies' system.

There were probably two factors that made Dallas the executive vice president and general manager of the Cubs. One was the uncertainty of the Philadelphia organization following the impending sale of the club from the Carpenter family to the group headed by Bill Giles. The sale became final two weeks after Dallas was hired by the Cubs.

A second major factor was the opportunity Tribune Company had presented Dallas. It would be his organization to build his way.

Finally, in early October, the Phillies were eliminated from the division championship series on a Sunday afternoon at the Vet in Philadelphia. Montreal's Steve Rogers had defeated Steve Carlton. The Phillies season had ended. Dallas bid adieu to Philly.

A day later the newpapers began confirming the rumors that had sprung up near the end of the season and that grew increasingly stronger through the divisional playoffs. Across the message board of the now-defunct Philadelphia Bulletin came the word: DALLAS GREEN TO TAKE OVER CUBS.

Philadelphia was taken aback. Chicago stood dumbfounded. The first major personnel move of the new ownership had taken place. Dallas Green became the executive vice president and general manager of the Cubs. The date was October 15. One week later, Dallas hired Lee Elia as his first manager, replacing Joe Amalfitano.

The first pieces were in place. Time would no longer stand still.

In his opening press conference, Dallas told the media one line that withstood the test of time. Dallas told Chicago that he "was no messiah."

He only claimed that no one would outwork him or the organization. Mistakes would be made, but it wouldn't be out of laziness or disregard for the game plan.

"Any losing organization has an attitude problem," he said. "We have to build pride, renew a dedication to change the attitude and outlook in Chicago. Losing breeds bad thinking on a ballclub. It breeds content with mediocrity.

I think the Cubs have some decent players, not all 25, but some decent ones. Just because a player has a big-league uniform on doesn't mean he's a big-league player."

The season before Dallas took over stood as a case in point. The best thing that happened to the 1981 Cubs was also about the worse thing that happened to baseball—the strike.

The 1981 Cubs were on a pace that would have made people forget about the 1962 (40-120) Mets. The Cubs were 1-13 on April 26 after losing to the Phillies. The Cubs won five of their first 32 games. On May 20 the club was 16 games out.

By the time the strike took place—June 12—the Cubs were 15-37 and 17½ games behind the division-leading Phillies. Psychologically, the team was finished. The club was in dire straits. The franchise was stuck.

On the eve of the strike Herman Franks sent Rick Reuschel to the Yankees in exchange for pitcher Doug Bird and a player to be named later (Mike Griffin). The Cubs also received $400,000 from the Yankees. It was a move to gain money more than talent. Otherwise, why trade the best starting pitcher the club had for the last seven years for a less accomplished pitcher? Reuschel was one of the few Cubs with any true market value.

Four days later, Tribune Company purchased the Cubs for $20.5 million.

The 1981 Cubs won 38 games and lost 65. They were 23-28 following the strike. The improved record was due in large part to much of baseball's nonchalant approach to finishing a season interrupted at its midpoint for 59 days. Despite the improved record, the club wasn't to be taken very seriously.

The on-field talent needed to be upgraded. The minor

league system needed a major overhaul. Wrigley Field needed improvements. The marketing of the Cubs needed spicing up. There was work to do on all levels.

From that starting point there was no way anyone could foresee Dallas building a division champion and a pennant contender just three seasons later.

At first glance in October of 1981, it appeared as if the task at hand would take nearly all of Dallas' five-year contract.

There was no way to do it except start over. He began assembling an expanded front office team.

For the first time the Cubs would begin a major marketing program. There would be an all-out campaign. One of the vice-presidents hired, Bing Hampton, came up with the slogan "Building A New Tradition." It was a catchy phrase although many people in Chicago were offended by the insinuation that what they had watched and supported for decades was inferior to what the Dallas Green regime would bring in.

The people had heard all the promises of rebuilding before. They had heard it and believed whether it was being said by someone sincere or someone who didn't care if the new program moved from square one. There was no way many of them could hear what Dallas was saying and feel it was any different than what they had heard before.

In the same vein, Dallas hadn't been a part of the Chicago depression and hadn't witnessed first-hand having his heart broken by the last 36 years of frustrating history.

"I know in my heart we will get the job done," Dallas said many times.

He was sincere. Incredibly sincere. A large portion of the public still had to be shown.

Soon after he arrived, Dallas was asked about the need for lights to be installed for night baseball at Wrigley Field.

People suddenly discovered that they were not dealing with a politician or someone who would speak around the issues. Ask Dallas a question and hold on for the answer, they learned. It may not have been what they wanted to hear but it was what Dallas felt in his heart. He was more concerned with honesty than diplomacy.

"All of baseball plays night games," he said. "If the Cubs are to contend and play under the same circumstances as the rest of the National League teams then someday lights will have to be installed."

The uproar was immediate and loud. The neighborhood people around Wrigley Field organized against the concept. There were meetings—loud, vociferous meetings.

It was the beginnings of a very rocky road, to say the least.

What did Dallas have to build from?

The team he inherited looked like this (players who played a majority of the season at the major league level):

The outfielders: Steve Henderson played left; Jerry Morales and Scot Thompson shared center; Leon Durham played right.

The infielders: Bill Buckner was at first base; Mike Tyson, Joe Strain, Steve Dillard and Pat Tabler played at least 20 games each at second; Ivan DeJesus was at short; Ken Reitz at third.

The catchers: Tim Blackwell was the Cubs No. 1 catcher until the strike. Jody Davis took over from that point.

The bench: Heitz Cruz, Tye Waller, Jim Tracy, Bobby Bonds and Mike Lum.

The starting pitchers: Doug Bird, Mike Krukow, Randy Martz, Ken Kravec and Mike Griffin.

The bullpen: Doug Capilla, Willie Hernandez, Rawly Eastwick, Dave Geisel, Dick Tidrow, Lee Smith and Bill Caudill.

In the span of two seasons, all but four players were either traded, sold or released.

Henderson played most of the 1982 season before being traded. Morales and Thompson also played in 1982 and most of 1983 at the major league level. Morales was released. Thompson was sent to the minors and opted for free agency. Durham remained.

Buckner was traded in 1984. DeJesus was traded in January of 1982. Tyson and Reitz were released before playing one game for the Cubs under Dallas. Strain was exiled to the minors. Dillard was released and Tabler, who spent most of the 1982 season in the minors, was traded in January of 1983.

The releasing of Reitz and Tyson was costly from a financial perspective.

"The worst mistake you can make is making the same mistake twice," Dallas said. "Just because they had big contracts didn't mean we were going to win with them and that we had to keep them and play them."

Rival general managers took note. The philosophy was sound. It may be costly in the financial department, but the action was correct for any team starting over.

Blackwell was signed as a free agent by the Expos. Jody has remained.

Bonds was released. Lum was released. Cruz played part of the 1982 season with the Cubs before being sent to the minors. He chose free agency. Waller was the opening day center fielder in 1982 and was traded at the end of the season. Tracy was traded before the 1982 season started.

Bird was the Cubs Opening Day pitcher in 1982 and was traded that December. Krukow was dealt in the winter of 1981. Martz was a Cub starter in 1982 and traded the following winter. Kravec pitched rarely in 1982 and was released. Mike Griffin was traded before the 1982 season.

Capilla was also traded before the 1982 season. Hernandez pitched all of 1982 and two months into the 1983 season before he was traded to the Phillies for Dick Ruthven and a minor leaguer. Hernandez had done a good job for the Cubs. But the Cubs needed starting pitchers and not in anyone's wildest dreams, not even Willie's, did there appear to be a Cy Young Award in his future.

Eastwick was released before the 1982 season. Geisel was traded. Tidrow lasted one season under Dallas and was traded along with Martz in Dallas' most controversial deal. Smith has remained. Caudill was dealt at the end of the 1982 spring training session.

The first roster didn't leave Dallas much to choose from. His marketable talents were Buckner and DeJesus among his infielders, Durham in the outfield, Krukow, Smith, Hernandez, Martz and Caudill among his pitchers. Although Smith, Hernandez, Martz and Caudill were all of questionable market value since none of the four had really had what could be called an outstanding season.

After Reuschel was traded in June, the Cubs only true starter was Krukow. He had some value. Bird and Tidrow didn't carry much value. Hernandez could help a club from the left side out of the bullpen with Smith being his right-handed counterpart. Geisel, Kravec and Eastwick also didn't hold much of any market value. In fact, Dallas had released both Eastwick and Bird prior to the Phillies' 1980 championship season. Martz and Caudill were both at key stages of their career. It was time for both to step forward and take control. Martz did for a season. Caudill apparently couldn't control his off-season weight and started off on the wrong foot literally and figuratively.

Caudill reported to his first camp under Dallas and Lee Elia overweight. Then he injured his foot. Dallas and Lee couldn't afford the luxury of waiting for someone to get in shape on the club's time. Dallas had made a very obvious effort to make that perfectly clear well in advance of the reporting dates.

Within a month of his hiring, Dallas wrote each player

saying, "physical conditioning the way I expect it to be done starts right now. Spring training is too late. Tony Garofalo (the Cubs trainer) and Lee Elia will be sending along their thoughts about conditioning and a program suggesting how they want things done.

"I'm telling you now, your job on the major-league level may well depend on this and one to two days a week in the winter won't get it. On this team, because you wear a major league uniform doesn't necessarily mean that you are a big leaguer . . . Come to spring training ready to work on fundamentals instead of spending time getting in shape."

The letter also voiced Dallas' opinion of the 1981 Cubs. Suffice it to say that everyone knew where they stood long before February of 1982; Caudill included.

That first spring training was a quick weeding-out process. It was a haven for free agents and a hell for free spirits.

At the end of spring training, Dallas sent Caudill to the Yankees who shipped him to Seattle for Shane Rawley moments later. Caudill went on to become a standout for the Mariners and then again for Oakland. But there was no guarantee that he would have done the same without the inspiration that he needed to prove himself with a new club.

Of the pitchers, only Lee Smith, who developed into one of the game's top relievers, remained from the 1981 club to celebrate 1984.

Of those 30 players, 16 never made it out of Green's first training camp. Of those 16, half never played in the majors again. Of the remaining eight, just four contributed to other clubs in 1982 (DeJesus, Krukow, Caudill and Geisel). Of those original 30, only Durham, Davis and Smith finished the 1984 season with the Cubs.

Of the 27 players who left the organization between October, 1981 and October 1984, only Hernandez, Henderson, Buckner and Tabler, along with the four players already listed, contributed to another major league club in 1984.

Of the 40-man spring training roster from 1981, only 17 made it back to spring training with the Cubs in 1982.

Of the 40-man spring training roster Dallas opened with in 1982, only six players were on the 1984 club—Sandberg, Durham, Smith, Bowa, Davis and Moreland. Gary Woods, who was a non-roster invitee, made it seven.

The minor league system and scouting department also underwent changes. For the most part the minor league system hadn't produced enough to give the Cubs a chance to grow from within. Of the 17 first-round draft picks the Cubs made since 1965 only 11 ever played for the Cubs, the most accomplished and well-known being Scot Thompson. Included in the list of those who made it to the big leagues with the Cubs from the first-round were pitcher Richard James, shortstop Terry Hughes and first baseman Jerry Tabb. Only the truest of Cub fans would recognize those names in a lineup.

Of the 16 first-round picks from the traditionally poorer winter draft, the Cubs have had two who made it to the majors, pitcher Alec Distaso and infielder Pete LaCock.

Of all the Cubs first-round picks from both drafts, only Don Schulze made as many as one appearance with the 1984 club. Granted that without Schulze and another former No. 1 selection, Joe Carter, the big seven-player deal with Cleveland would have never come off. But would the Cubs have won the National League Eastern Division without trading Schulze, Carter, Mel Hall and Double A pitcher Darryl Banks? Not likely. Sutcliffe, George Frazier and Ron Hassey obviously played a much larger role with the 1984 Cubs than the kids would have.

On the 1984 Cubs playoff roster only Lee Smith and Henry Cotto had played their entire pro careers in the Cubs system. Of those players who played most of the season, only Rich Reuschel's name could be added to the list of Cub farm-team products.

Between Dallas' own observations as a rival manager and

what he heard from other baseball people, he knew the rebuilding wouldn't come quick. But no matter how prepared he may have been, he was still stunned by the overall picture. Yet, history told him, it could be done.

"This team reminds me so much of the Phillies when we (Paul Owens as the general manager and Dallas as the farm director) took over in 1972. We were 33½ games behind the league leaders. There were no promising prospects. The team on the field was not competitive and had no hope of being so. There are so many similarities between the 1972 Phillies and the 1982 Cubs. It is intriguing and exciting and I'm looking forward to it.

"I don't have a good feel for a timetable. But don't sell what we do short. I'll guarantee you, we'll wake some of them up."

His first moves involved his marketable commodities, Krukow and DeJesus. He also went looking for new utility players, players who had played on winning teams.

He acquired Woods from Houston, the team Dallas' Phillies had to take to five electrifying games in 1980 to make it to the World Series. He also added Junior Kennedy. Junior had spent the 1970s with two organizations, the Baltimore Orioles and the Cincinnati Reds, two of the best in that decade.

While all the changes brought improvement, nearly all the trades brought skepticism. Few people ever looked at the total picture.

Not even on June 13, 1984 when the seven-player deal with the Indians took place did the deal meet with mass appeal even though only one player from the Cubs major league roster—Mel Hall—was included.

Certainly, the future of that trade may change the first-year complexion. But at the outset, it proved to be the trade that made the Cubs division champions.

Nothing came easy. Every move, while well calculated

by Dallas, was perceived as a hair-trigger response to removing the old and bringing in the new—mostly Phillies. But what was the man to do?

Who knew the calibre of the Philadelphia organization better than the man who helped build it? Why not go back to the players he knew best?

It was the Phillies that Dallas went back to first. The first big trades were made with Philadelphia. The trade that spun the Cubs in the right direction in the spring of 1984 was also made with Philly. Amid all the Chicago criticism, there wasn't a team in baseball that took the Cubs' success in 1984 harder than the Phillies. There must be a reason for that.

On September 24, 1984, did anyone in Chicago really care who the former Phillies were? All Chicago should have cared about was who the National League Eastern Division Champions were. They were the Cubs.

The first player Dallas added to the Cubs was Junior Kennedy, the first he released was Bobby Bonds. Then he hired Lee Elia, his third base coach from the Phillies during the 1980 and 1981 season. Lee had been to Chicago before. He played for Durocher in 1968. Actually, he watched a lot more than he played. He had 15 at bats in 17 games that season. Dallas knew him well. He knew Lee was good with kids and he knew he could be fiery. It was Lee's first major league managing job. Dallas signed him for three years.

"I figured it would take at least that long," Elia said. "We weren't starting with much and I wanted to be sure I'd be given the chance to work some of the problems out."

The winter meetings were held in Hollywood, FL in December of 1981. With not much more than loose change in terms of marketable talent, Dallas began putting the club together.

His first major deal was made on December 8. His best

pitcher was Krukow. He traded him to the Phillies. In return he received Moreland along with Dickie Noles and Dan Larson, two pitchers.

Chicago looked at the deal and wondered aloud how Dallas could deal the only true starting pitcher he had. Sure Moreland might hit 25 homers at Wrigley Field but where is he going to play? He had caught for the Phillies sparingly. But the Cubs fans had fallen in love with Jody Davis. One of the few bright prospects the Cubs had was suddenly cast into a secondary role by someone who had never caught full time in the big leagues. That, coupled with Noles and Larson never having proven themselves, caused the first stir.

Dallas remedied it slightly when he signed Fergie Jenkins as a free agent. Only the A's and the Cubs had shown any interest in Jenkins, who turned 38 five days later. Dallas also signed free agent reliever Bill Campbell.

The next day he traded Jim Tracy to the Astros for Woods.

Big deal, Cub fans shrugged. They had no idea who Woods was. Dallas did. He had watched Woods come up in September of 1980 and help the Astros to the playoffs. He also saw Woods get two hits off Carlton in the opening game of the League Championship Series. Granted he was a part-time player, but at least he was a part-timer who had proven he could play for a winner.

To Dallas, that was a big deal.

It was six weeks later when Dallas went back to the phone lines and dialed Philadelphia. He knew that Larry Bowa, a Philadelphia fixture for a dozen years at shortstop, was at odds with Giles and Owens. Bowa's contract was a major bickering point. The sides were miles apart. Bowa wanted out. The Phillies wanted him out.

Dallas called Philly and told them he would send them the shortstop (De Jesus) they needed to maintain their lofty Eastern Division standing. In return, Dallas would take the problem (Bowa) off their hands. The Phils said it sounded great. Dallas and his new minor league director Gordon Goldsberry, said throw in the kid Sandberg and you've got a deal. The Phils balked. Dallas put them on hold. The Philly brass debated. Deep down they weren't certain Sandberg would ever become a good major leaguer. The Phillies already had Julio Franco and Juan Samuel in their system—two players that ranked higher in their eyes. They questioned their people again. The word came back that Sandberg was expendable.

The Phillies needed to make the playoffs to make their checkbook balance. It was that simple. Baseball salaries had put the Phillies in the same situation it had put many of the good and high-payroll teams—the Phils had to win this year in order to keep the program flowing. DeJesus could do that for them. He was younger than Bowa by seven years. His range and his arm were better. And the opportunity to play on a contender where he wouldn't be considered one of the top players might move him up another notch production-wise. Plus, he would be reunited with his former double-play partner with the Cubs—Manny Trillo.

And what of Sandberg? Where was he going to play for the Phillies? The kid wasn't going to play his natural shortstop position with DeJesus there. He wasn't going to play second with Trillo there and he wasn't going to play centerfield with another Gold Glover—Garry Maddox—riveted to that position. Simply, he wasn't going to be in Philly any time soon.

What Dallas was getting was the fiery Bowa, the first step toward leadership, a guy who had won, who had taken his talents and stretched them as far as anyone ever did. Along with Bowa, Dallas had pulled in a prospect. Not just any prospect but one of the top prospects from an organization that had been built from its own system.

The people of Chicago, the media, the experts, couldn't

believe it. In his first two major trades, Dallas had traded away the team's best pitcher and one of a handful of talented everyday players for a player without a true position (Moreland), two pitchers who had won a total of 16 major league games (Noles and Larson), an aging shortstop (Bowa) and a kid that the Phillies didn't want (Sandberg). This, the people asked, was an improvement?

The first impressions were far from assuring to Cub fans. What had Tribune Company done? The impression of Dallas was, a) he didn't care for the years of tradition that belonged to the Cubs, b) he didn't care that much for antiquated and lightless Wrigley Field, and c) he was making the same type of deals that took on the suspicious look of Pafko-for-Miksis; of Brock-for-Broglio; Madlock-for-Murcer; and Trillo, Gross and Rader for Foote, Martin, Sizemore, Botelho and Mack.

The phones at Wrigley Field rang and rang.

And Dallas stood steadfast.

What, he wondered, were all these people so proud of? What had their Cubs accomplished in the last 36 years? What indeed, when the year that stood out in every Cub fan's mind was 1969—a year that team went down the chute the final six weeks and finished in second place, eight games back? Finishing second, finishing eight games out of first was something to be proud of?

If the people of Chicago couldn't take Dallas' first three months seriously, how could he take those same people seriously?

There were few bright moments during the spring. Dallas began buying up contracts and he and his baseball people began making evaluations of the young talent. There was a quagmire of players and a minimum of pennant-contending talent.

Many decisions were made. Sandberg would move to third and get a chance to play every day. With two weeks to go before the season opener, Dallas traded for Bump Wills, certainly not a Trillo, but a stopgap second baseman who could help. Bump would lead off and Sandberg would bat second, followed by Buckner, Durham, Moreland, who was given the catching job ahead of Davis, Steve Henderson, Tye Waller and Bowa.

It was the beginning of a pretty good offensive club. But good pitching was still something everyone else had and the Cubs only saw against them.

The 1982 season would be remembered for a number of reasons — very few of them positive at first glance. The season opened with a Bump Wills homer in his inaugural at bat for the Cubs. Bump homered off Mario Soto in the traditional National League opener at Cincinnati. The Cubs won. Lee won his first game as a big league manager. And a good luck telegram greeted the Cubs in the visitors clubhouse at Riverfront Stadium. It was from Mike Lum. Lum was playing in Japan. He had spent less than one full season with the Cubs yet he offered hope and praise for what was trying to be accomplished.

After the thrilling win in Cincy, the year took a turn for the worse. 1982 was the year the Cubs lost 13 straight, tying their own record for futility.

It was the year the Cubs bought out a couple of million dollars in contracts and traded Bill Caudill, who went to Seattle and won a dozen games while saving 26 more. The Cubs leading pitcher was 38-year-old Fergie Jenkins, who won 14. The leading reliever was Lee Smith, who saved 17.

It was the year Sandberg started off 1-for-32 and Elia stayed with him, never letting the kid's confidence break even though 99.9% of the managers in the game would have benched him or sent him back to the minors.

In May, Buckner and Elia tussled in front of 8,635 fans in San Diego. It was as if Buckner represented the earlier Cubs and Chicago while Elia stood for everything new and all the ex-Phillies. A small melee spilled onto the field between innings that evening. At that point, it was the biggest news the Cubs had made all season.

Buckner had pushed Elia too far and Lee wasn't about to let the players watch him be swallowed up. He went after Buckner after Bill said a few choice things and lunged toward Lee. The results weren't pretty.

Elia questioned Buckner's value as a team player. Buckner apologized a day later, The players backed Elia in print in a rare display of management support.

Before long, the 13-game losing streak hit. The Cubs fell from the race. They were 21-39, in last place, 14½ games back when it finally ended. The jury was still out.

It was after the 13th loss that the Cubs returned home to Wrigley Field. It was a Sunday night, June 13. A few players had family members pick them up at O'Hare airport. Others came downtown, to Wrigley Field.

Noles was one of the players who came back to the park. In the quiet of the evening, in the solitude of the bleachers, Noles sat and cried. The losing was getting to every one. There was Noles, the pitcher credited with turning around the 1980 World Series when he separated the Royals' George Brett from his helmet with a knockdown pitch. Noles typified the Dallas Green player—tough, hard-nosed, a great competitor. As darkness fell, Noles sat in the bleachers alone and cried.

The Cubs went on to finish fifth with a 73-89 record. The Cardinals won the East and also the World Series. The Cubs finished 19 games back.

"This is all a big test," Vukovich said over and over.

Lee found himself in deep trouble when he spoke his mind to a *Tribune* writer who began covering the club the second half of the season. Looking for insight into what had gone on during the first half of the season, the writer, without pen or tape recorder, asked Lee for his summation position-by-position.

By then Lee had already become disenchanted with Wills' play at second base. He said that Bump had cost the club six wins already with his defensive shortcomings. It made headlines the next day.

Elia almost fainted when he left his Des Plaines apartment and went to the store to pick up the morning papers. He was stunned. He made the comments off-the-record. Suddenly, all Chicago knew how he felt, including his players, including Bump.

For all the trials and tribulations Elia and the Cubs went through there were still signs that a change might be in the wind.

Sandberg went on to play great at third base. He batted .271. In May, Jody replaced Moreland behind the plate. After jockeying between relieving and starting and relieving again, Lee Smith was finally given the role as the No.1 reliever. He came through with 17 saves and made the rest of the league take notice.

Fergie returned to the Cubs and won 14 games. He also became the seventh pitcher in baseball history to strike out 3,000 batters when he fanned San Diego's Garry Templeton the night after Elia and Buckner squared off.

Moreland switched to the outfield and played his first full season. For the first two months of the season he was one of the best offensive players in the league. Durham became the first Cub in 71 years to have 20 or more homers and 20 or more stolen bases in one season.

The team began to come together the last two months. Elia was more comfortable and so were the players. From August 1 through the end of the season only the Giants played better in the league and only three American League teams had a better record than the Cubs' 33-24 mark. It was the second best post-August 1 record of any Cub team since 1945. That, at least, was a breakthrough.

It was still far from perfect. The pitching rotation Connors was left to mold into a major league outfit consisted of Jenkins, Noles, Martz and Bird.

At 38, Jenkins' every outing was a question mark. Noles was great at times, like when he shut out the Reds on one hit in April, and he was awful at times. Martz rarely made it past the fifth inning and Bird seemingly lost interest.

Then there was Allen Ripley. On the final day of the 1982 spring training session the Cubs played the Brewers in Sun City, Az. Following the game the Cubs were set to depart for Chicago. Ripley was a no-show until 15 minutes before the plane took off. No one saw him all day. It seems he went to visit relatives in Tucson the night before. It's a two-hour ride from Tucson to Phoenix. On his return trip Sunday morning, his rent-a-car broke down perhaps a half-hour into the ride. He left the car and began walking and hitch-hiking. It took him all day to make it back through the desert.

For all anyone knew, he could have been dead.

Al struggled early in the season. He would pitch one inning that would last four runs and 25 minutes, another inning that would last five runs and a half hour and so on. He was struggling. Before Lee could pull the trigger on him, he went into Lee's office. He told Lee he would really appreciate one opportunity to start to see if he could get his act together before Lee released him. Lee looked at him and said, "I've watched you spend a half hour getting three guys out a number of times already this season and now you want to start a game? Well, Allen, I'm not sure anyone on this club has got that much time to watch you work five innings."

Ripley was also the pitcher whose wife didn't believe he

was going to the park one day for an off-day workout. He told her to come along.

After the workout, his wife grabbed a bat and said she'd like to hit off her husband. Rip complied. She hit something like four of his five pitches.

"That's when I knew my career was really in jeopardy," he said.

Ripley's father had pitched for the Red Sox in 1935. On August 6, Allen beat the Phillies at Wrigley Field. He went on the post-game television show and dedicated the victory to his father as a Father's Day gift. Father's Day had passed two months earlier.

There were some light moments later in the season also. After Elia once again blew up at Bump Wills and was quoted as saying he was sick of seeing all the garbage, the players flew off on their final road trip wearing garbage bags as the plane taxied.

It was Wills who probably irritated Elia the most that season. Bump, who committed 19 errors at second base and turned only 45 double plays (compared to Sandberg who had six errors in 1984 and turned 102 double plays), was asked to come out on an off-day and work out at second base. He showed up eating his breakfast at second between grounders.

Bump was also on the final year of his contract. His proposal to the Cubs was very high. The Cubs decided to play Sandberg at second through September and let Bump try free agency. Bump ended up playing in Japan. Sandberg ended up leading the league. But when all was said and done, the Cubs still finished fifth, a lengthy distance from the top and only a shade better in terms of respectability.

The organization and Dallas realized a few of the holes had been plugged for the 1983 season. Buckner was still at first, Sandberg had become a fixture at second base and Bowa was at short. Davis, who had an outstanding season defensively in 1982, would continue to catch. With Buckner at first, Durham was still out of place defensively in the outfield, but his bat more than made up for his play in the field. Moreland had fallen into the right field position and began accepting it and working at it. His offensive production had tailed off in the second half, but his defense was improving to the point where it was acceptable.

The problem areas were at third, with Sandberg moving to second base, center field, where there was some question about whether or not rookie Mel Hall could play every day, and of course, the pitching staff.

As fall changed into winter it was apparent that Dallas had to make some type of move. The best bet for a quick fix was the free-agent market. The Dodgers and Steve Garvey were parting ways.

What would Garvey's presence be worth? If Garvey played first, Buckner would have to move to left field and Durham would have to play center. Or, either Buckner or Durham would have to be traded. Would signing Garvey add that much credence to make it worthwhile?

Dallas decided it would. By signing Garvey it would give the Cubs that much more talent whether it was used to field the 1983 club or to be used on the market at the upcoming winter meetings. The Cubs selected Garvey in the November re-entry draft.

In the interim, the Cubs re-signed Jenkins for two seasons. Dallas said publicly that Fergie had two goals remaining. One was to pitch in the World Series and the second was to win 300 games. Fergie entered the 1983 season with 278 wins. Privately, Dallas felt that only if the Cubs signed Garvey and made a blockbuster deal would Fergie ever have a chance to pitch in the Series. Time was running out on Jenkins and the prospects of winning something as grand as even the N.L. Eastern Division seemed distant.

The Cubs were not the only team that felt Garvey could

add to their club. The Yankees, Giants, Astros and Padres were also coming heavy after him.

The Cubs invited Steve to town. They put on a lavish press conference for him and his agent, Jerry Kapstein. One writer commented that the press conference, complete with a seafood buffet, was so extravagant that if the Cubs did sign Steve the proper way to bring him into town would be on the back of an elephant right down Michigan Avenue.

After the conference, Garvey, Dallas, Kapstein, Andrew McKenna and a couple of members of the Cubs front office staff dined in a private room at the Chicago Sheraton. All systems pointed to signing Steve.

The money was good, the relationship between Garvey and Dallas, Kapstein and Dallas, Garvey and Kapstein and McKenna seemed very affable.

After his Chicago stop Garvey went to Houston and San Francisco and finally to San Diego for more of the royal treatment.

The negotiations carried on into December. Garvey would say the Cubs offered him a chance to play in a great city. . . but San Diego offered him a chance to stay in southern California where he would like one day to run for state office. It went on and on. Dallas left for the winter meetings in Hawaii with nothing concrete. He had the feeling that if Garvey could be shown that the Cubs were closer to winning a title, it might be enough to sway him to Chicago.

At the meetings, the Cubs tried to improve the pitching staff with three deals. They sent Bird to Boston for Chuck Rainey. With intentions of releasing Steve Henderson, the Cubs went to Seattle in one last effort to, a) save on buying-out Henderson, and b) acquire another pitcher. Seattle offered the Cubs Rich Bordi. Dallas took him. Bordi was still young enough and had enough raw talent that he now became one of Connors' pet projects.

In another minor deal, the Cubs acquired Reggie Patterson from the White Sox for outfielder Tye Waller. With Waller traded and Reitz released, only Durham remained from the Bruce Sutter deal of December, 1980.

There wasn't much else Dallas could do to improve the pitching staff. With an eye on Garvey and an eye on trying to deal for strength through a weakness, Dallas' options weren't many.

Then came a monster proposal. The Phillies came calling with a reported 5-for-2 package. The Phillies wanted Durham and Hernandez.

In exchange they would give the Cubs a starting pitcher (Ruthven), a second baseman (Trillo), a center fielder (Dernier), a left fielder (Matthews) and a minor league pitching prospect (Jay Baller).

There were both negatives and positives. A few of the negatives included Trillo being a year from free agency, Dernier's inability to hit major league pitching in the short trials he had in the big leagues and Matthews' contract and age. The biggest question, however, was whether or not to deal Durham, a franchise cornerstone type player?

The positive ramifications could be an improved club overnight and also a sign to Garvey that the Cubs were serious.

The deal would also give the Cubs a surplus of talent, especially if Garvey decided to sign.

There had been rumors that the Texas Rangers had shown an interest in Moreland. Would they have parted with lefty starter Rick Honeycutt, who they later traded to the Dodgers? At one point the Yankees were interested in Buckner. Could the Cubs get another starter from New York? Maybe Shane Rawley or Dave Righetti? The possibilities were endless.

Would this batting order plus Jenkins and either Honeycutt, Rawley or Righetti put the Cubs in a position to contend: Dernier, CF; Sandberg 3B; Matthews LF; Garvey 1B; Moreland RF; Davis C; Trillo 2B; Bowa SS?

It was certainly inviting. But the lingering question remained. Do you trade Durham at 25 and possibly on the verge of stardom? The Cubs thought about the proposal long and hard. Finally, their decision stunned Philly. The Cubs would not trade Durham.

A day later, the Phils traded Trillo, Baller, George Vukovich, Julio Franco and Jerry Willard, the last two being top prospects, to the Cleveland Indians for outfielder Von Hayes. The Phils had obtained the left-handed hitter they were after. The Cubs had stood pat. Could they afford to stand pat? Would this ultimately affect the Garvey decision?

Just a few days before Christmas of 1982, Kapstein, based in San Diego, made an appearance on Monday Night Football during a Charger game. Kapstein announced to the world that Garvey would sign a contract the next day.

The Cubs hadn't made any press conference plans. The race was over. Garvey signed the next day with the Padres for five years at approximately the same terms Dallas offered.

The winter meetings were over. Garvey was a Padre. The winter had yet to fulfill Dallas. He returned from the meeting, from the Garvey chase, with a distant look on his face.

Into January, Dallas was quiet. His mind was working, wondering, questioning what to do next. After the trials of the last season, the second-guessing for all his deals, the wrath of the public that landed on him following the dismissal of front office people and the two deals that nearly came off but didn't, Dallas needed to regroup. The team that finished 73-89 would only be better if Hall could play everyday, if another rookie, Pat Tabler, could play third and if Rainey turned out to be a better pitcher than Bird.

The trio of longshots didn't allow Dallas to rest any easier. Hall would probably be satisfactory in center field. Tabler remained a big question. He had come over on the coattails of the utterly complicated Rick Rueschel deal of June, 1981 and never convinced Dallas and his staff that he could play either second or third base. And Rainey had never looked like a stopper. He was another pitcher, a little younger than Bird and with a better attitude. There hadn't been enough moves to satisfy Dallas.

Basically, the Cubs would have gone into the 1983 season with just as many questions as they had after the 1982 season. There was no sure-fire, quick-fix solution. But Dallas kept looking. There was a need to make a move that would at least change the look of the club slightly as well as fill one of the holes. As spring training inched closer by the day, Dallas went back to the drawing board in search of a deal.

Al Campanis of the Dodgers and Dallas had talked during the winter meetings. The Dodgers were going to continue moving in the direction of younger players. Los Angeles felt Greg Brock was ready to play first and that Garvey was expendable. They also felt that Pedro Guerrero could move to third to allow Mike Marshall, another hot prospect, an opportunity to play the outfield. That move would make Ron Cey free. Cey was nearing the end of his contract. He had one year to run and then the Dodgers were prepared to let him move the way of Garvey.

Cey was holding up the Dodgers' plans. He was available for a couple of minor leaguers. Dallas and Gordon Goldsberry went though the Cubs' system. The Cubs offered outfielder Dan Cataline and the Dodgers said that Cataline was fine but they also wanted left-handed pitcher Vance Lovelace.

Lovelace was one of the few pitchers in the Cubs' organization that had solid major league potential. Considering that the only lefties on the Cubs staff in 1982 were Hernandez and seldom-used Ken Kravec, it was obvious that southpaws in the Cubs' organization were at a premium. At this point in time improving the parent club was the first and foremost priority. Lovelace was a minimum of three years away. By then the whole plan may have gone up in smoke. The Cubs approved the Dodgers bid. The only matter left was satisfying Cey.

The negotiations continued on. The Cubs still had the financial commitment of Tribune Company earmarked for the Garvey deal. The deal for Cey was set. On January 20, Dallas filled an important hole at third and added power to the lineup.

Cey's presence moved the lineup into a positive direction. He could still produce offensively even though the Dodgers had moved him down to sixth in the batting order. He was in great shape and just what the Cubs needed to add some hope to their depressed winter of rebuilding.

As had been the general reaction to all Dallas' dealings, people wanted to know how good the prospects must have been to pry Cey away. Was Lovelace another Gura? Cataline another Brock?

"If people would just relax a little and let Dallas do the job, I know they'd see that this thing will work out," Vukovich said. "I know the man. It will happen here."

The outcry continued. There was speculation in the media that Dallas had given Cey an incredible contract. No one knows for sure except Cey, Dallas and Cey's attorney. Nevertheless, once again the second-guessing grew louder and louder.

It was as if the fans asked themselves if they hadn't seen this all before? They questioned not acquiring Garvey and then turning around and giving Cey a great contract. They came down hard.

They said it was just like when Bill Madlock wanted a substantial raise in 1976 after leading the league for the second time in hitting. The Wrigley family said they wouldn't pay that much. So Madlock was traded to the Giants for Bobby Murcer. The Wrigleys reportedly paid Murcer as much as Madlock wanted. Madlock continued to be one of the toughest hitters in the game. Murcer had one good season with the Cubs, one horrible one and halfway through his third season was dealt to the Yankees for a minor league pitcher, Paul Semall. Semall never pitched an inning for the Cubs. Was this the same old song, the fans wondered?

It was only a couple of days after the Cey deal when more fireworks went off. The White Sox had lost Steve Kemp through free agency. Because the Sox had lost Kemp, a type A free agent, they were allowed to select a player from the participating clubs' unprotected list. On January 20, the same day as the Cey deal, the White Sox selected Rudy May from the Yankees.

The White Sox learned later that May had a no-trade clause. They would have to select again. They called Dallas and told him they might consider taking Jenkins.

When the news hit the streets it became a battle of North Side vs. South Side. Fergie had been the Cubs most successful pitcher in 1982. He was closing in on 40 years old. He had also just signed a two-year contract. At his age, that length of a contract should have been a deterrent. It wasn't.

The Sox threatened to take Jenkins. The media wanted to know how Dallas could leave Fergie unprotected. It didn't matter to them that the Cubs could only protect 26 players from the entire organization.

On the other hand, what did the Sox want with another pitcher? They had just signed free agent Floyd Bannister to go with Richard Dotson, Britt Burns and LaMarr Hoyt. The Sox were pitching rich. Another pitcher, especially an aging veteran, shouldn't have been very high on their priority list.

Shortly before 9 a.m. on January 26, the Cubs traded reliever Dick Tidrow, starter Randy Martz, shortstop Scott Fletcher and infielder Pat Tabler to the White Sox. In return the Cubs acquired Steve Trout, a left-handed starter (their first in more than a couple of years) and reliever Warren Brusstar.

Moments later, the White Sox chose Steve Mura from the World Champion Cardinals in the compensation draft.

The media howled. Dallas, it was written, had been taken. The White Sox had forced Dallas to cry uncle, they wrote. The White Sox had exposed the fact that the Cubs and Dallas had left Jenkins unprotected and then forced the Cubs into a one-sided deal.

No where was it written that the Cubs had no choice except either to take a chance with Fergie or possibly lose a prospect. No where was it written that players like Pete Rose, Willie Stargell and Carl Yastrzemski had been left off the same list, but other teams, adhering to their own conscience and the ideals that a player of that stature and age should have the honor of finishing his career in the city of his choice, backed off.

For a week the city turned its attention against Dallas. The radio talk shows, the newspapers and newscasts hammered him hour-by-hour. The *Chicago Sun-Times* berated Dallas and the trade for a week and then asked its readers to give their opinions of the deal. Naturally, the readers kept the ordeal going by an 18-1 margin in the White Sox favor.

Now, two years later the results are slightly different. Tidrow was cut loose after one season and later released by the Mets. Martz pitched one game for the White Sox and was released. Tabler was traded in spring training for Jerry Dybzinski, who platooned with Fletcher at shortstop. In 1984 only Fletcher remained with the White Sox.

Trout's record with the Cubs through two seasons was 23-21. He matured into a good pitcher who went 13-7 in the Cubs' championship season. He was then selected by 17 clubs in the re-entry draft before re-signing. Brusstar pitched two years of relief for the Cubs through the 1984 season.

The city, the fans, the media had again taken it to Dallas. The man remained steadfast. He had sought a lefty starter throughout the Winter Meetings so Trout filled that requirement. He also knew Brusstar could fill a role in the bullpen.

Certainly, the pressure would be on. But there were no odds Dallas liked better than one against the world. The day the deal was made the skies were gray, the Cubs' world overcast.

The phones at Wrigley Field rang incessantly, "What," they all wanted to know, "was Dallas doing?"

It was another trying time for the organization. Dallas took a deep breath and went back inside his office. Spring training opened in a month. The world would see what this winter of question and discord had evolved into.

Elia's second spring training moved along well. The cynics wanted to know if the Cubs wanted to sign any other ancient players. They had Fergie who was 39, Bowa at 37, Jay Johnstone at 37, Cey at 35 and Buckner at 33.

Lee laughed it off. He had himself a pretty good team offensively. The combination of adding Cey to the middle of the lineup with Durham and Buckner along with Moreland and Davis and Sandberg certainly made the Cubs interesting offensively.

Defensively, the left side of the infield had some age to it. The outfield held some concern with Moreland and Durham not being natural outfielders along with the question mark in center field—Mel Hall.

The pitching staff would be slightly different. Trout replaced Martz and Rainey replaced Bird. Ripley was gone, but not to be forgotten.

The bullpen had remained sturdy with Smith, Hernandez and Brusstar along with Mike Proly and a newcomer, lefty Craig Lefferts.

This club wouldn't be outstanding, but it was a definite improvement over the 1982 club and an incredible facelift from 1981.

It had been a long, arduous process. Not every piece of the puzzle fit perfectly. But at least there were a few more pieces to work with.

The naysayers remained within striking distance of Dallas. They wanted to see improvement, practically overnight changes. No one wanted to see it more than Dallas. No one.

"I have a lot of faith in my ability," Dallas said in retrospect. "When I came to Chicago I was at the peak of what baseball is all about because we accomplished something in Philadelphia that hadn't been done.

"Everyone there respected me, but then I came here and didn't have the same respect. That boggled my mind more than anything else. I didn't understand why I didn't have the same respect in Chicago, why all of a sudden I was perceived as less a baseball man.

"I understand a little about having to earn your spurs, but it just hurts a little bit when people don't recognize you're doing positive things for the Cubs' organization despite the won-loss record.

"I was trying to make us a winner."

"The Cubs are coming out of hibernation," the new marketing motto claimed. But were they?

The second season opened a day late and probably a couple hundred thousand dollars short. Opening day was supposed to be played in the Wrigley Field splendor with 40,000 baseball hungry fans looking on as the Cubs started off right by beating the Expos and Steve Rogers.

Instead, the opener was rained out sending the 40,000 fans back to work and bringing out 4,802 paid for the day-late season opener. Rogers was one of those who went to work the second day. He shutout the Cubs 3-0 behind homers by Al Oliver and Gary Carter.

It also marked the first game in a Cub uniform for Cey. Cey's transition would, at times, be difficult. Opening day had to be a new, sobering experience for Ron. Usually, Ron was accustomed to home openers being played in 75 degree weather with nearly 50,000 in gorgeous Dodger Stadium. Instead, he stood in a constant drizzle made worse by a gusty north wind that made the 40 degree weather report nothing more than a misleading thermometer reading. He watched along with not-quite 5,000 fans.

To make matters worse, he hit a shot to left field that Tim Raines went high against the wall to grab. Ron found out in a hurry that the wind doesn't always blow out at Wrigley Field.

The next day the Cubs dropped another game and promptly departed for an Eastern swing through weather that made the last week look good.

What would Elia's second club look like? Not much at first.

The trip opened in Cincinnati where the Reds, destined to finish last in the National League West, swept the Cubs in four straight. By the time the Cubs left Cincy, four straight losses to the Reds and six in a row to start the season would seem petty compared to the extra activities in Cincy.

After a Saturday night gathering of media and Cubs brass, Dallas received a call that Noles was in deep trouble.

Noles and a former teammate in the minors, Scott Munninghoff, were involved in a barroom fight. Noles allegedly took his final swings of the evening at a police officer. All hell broke loose.

Dickie injured his knee in the altercation. He went to jail. The next day the media was all over Dickie. It didn't take long for the 1983 season to turn ugly.

As far as the Cubs were concerned in general and for Noles in particular, happiness was seeing Cincinnati in the rear-view mirror.

Less than one week into the season the Cubs had six loses and one pitcher out on bail.

After the sweep was complete the Cubs were off to frigid Montreal. On the way through Canadian customs, Bowa was asked by the agent what he had to claim. Bowa said, "Zero-and-six and I'm not proud of it. And yes, I wouldn't mind leaving it here."

A day later, Trout ruined the Expos' opener by working 8.1 innings before Smith closed a 5-0 victory.

Did the Cubs need a lefthanded starter? Just consider that Steve's win was the first by a Cub lefty starter in more than a season. Dave Geisel was the last lefty before Trout to earn a victory as a starter. Geisel accomplished the rare feat in September of 1981.

The cold weather hung on. Pittsburgh was next and it was no better. There was snow and John Candelaria in Pittsburgh where the Cubs won one game, lost one game to the Pirates and Candy, and lost two games to the weather. The first game of the Sunday doubleheader had to be delayed because of blizzard conditions. It was on to Philly after that.

Nothing much changed. In the first game of the series, John Denny, on his way to the Cy Young Award, knocked the Cubs off. The next night's game was called because of cold weather. It could have been called due to snow, sleet, hail or temperature. Any of the four qualified.

Nothing was going right for the Cubs. Because of the cancellation, they were forced to face Steve Carlton in the makeup game the next night. Lefty dropped the Cubs to 2-10.

Barely two weeks into a season, the Cubs were eight under .500 and 6½ games back. Just 15 days earlier they had left Arizona with hopes of prospering and making strikes toward respectability.

"It's tough sometimes," Moreland said in Philly. "There are a lot of guys on this team who have played on winners. Look at Bowa and Cey. Last year Larry and myself had to adjust to losing. Right now Cey is going through it. Basically, getting your ass kicked takes some getting used to. None of us like it."

Bowa's approach to the game and his dislike for losing

was one of the main reasons Dallas went after Larry. "I know Larry is 37 years old," Dallas said. "But he is the epitome of what I'm talking about—his attitude, his work habits. And I know what he has done for this club. He believes what I believe; that you can never, ever accept losing as part of the deal. Ever."

It was time to regroup. The Cubs took off for Chicago. The frustrations continued to build until Elia exploded following the Friday, April 29th game against the Dodgers in Wrigley field.

The Cubs record was 5-13 before the game. The Cubs were in position to knock off the Dodgers this day. Then Smith came in and threw a wild pitch in the eighth inning allowing the winning run to score.

At 5-14 the Cubs weren't in the best of moods and neither were the 9,000-plus who paid to watch. They booed and howled. All tempers were short. For a second it got to Moreland who had thoughts of going into the stands after a handful of hecklers.

Elia held a clubhouse meeting immediately after the game. Soon after, the press entered. Elia let loose at both the fans and the media. The tape recorders rolled on. The reporters let Elia go and off he went. In the baseball tape library, in the purple language section, sits a tirade that ranks at the top.

It was nearly crushing. Lee apologized less than an hour later but most of the damage had been done. Throughout the week and into the summer, radio stations wouldn't let the subject drop. Not a day went by that some radio station didn't drop in the tape of Elia.

It was unfortunate for a number of reasons, one of which was the opinion of Lee people derived from hearing the tape. In most every situation, there are few finer people than Lee Elia.

His outburst was the culmination of many things. One was breaking spring training with confidence and leaving beautiful weather only to come north and start the season not only in a team slump but in rain, cold and snow.

Another was losing and being subjected to the booing fans at home.

Those two facets, coupled with Lee's strong desire to make the program very successful, very quickly, turned the afternoon's press meeting into a catastrophe and a national story.

The team rallied around Elia the next day. Rainey went out and beat Fernando Valenzuela. Rainey was struggling in the seventh when Lee took the long walk to the mound to pull him. As Lee emerged from the dugout, the fans let him have it. Rainey looked at Lee and said, "Lee, I am really sorry I had to make you come out here and get me."

"Don't worry about it," Lee said. "I had to do it sooner or later."

There were those who contended that Elia's managing changed, that he began managing too cautiously. It ultimately cost him his job.

The Cubs followed with a road trip to the West Coast with Lee's job reported to be in jeopardy. But Dallas wasn't about to pull the trigger. The players hadn't quit on him. The record had been the end result of many things, none of which had to do with too little talent or a lack of respect for the manager. If anything, the players liked Lee too much and Lee worked too hard at trying to be the players' friend as well as their boss. Time and again he would threaten to lay the law down and rip a player to the press. But he rarely did.

It seemed as if everything had turned bad. Cey, for example, hadn't homered as April turned into May. He had a handful of RBIs and was hitting .200. The West Coast trip proved to be his lowest ebb of the year. Especially a game against the Giants at Candlestick Park. The transition for Cey was never tougher. He was charged with two errors and could have had a third.

"I cost the team the game," he said. "The next day I wasn't

sure I even wanted to go to the ballpark. That's never happened to me before. I was that embarrassed. That was the low point."

It wasn't until June that the Cubs started to draw positive attention to themselves. They rallied to open the month with seven straight wins and nine wins in 11 games. Montreal, Philadelphia and the defending champion Cardinals were struggling while trying to establish a dominant pace.

The Cubs closed a 13-game homestand with a three-game series against the Cardinals. With the weather finally turning into summer the Cubs went out and played in front of crowds of 37,024, 40,448 and 38,635, the largest three-game series attendance total in Wrigley Field history.

On Saturday, the Cardinals jumped to an early lead in an NBC televised game. With the capacity crowd chanting "Joo-Dee, Joo-Dee, Joo-Dee," Davis responded with a long homer bringing the Cubs back into the game. It was an incredible scene. It was not a storybook finish, however. Sutter came on to beat the Cubs 5-4 in 10 innings.

But if nothing else, the day's drama brought a new, vocal following for Davis, who had emerged as one of the cornerstones in Green's plan.

The following day, Davis completed the hat trick with a majestic grand slam giving the Cubs a 6-3 win.

The Cubs had climbed back from the dead, but it remained to be seen whether or not they could continue it on the road. Following the Cardinal series they left for a 15-game, four-city trip through four division rival cities. They opened in New York and took two of three.

The game they lost was one in which Lee made the mistake of forgetting Rusty Staub was still available for pinch-hitting duty. With struggling rookie Darryl Strawberry batting in the 10th inning, Elia decided to have Smith walk Darryl.

With runners on first and second, Staub came forward.

Rusty promptly took Lee Smith's fastball to the opposite field for a single scoring the winning run.

The Cubs rallied to take the rubber game of the series and then departed for St. Louis. After Bob Forsch beat the Cubs in the opener, the Cubs received back-to-back complete game victories for the first time in a couple of years. Dick Ruthven, who the Cubs acquired on May 22 for reliever Willie Hernandez, stopped the Cards on two hits Saturday. The next day, Trout allowed four hits and beat the Cards 10-1. The champion Cardinals were still trying to figure out what hit them.

But next was Pittsburgh. The Cubs were forced to play five games in four nights because of the April snow-out. After sweeping Chuck Tanner's team at Wrigley Field four straight 10 days earlier, one would assume the Cubs could manage a couple of victories in Three Rivers Stadium. By now, the Cubs had moved to within two games of the .500 mark and were only three games from the division lead. It was late June and the Cubs were still in the race after the nightmare start.

Suddenly, the nightmare came back into focus. Pittsburgh stunned the Cubs. The Pirates swept all five including a Monday twi-night doubleheader. Pittsburgh won both games in extra innings, both off Bill Campbell. Game 2 ended at 2 a.m. Game 1 ended when Richie Hebner hit a pinch homer.

The Cubs were hurting again. Montreal was next. A Players Association rule stipulates that if a team has to fly to a city and play a game that begins before 6 p.m. then that flight cannot be any longer than 1 hour, 30 minutes.

The Cub players protested the schedule that found them playing a holiday day game in Montreal following the finale in Pittsburgh the night before.

The problem was averted when the plane touched down at Montreal's Mirabel Airport with 10 minutes to spare. Unfortunately, the Players Association contract does not take into consideration the bus ride from Mirabel to downtown Montreal. It is practically a 45-minute trek through the desolate north. Usually, a team flies to Dorval, the metropolitan airport. Mirabel is only used for late arriving or departing flights. Normally, this wouldn't present a problem. But this was not a normal day or week for that matter.

The Cubs managed to win two of four from Montreal and returned with a 6-9 record for the 15-game trip. They were in fifth place, seven games back. But in the N.L. East that wasn't that far from the front.

Before the All-Star break the Cubs had three more games against the Pirates at Wrigley Field followed by five against the Expos.

True to form, the Cubs swept the three from Pittsburgh at Wrigley Field setting up the big series against Montreal.

The Cubs continued to play well with Noles, Rainey and Trout winning the first three games.

On the morning of July 4th, the Cubs were a mere game under .500 with a 38-39 record and only two games off the pace.

They were close . . . but not close enough. Rogers and Scott Sanderson buried the Cubs in a doubleheader sweep.

The Cubs hit the break in fourth place, four games back.

The party was all but over. The season that started horrendously and then had exhibited signs of a possible major upset, settled into a slow, laborious trek to the finish.

The Cubs opened the second half on the West Coast and lost eight of 11. There were only two highlights, Bowa getting the 2,000th hit of his career off Fernando Valenzuela, and Noles, firmly on the way back from a long, soul-searching trip through an alcohol rehabilitation program, pitched great in shutting out the Dodgers.

Ever so slowly the Cubs fell from the race and Elia fell from grace. The fans had all but forgiven him when the Braves came to town in late August. They had a new player named Gerald Perry. Perry beat the Cubs one day and when asked about the scouting report on the Braves rookie, Elia claimed he hadn't received one. Dallas was furious.

Two days later, Elia was fired.

It had to be one of the toughest days in Dallas' baseball career. He had handpicked Lee both as his third base coach with the World Champion Phillies and also as his first manager. Dallas and Lee shared the same vision—to bring a championship to the Cubs and Chicago. The vision was gone. They had dreamed together of bringing glory to the city. On August 22, Lee, dressed in his uniform, was called to Dallas' office and removed as the Cubs' manager.

Dallas looked weary as he made the announcement to the press. Charlie Fox would take over the club. Speculation in the media began. Who would manage the Cubs in 1984? Would it be Jim Fregosi, who was managing the Cardinals' Louisville club? Would it be Charlie? Would it be Gene Mauch? How about Jim Frey?

On the day of the firing, Lee did not meet with the press. Instead, in a show of extreme class, Lee asked that they return the next day. By then his thoughts would be collected, his emotions on an even keel.

The man went out with dignity. It may have been one of the few times in baseball history that a manager who had occasionally feuded with the media nearly brought that same media to tears upon his departure. Lee left the room and went back to Des Plaines. He returned to Florida that afternoon with his wife Penny and daughter Tana.

"I think everyone in Chicago who has said that Dallas

is so Philly-oriented and biased should take note of this,"
Bowa said. "What Dallas did today was something not many
people anywhere could do—fire one of his best friends. It
had to be one of the toughest things he's ever had to do."

The first chapter of the Cubs had been completed. Charlie
Fox picked up the pen and began writing chapter two.

One of the first moves Fox made was the call-up of
Carmelo Martinez from Iowa. Carmelo was playing first base
for Iowa and tearing up the pitching in the American Association. Cub fans desperately needed someone to look forward to. The 1983 season had turned from a spring prom-
ise into an experience not unlike the 30-plus previous attempts at a championship.

Carmelo had a flair and charisma. In his first major-league
at-bat he walked. In his next plate appearance he homered.
From that moment on he had the Wrigley field fans in his
pocket. In early September he hit a three-run eighth-inning
homer to break a tie and give the Cubs a 9-6 victory over
Houston at Wrigley Field. The crowd was delirious. Carmelo
came out for one of the few bows of the season.

In Fox' third game, Rainey took a perfect game into the
seventh inning before Eddie Milner walked. With two outs
in the ninth, Chuck still had a no-hitter. Once again, Milner
ruined it with a single to center.

Rainey settled for a one-hitter. Milner had once again put
his mark on history. It marked the third time in two seasons
that he had ruined a no-hitter. The previous two pitchers
were Noles in April of 1982 and Los Angeles' lefty Jerry
Reuss.

"What," Milner wondered aloud, "was the matter with
pitching a one-hitter?"

Momentum was something Philadelphia finally caught
in a bottle. The Cubs and Mets tangled down the stretch

for the usual indignity of finishing fifth and sixth. The Cubs did prevail.

On September 29, the final irony developed as Hernandez and the Phillies clinched the National League Eastern Division at Wrigley Field. The Phils beat Ruthven 12-6. The Cubs went on to St. Louis for the final three-game series. They entered the series with a 71-88 record. Three victories would give them a 74-88 mark, one win better than Dallas' first Cub team.

The Cards swept leaving the Cubs 71-91, two games behind the 1982 club.

It was eight days earlier that Tribune Company made a major move at finishing off the Cubs' front office staff. On September 21, Tribune Company announced that Jim Finks, long involved in every aspect of pro sports and a fixture in Chicago sports for the last decade, would take over as the President and Chief Executive Officer of the club.

Finks had resigned from his position as the Executive Vice President and General Manager of the Chicago Bears just a month earlier.

Finks would give added direction. He would also allow Dallas to spend more time trying to develop the on-the-field product. Jim Finks would take care of the off-the-field segment of the organization.

The initial response from the media was that the two would never get along. The press contended that they were too much alike. But as time wore on, it became evident that Dallas and Jim complemented each other perfectly.

In retrospect, the 1983 season was certainly one of advancement, although record and the managerial change made the first impressions seem just the opposite.

Yet, there were reasons for some of the failure and there were also reasons to think positively.

The Cubs had been beset with injuries most notably to Hall and Durham, who spent a combined total of 112 games away from the club. Noles also missed considerable time as he tried to correct his off-the-field problem.

Still the Cubs established themselves as a club that lacked only pitching. Offensively, they led the league in slugging (.401) and were second in runs scored (701) to Atlanta.

Cey rebounded for 24 homers and 90 RBI and Davis suddenly became one of the Cubs' greatest offensive catchers with 24 homers and 84 RBI. Moreland worked as hard as anyone to get a grip on playing right field. He also led the club with a .302 average and had 16 homers and 79 RBI. The Cubs had 140 homers, their best total in a decade.

Defensively the club also showed improvement. They led the league in fielding. Sandberg turned from a very good third baseman his rookie year to an outstanding second baseman his second year. He won the first Gold Glove by a Cub since 1970 while leading the league in percentage (.986), assists (571), total chances (914), double plays (126) and games played (157). He became the first player in the National League to win the Gold Glove in his first year at a new position.

He was gradually grabbing the attention around Chicago. Soon it would come on a national level.

Bowa worked daily with Sandberg. It not only helped Ryno win the Gold Glove it also helped Bowa lead the league's shortstops in fielding percentage (.984). The club finished with a club record low 115 errors.

On October 6, the guessing game ended. The Cubs announced Jim Frey would take over as the Cubs' manager. Frey had been Earl Weaver's right hand man for 10 seasons. He managed the Kansas City Royals into the World Series in his first year as a manager (1980). His Royals lost to Dallas' Phillies.

He was fired during the 1981 strike season. He spent the 1982 and 1983 seasons coaching for the Mets. Frey had been credited with much of the development of Darryl Strawberry. Jim also had the chance to watch the Cubs the last two seasons. He, at least, had a feel for what had gone on.

It was during the Mets last visit that Billy Connors, Frey's pitching coach with the Royals, brought Frey up to Dallas' home in Winnetka for a meeting.

The die was cast. Frey would lead the Cubs. All signs pointed to a brighter 1984 if only because the Cubs were due for some breaks.

In his inaugural press conference, Frey began captivating the media that had known very little about him when his name first came up in August.

When someone asked about challenges, Frey responded, "I'll tell you what a challenge is. A challenge is being too short to play, not being able to see real well and wanting to play in the big leagues. I know all about challenges.

"I know Dallas is going to go out and get me the players I think we need to win. I don't know how many games we'll win. All I know is that I'm not afraid to go out there every day, day-by-day, and win as many as possible."

The winter meetings opened in Nashville at the Grand Ole Opry hotel. The Cubs had established themselves as a good offensive team and an above-average defensive team. All that was lacking was pitching and every team in baseball knew it. Give the Cubs a few good arms and there was no telling what trouble they might cause.

Again the Cubs' main marketable player was Buckner. Martinez' exciting play in September at first base coupled with the Cubs' desire to have Durham play first, squeezed an already tight position. Buck was the oldest and the highest paid. It made sense to try and bring in a pitcher for Bill.

But the Buckner deal would have to wait because the interest never reached a serious level. Dallas wasn't going to give Buckner away just so he could move him. Buckner stayed and the heir apparent at first, Durham, again found himself waiting for the first shoe to drop.

The one deal Dallas consummated at the meetings was a big one. San Diego General Manager Jack McKeon kept close watch on Dallas. McKeon was only a player or two away from a team that could win the West and he knew that while most of the other teams were going to stand pat, the Cubs and Dallas wouldn't. Make Dallas an offer, McKeon reasoned, and anything was possible.

After a couple of days of deliberating McKeon came up with a deal that would send the Cubs the starting pitcher they desperately wanted—Scott Sanderson. To get Scott, the Padres had to send lefty reliever Gary Lucas to the Expos. The Padres, who had cornered the market on left-handed pitching, found Montreal eager to get Lucas. The Expos had gone most of the 1983 season with only one lefty—reliever Dan Schatzeder.

McKeon needed Sanderson like San Diego needs more sand. What McKeon wanted was one of the Cubs' prime kids, Carmelo. With Martinez being basically a one-position player and with that position being first, currently occupied by not only Buckner but also Durham, Dallas would let Martinez go. McKeon also wanted lefty reliever Craig Lefferts from the Cubs to replace Lucas. Third baseman Fritz Connally, the big power-hitting minor league third baseman was also shipped to McKeon. Connally could crush minor league pitching but as soon as the fastball made the jump from 88 to 92 miles per hour his bat speed couldn't keep him from heading south.

The deal was complete and as usual the fans and press howled. Here Dallas was giving away another prize kid (Martinez), the only lefty reliever (Lefferts) on the club and another potential prize (Connally).

Nobody ever bothered to ask, where were the Cubs go-

ing to play Martinez? Where had they finished the season
before with Lefferts in the bullpen? And who in the big
leagues was Connally going to be able to hit against with
success? More importantly, few took into account that the
1984 Cubs could not start out with the same pitching staff
that the 1983 Cubs finished with.

If nothing else, Sanderson took over as the No. 1 starter
and pushed the whole staff back a notch, making at least
a few pitchers more comfortable in their more accustomed
role and, of course, making more than a few pitchers aware
that unless they produced in spring training the only way
they would see the Cubs would be on cable television.

The Cubs had tried to go to Boston with a Buckner deal.
The names thrown around were lefty John Tudor or his
pitching teammates Dennis Eckersley or Bob Ojeda and even
Bruce Hurst. Boston instead went to Pittsburgh trading
Tudor for Mike Easler.

The Cubs' other major pre-spring training acquisition was
outfielder-infielder-pinch-hitter Richie Hebner. Hebner
wasn't going to re-sign with Pittsburgh. Dallas knew Hebner's style and record from the days they spent together
in the Philadelphia organization. Hebner had played on
seven division champions. He knew how to win, how to
play hard and how to make people laugh. Dallas figured
he didn't have enough players that possessed all three char-
acteristics so he went after Hebner.

If Hebner did nothing all season for the Cubs, people
figured it was a good deal because Hebner had lifetime stats
against the Cubs that, carried out over an entire career,
would have made Hebner one of the all-time baseball greats.
He hit 30 homers against the Cubs and batted .330. If
nothing else, he couldn't kill the Cubs in 1984.

The other changes were in the dugout. Frey went after
the best baseball man he knew to coach third—Don Zim-

mer. Zim had coached for the Yankees the year before and had had enough of George Steinbrenner and Billy Martin and all the side shows.

Frey and Zimmer had known each other since their high school days at Cincinnati's Western Hills. They'd known each other and each other's family for 40 years. When building a coaching staff, the manager has to look at how that group will relate to him and to each other. Seeing eye-to-eye is imperative for the coaching staff. Nothing says they all have to get along and agree with everything that is said and implemented but they had better realize each other's role and respect the knowledge each one brings to the park everyday.

The hiring of Zimmer meant Frey was getting a great friend and the equivalent of a second manager in the dugout. Whenever a managerial job came up, Zimmer's name was always one of the first mentioned.

The Cubs also brought in Johnny Oates to serve as the bullpen coach and work extensively with Jody. In 1982, people were saying that Jody's defense was good enough that anything he hit was a bonus. The next year his offensive production rose, making him one of the best hitting catchers in the game. Unfortunately, his defense crashed. His percentage of throwing out baserunners attempting to steal dipped drastically. He also committed a league-leading 21 passed balls for a pitching staff that didn't need any more obstacles.

"It was my concentration," Davis said. "I've got to work on putting two good aspects of my game together in one season. I know that now."

Frey's first spring training with the Cubs opened on February 15. At first, he didn't know what he had. There were positions to fill, but by-and-large the everyday players were set.

Nobody was going to move Cey off third or Bowa and Sandberg from the middle of the infield. Jody was a fixture behind the plate.

The outfield was a little less settled. Durham was in left begrudgingly. Hall was in center field and Moreland in right field. There was also Joe Carter, the Rookie of the Year in the American Association in 1983, and Henry Cotto, a quick, defensively-strong outfielder.

Carter was the player who deserved the longest look in spring training. Cotto was nothing more than a longshot at the outset, but slowly played his way onto the team. While the three regular outfielders continued to have trouble with easy fly balls, Cotto did nothing wrong.

"Our main objective," Frey said, "is to get our pitching staff in order. It's a must."

The rumors began early with Buckner once again being in the spotlight. The rumors had Buckner going to San Francisco. The Giants reportedly offered pitcher Bill Laskey. Dallas said they had to come up with more.

The Cubs liked Chili Davis, who had an exceptional rookie season in 1982 before winding up in Frank Robinson's doghouse. The Giants at first wouldn't consider moving Davis. Finally, a package seemed to be ready: Buckner and Carter to the Giants for Laskey and Davis.

Practically everyone accepted the deal. Reportedly, the only party who didn't was Bob Lurie, the only real party on the Giants' side of the table that had the ultimate say. Lurie owns the ballclub. Chili Davis wasn't going anywhere, as far as Lurie was concerned. The deal fell through.

Within a couple of days, the Giants found the first baseman they had been looking for. They acquired Al Oliver from Montreal for pitcher Fred Breining and a player to be named later, Max Venable.

Buckner would not be a Giant.

The first spring training uproar was about to start.

Buckner, who had the right to veto a trade, told Dallas he would only accept a deal if it was made before spring training. Dallas said he would do all he could, but it takes two to tango. Would Buckner turn down any trade offers even though spring training was past the early stages?

Dallas went on record saying that Buckner had better approve an acceptable deal or be prepared to spend the season sitting on the bench. A no-trade clause would not hold Dallas up from trying to build a pitching staff. The Cubs had made the decision that Durham had to play first. The amount of time Leon had spent on the DL was always going to stand in his way and the club's way. If he played first his chances of pulling up lame would be decreased.

When the spring games finally began, Frey couldn't believe what he was watching. Had he been in the stands scouting for another organization he might have laughed. Unfortunately, this was his club.

After a week of spring training games the team looked set—set for disaster. An 11-game losing steak was in progress, an incredible feat considering that spring training is a tough place for any team to lose that many games against teams playing a conglomeration of minor and major league talent.

On Saturday, March 10, before a game against the Brewers in Mesa, the Cub pitchers were standing in the outfield shagging flies. In right field, two minor league pitchers on the big-league roster, Bill Johnson and Reggie Patterson, started talking. Suddenly they were no longer talking. The first fight of the spring camp had erupted.

Not only did the ball club look ragged in the early going, but there were two pitchers with major league potential trying to dismember each other.

On March 17, an era ended. Fergie, who had been ineffective in a handful of "B" games, was called into Dallas' office on a sunny, Saturday morning. He knew what the meeting was about. Fergie was told he was being released.

"Releasing him at this point gives Fergie an opportunity to catch on with another club if he wants to," Dallas said.

Fergie went back to the Mezona Hotel. He flipped on an NCAA basketball tournament game and began packing.

"I've got no regrets," he said. "It's been a long, fulfilling career. Sure I would have liked to have won 300 but I still have a lot of great memories that no one will ever be able to take away."

Fergie Jenkins was finished. His record was 284-226. A new life began for Fergie at 40.

"At least now I can start playing in all the Old-Timers Games like the rest of the guys I came up with are doing. Nothing lasts forever."

Ten days after the first fight, the Cubs were in oven-baked Yuma for a game against the Padres. There were perhaps 500 people in the stands watching the Cubs take batting practice at Desert Sun Stadium. Ruthven was standing behind second base putting batting practice balls into a container.

Hall was standing in the outfield fooling around when Rufus asked Mel to pick up a couple of baseballs. The unprintable was spoken and soon Ruthven, a million-dollar pitcher, and Hall, an aspiring outfielder, were rolling around in short-center field. Players came from all directions trying to restore order.

It happens, everyone agreed. Maybe once a year.

"I've seen it happen before," Bowa said. "But never on the same team . . . in spring training . . . ten days apart."

Frey, who had spent more than three decades in the game called a meeting immediately—right in short-center in front of the Yuma fans.

"The fighting," Frey said, "is over. From now on we'll do it on the field in trying to win some ball games."

The talk was successful in cooling the fistiana. It didn't do much for the losing streak. That day Carmelo Martinez took Lee Smith over the wall in the ninth inning for a game-winning homer.

It was on to Palm Springs, another four hours by bus through California's answer to Hell's Kitchen. The Cubs were on a road below sea level to Palm Springs. They were also playing well below sea level.

The Cubs played one game in Palm Springs against Gene Autry's Angels. The Cubs lost. It was time to get back on the bus and drive six more hours back to Phoenix and Mesa.

The losing continued. On March 25 the record was 3-18. At one point the Cubs had more fights than wins. Sanderson was getting clobbered, fights were breaking out, outfielders were running fly patterns into each other and Dallas was running up an incredible phone bill.

"We've got a plan," Frey said one day. "Everything will be alright. Trust me." It was an obvious attempt at self-hypnosis.

Then the pieces began fitting together. According to later reports, the Phillies had decided sometime earlier that, in the event catcher Bo Diaz was ever sidelined for any length of time, Ozzie Virgil wouldn't be able to catch every day.

The Phillies went looking for a back-up catcher. They liked John Wockenfuss of the Tigers. John was a versatile, experienced player. The Tigers wanted Greg Gross, basically the same type of player and close in age to Wockenfuss. Gross, reportedly, vetoed the deal through the five-and-ten rule.

The Phillies were still interested in Wockenfuss. The deal grew until the Tigers, Phillies and Giants sprung it on the baseball world.

On Saturday, March 24, the Giants sent first baseman Dave Bergman to the Phillies for minor league outfielder

Al Sanchez. The Phils turned around and traded Bergman and reliever Willie Hernandez to the Tigers for Wockenfuss and outfielder Glenn Wilson.

As the players were announced, Dallas held his breath. Finally, all the names were public. Dallas was ecstatic. His plans had not been jeopardized. In fact, the chances improved on two accounts: 1) Philadelphia had acquired another outfielder in Wilson, and 2) they had lost a solid reliever in Hernandez.

The Phils were looking for a reliever and trying to ease the outfield jam they had created.

Dallas soon finalized the first deal of the spring. On Monday, he acquired Tim Stoddard from the A's in exchange for two minor leaguers—Stan Boderick and Stanley Kyles. Stoddard had been with Oakland only a couple of months. He had been acquired during the off-season from the World Champion Orioles in exchange for third baseman Wayne Gross.

Frey knew Stoddard from his days in Baltimore. At one point the former college basketball player (he played on the N.C. State NCAA championship team with David Thompson), was considered one of the best relievers in the game. Somewhere he had lost it. Frey had faith that Tim could get it back together. With that deal complete, the team departed on the two-hour drive to Tucson to play the Indians. While every pitcher and every reliever in camp wondered what Stoddard's arrival meant, Dallas was back in Mesa running up the phone bill.

Not making the trip to Tucson was Buckner. Bill instead made a trip into Dallas' office where he was told of the latest proposal. Dallas had another chance to deal with the Phillies in what would change the look and style of the team. The Phils wanted Buckner. A deal that would increase Buckner's bank account was possible, very possible.

But Dallas warned, "don't try and hold the Phillies up for too much money in compensation for approving the deal. The Phils won't go too high."

While Buckner contemplated, the names remained on the table. Buckner and Bill Campbell would go to the Phillies for outfielders Gary Matthews and Bob Dernier and pitcher Kevin Gross. The trade came out in the Philadelphia newspaper. Then Buckner's demands hit Bill Giles. Giles flatly refused to make the move.

In the meantime, Dernier and Matthews had said goodbye to many of their former teammates. Both loved playing in Philly when they played, but neither was playing.

Just a couple of days earlier, the Phils tried to send Dernier back to the minors again. After trying to pass him through waivers they discovered Dallas still coveted the leadoff portion of the Dernier-Sandberg tandem that tore up three minor leagues. When Dallas claimed Dernier, the Phillies were forced to either trade Dernier or keep him on the outfielder-packed major league roster. Their hands were tied. Dallas was about to land his catch.

The big question that remained was who would go to Philly instead of Buckner. The Phillies selected minor league first baseman-catcher Mike Diaz. Philly pulled back Kevin Gross and threw in reliever Porfi Altamirano. Diaz had shown the Cubs two things during the spring. First, it looked as if he could hit and hit with power. Second, it didn't look like he could catch every day or play first every day for the Cubs.

In Philadelphia the fans were furious. The radio talk shows were calling for the scalps of Huey Alexander, the Phils' chief scout, and Paul Owens. People were livid. Once again, Dallas and the Cubs had dealt with the Phillies and the people felt the Cubs had once again come away with loaded pockets.

As one Philadelphia fan wrote, "Dallas can never be satisfied with just getting one player for one player. No, he has to have two-for-one (Sandberg and Bowa for DeJesus), three-for-one (Moreland, Noles and Larson for Krukow) and now three-for-two.

"Dallas," the man continued, "when you won the World Championship in Philadelphia in 1980 we loved you. But now you're nothing but a thief."

Another fan considered the inevitable to have just taken place. "I knew that one day the Phillies would do it," he said. "They've traded for a player they already had (Diaz joining catcher Bo Diaz)."

What didn't help matters was the first report that Buckner was coming to Philly. The fans could accept that deal. Buckner would more than replace Pete Rose at first.

But Buckner was still a Cub. In a column the day after the aborted trade, Buckner took off against Dallas. After Dallas hung the column on Buckner's locker, Bill went after the author, the *Tribune*'s Bob Verdi. Buckner claimed Verdi had misquoted him. The furor died down during the next couple of days.

Through all the extra events, the Cubs had suddenly found themselves as an overnight contender. Dernier filled a couple of voids—one as a leadoff hitter and the other as a bonafide center fielder. Matthews not only filled Durham's left field spot—allowing Bull to move to first—but he also provided the Cubs with the No. 3 hitter in the lineup—Buckner's usual position. Most important, though, Matthews was bringing with him great leadership qualities. No matter how talented a club is, it must have that leader, that guy who anyone can talk to, the guy who goes out of his way to say hello to the new kid and who plays day-in, day-out as if each game were his last game. Matthews was it. The first Cub leader since Bill Madlock.

An hour after the deal, Matthews and Dernier dialed Dallas. First the Sarge got on the line, "Dallas," he said, "what took you so long?"

The surface improvements were many. The underlying improvements were also becoming more-and-more evident. For the first time in years, nay decades, there was competition on the club for starting positions. The bench would have Buckner on it as well as either Hall or Moreland and Hebner.

Dallas had not only called Buckner's number, he had taken a secure situation for many players and suddenly put them all on call. There were no more free jobs. It was indeed unique for a Cubs team to be so well fortified.

The problem of upgrading the pitching staff was still unsolved. But now at least Dallas had two wild cards left in his hand—Buckner and either Moreland or Hall. He also had another ace up his sleeve in Carter, who was whisked out of the picture by Matthews' arrival.

The players were irate. Buckner was hot. Moreland and Hall were dejected. It was as if Dallas had broken up the 1927 Yankees. Some players and fans must have forgotten that this Cubs team was 71-91 in 1983 and was utterly terrible and unpredictable in spring training. What was Dallas to do? Sit and watch the third year follow the path of the first two?

"I can sit back and tell people I'm trying and not do anything," he said. "I've got a five-year contract. I could just sit back and let them pay me. But that's not me. I'm determined to get this job done."

Besides Carter, Don Schulze, the strong-armed righty of the Cubs' Iowa staff, was returned to the minor league complex. At first, he balked but later reported to Fitch Park, three blocks south of the major league park, HoHoKam.

"It takes a kid two minutes to travel the three blocks from the minor league complex to the major league complex," Cubs trainer Tony Garofalo said. "But it takes them two days to find their way back."

It also took a few days for Matthews and Dernier to arrive in Arizona from the Phillies' Clearwater, Fl camp. In the interim, there were some players who wondered where they fit in.

There were also fans in Chicago who were disturbed that the deal landed Buckner on the bench.

But overnight the job had been done. Suddenly, there was a new intensity. Suddenly, everyone felt the Cubs could not only compete, but also possibly contend. There were now too many players who wouldn't let it be any other way. Dallas knew he had acquired both a very good player and a leader in Matthews. He only hoped Dernier's talents hadn't been frozen through inactivity.

"If he hits .240 and plays great center field," Dallas said, "we'll be thrilled. I just hope that he hasn't rusted away his hitting talents by sitting most of the last couple of years."

Time would tell.

In the final few exhibition games, the Cubs began putting it together. This would be an interesting team. It had balance, it had speed, it had power and it had youth and age.

They also had become a group bound and determined to prove they could contribute. Bowa, Cey and Matthews had all been cast aside by winning teams. All had been told that they no longer fit into the plans of their former clubs. All three have great pride and they made it their personal unspoken crusade to prove them wrong.

There was also Moreland and Hall who were trying to prove that the Cubs were wrong in trying to deal them out of a job. There was Davis, Durham and Sandberg, the young guys who found themselves vital parts of the blend. Matthews and Dernier were both out to prove Philly wrong. In the resulting domino effect, they pulled the club up a notch on the intensity level. Cey, for one, noticed the changes in attitude on the club. He was more comfortable. By the time spring training was over, Cey had drawn a bright conclusion.

"I don't see as much of the negative attitude as I did last

year," he said. "When I was with the Dodgers the questions were always how we were going to stay in first place. I never heard that here the first season.

"This year I've got a greater overall outlook. I'm not one to sugar-coat. I'm honest and outspoken. But I look at what we have and who we have to play against and I think we'll be right in the middle of it. I wouldn't say that if I didn't feel it.

"Frankly, I've gotten tired of hearing how the Cubs haven't won for 39 years. We have nothing to do with that. But the only way to change that is to go out and win."

Amid the turmoil and new faces, the Cubs broke camp Sunday, April 1 and departed for San Francisco and the season opener on Tuesday. They left Arizona with a 7-20 record, the worst in baseball. But that record meant nothing now.

The Cubs were starting fresh and heading for the West Coast where, ironically, an astrologer had predicted an incredible year.

The astrologer predicted in January that 1984 would be the year of the Cubs. The prediction contended that there would be turmoil and tension in the clubhouse. But by August the team would jell and become awesome and would win a title.

At first glance, the astrologer was already right. The turmoil and tension was there as the Cubs' United Airlines charter lifted off the runway and headed into the sunset, off to catch the sun that was dipping into the mighty Pacific.

It was off to San Francisco. The great chase, the greatest of all sports marathons, was about to begin.

2 1984: A Journal

The opener.

Openers are always beautiful. They are like newborns. For one day, everything about the season is perfect. Everyone starts even—from dynasties to doormats. Every team takes its first step. A baseball season awakens like a child opening its eyes. On to San Francisco.

The Giants knew the Cubs and the Cubs knew the Giants. They had met numerous times during the spring. There would be no surprises.

Once San Francisco's Huey Lewis & the News opened the day's festivities with the National Anthem, the Cubs proved that maybe, just maybe, the club would be respectable.

Dick Ruthven earned the starting assignment for the Cubs. It was the first for Rufus even though he had been in the big leagues more than 10 years. There was no Carlton to shield the spotlight from him.

The Giants opened the scoring in the first but the Cubs came back with a single run in the fourth and took the lead in the sixth on Moreland's homer. After the Giants tied it in their half of the sixth, the Cubs came back with two more runs in the seventh with Moreland again contributing. Davis had the big hit—a two-run double. Cey's homer in the ninth gave the Cubs a 5-2 lead and the insurance they needed. Everything went as planned as Frey brought in Smith for the first save of 1984 and a 5-3 Cubs victory.

First place. In a blink of the eye the Cubs led the National League East. Of course, they had company since two other teams were 1-0. But why not brag? The last time the Cubs were in first was opening day two years earlier.

After the April 3 opener, the Cubs took the next day off. Frey put the club through a workout at Candlestick just prior to the 3 p.m. wind song off the ocean.

Frey is told that both Moreland and Hall as well as Buckner are not happy about their roles as platoon and bench players. Frey spits tobacco juice on the grass, digests the question and utters, "Who gives a damn? I don't care who is happy. All I want is for everybody to play hard when they are in there. That's all I care about."

And so the great summer was on. Frey had everybody in a place and a place for everybody. Funny how it all came together so quickly. Just a week earlier he was on a bus to Tucson awaiting word that the Cubs had added Tim Stoddard to the bullpen. He was also awaiting some semblance of an outfield.

"Just give me somebody who can catch the ball," he said. "At least once in a while."

Also on the off day, Matthews and Durham, the veteran and the rising star, run lap after lap in Candlestick. A friendship has already begun to grow.

It wasn't until Thursday night that the Cubs and Giants met again. Once again the Cubs prevailed, stopping their former teammate Mike Krukow with a six-run fifth inning.

Check that. Few of the 1984 Cubs could legitimately call Krukow a former teammate. As the season opened there were only four players left from the team Dallas inherited— Buckner, Smith, Durham and Davis. Hall played only 10 games for the 1981 club.

The plane takes off for San Diego and a date with the favorite Padres. San Diego has loaded up over the winter.

They have a great balanced pitching staff, outstanding speed, a great young outfield and enough veterans to make it work.

Arrival in San Diego is 2 a.m. Thank goodness the airport and the hotel are practically adjacent. There is one problem, however. The hotel is undergoing massive renovations. It will be wake-up call by jackhammer in the morning.

The Cubs and Padres battle until the end in their first meeting. The end came in the bottom of the ninth when pinch-hitter Champ Summers hit a slicing double into the Padres' bullpen at the base of the left-field foul pole. Garry Templeton, who had singled with one out, kept right on running. Bowa's relay throw from behind third was right on the money. Moreland, who replaced Davis behind the plate, thought he had Templeton out. But Lanny Harris, who came from his first base post to make the call at the plate, disagreed.

"We got robbed," Moreland said. "There is no way he's safe."

The decision stayed and cost Frey the first injury of the season.

"I pulled a muscle running out to save Moreland and to argue," Frey said. "I'll be alright. I just wish we would have got that call. It could have gone either way."

It was the Cubs' first loss of the season. The Padres, favorites in the West, were the only remaining undefeated team in the league.

The game also featured the debut in a Cub uniform of Sanderson. He went six innings and didn't pitch badly. The Cubs just couldn't get anything going against lefty Tim Lollar, which should come as no surprise. He has beaten the Cubs a few times the last couple of years.

The Cubs could have averted the loss in the ninth when they rallied. But after Sid Monge walked Henry Cotto to fill the bases and followed that by walking pinch-hitter Richie Hebner forcing in the tying run, Sandberg fanned.

Saturday in San Diego. An afternoon at harborside. This place is almost too relaxing.

The Cubs grab a 4-1 lead against Ed Whitson. Trout is breezing along until the third, fourth and fifth innings when he looks like he did in 1983. The Padres take a 5-4 lead in the fifth and add two more in the seventh off Porfi Altamirano.

The guy who killed the Cubs was Kevin McReynolds. He doubled in two runs in the fifth and then delivered a two-run triple in the seventh. This guy can play. With McReynolds, flanked by Martinez in left and Tony Gwynn in right, the Padres have the youngest outfield in the league and probably one of the best offensively.

Even down 7-4, the Cubs came back in the ninth to make it interesting. The Cubs loaded the bases in the ninth off Rich Gossage with one out. Moreland flew to Gwynn. With two outs, Davis drilled a single to right scoring Sandberg and Buckner bringing the Cubs to within one. But Goose got Tom Veryzer to ground into a forceout.

With Eric Show working on Sunday it looked like the Padres had a great chance to sweep. Show came into the game with a lifetime record of 4-0 and a 1.96 ERA against the Cubs. No pitcher in the league handled the Cubs better than Show in the last two seasons.

For six innings, it was a grand pitching duel with Ruthven matching Show. The score was 1-1 after six and then suddenly all that good pitching went south.

The Cubs took a 2-1 lead in the seventh, the Padres countered with two runs and a 3-2 lead a half-inning later. The Cubs tied it in the eighth on Hall's first homer of the season.

In the ninth, the Cubs pulled away with two runs, both walked in by Monge. In two games he walked in three runners. That's pretty tough to do.

The Padres, to their credit, stayed with it. They retied it in the ninth with a pair of runs that scored on ground outs. The game moved into the 10th.

With two outs and a runner on second, Cotto hit a grounder to Templeton. Garry isn't the great shortstop he once was, but he is still very good. He must have taken his eye off the ball because he never came up with it. Lake, who was on second, stopped at third. Sandberg followed with a triple to deep right-center scoring both runners. Ryno then stole home. The 8-5 lead held up.

"What I liked most about this game was the way we came back and kept coming back," Frey said. "Sure they did the same thing. But you've got to like what we did today. We could have just said the hell with it."

Another plus was the play of Cotto. He didn't do anything to make anyone miss Dernier. Bobby injured his arm running into the center field fence at Candlestick in the second game. He'll be out for a little while. At least it's early and it won't hurt to see Cotto play.

The Cubs bus to L.A. with a 3-2 record. Not bad at all. The consensus before the trip was that the Cubs should be satisfied with a 3-4 West Coast swing. There was speculation at one point that a 0-7 trip was a possibility. A possibility that would have made everyone a mite leery about returning to Chicago.

The Dodgers throw Jerry Reuss in the first game of the two-game series and Rick Honeycutt in the second game. They win both with great pitching performances. The Cubs' offense sputters but, all things considered, it could be worse. Cotto, playing in center, makes two great catches. Where did he come from?

The Cubs arrive back in Chicago with a 3-4 record. It's daybreak in the Windy City. Those players who live in the city during the off-season haven't been home since mid-February. The plane lands. It is April 12.

The home opener. Friday the 13th. Thirty-nine years without a pennant. Why does superstition want to creep into the picture? As usual, the goat makes its Wrigley Field appearance. As legend has it, the Cubs wouldn't let a restaurant owner's goat into the ballpark for the 1945 World Series. The owner put a hex on the club and for that reason and that reason alone, the Cubs haven't won anything since.

Forget porous infields and 5.33 ERAs and catchers with long, bizarre names. Forget all that meaningless garbage. It was the goat and only the goat.

That taken care of, the Cubs got their first look at the Mets and their phenom Dwight Gooden. The kid struck out 300 batters in 191 innings last year in the minors. Anyone who strikes out 300 in any season against any competition, even goats, is worth taking a look at.

The Cubs counter with Trout. A crowd of 33,436 comes to Wrigley Field for the 70th opening day in the park's grand history. Under a dishwater gray sky, the Cubs start off against the kid.

They score in the first with Matthews singling home Sandberg who doubled. In the fourth, the Cubs explode and take advantage of the tentativeness of Gooden. Having stolen two bases already, they steal two more in the fourth and add five runs, knocking out Gooden and leaving him with a distinct dislike for Wrigley Field. "For the rest of my career, the Cubs are on my list," he threatens.

The Cubs romp in the opener 11-2. Trout, believe it or not, goes the distance. He says he has rededicated his career after the birth of his first child, a daughter Tatum Ashley. Of course it helped that Connors had warned Trout that this season was his last shot. One more reason was a huge salary that could be his after the season as he would test the free agent waters for the first time.

"I feel great about what I did today," he says. "I haven't had the greatest amount of success."

The worse part of the day was the fans reaction to Durham. They were booing Durham because Buckner wasn't playing. It got real tough when Bull struck out for the third time. He finally silenced them with a triple.

"I'm pulling for Bull," Buckner said. "I wish the fans would stop booing Bull. I realize it is in appreciation for what I've done, but it's not a good situation."

"I'll have to deal with it," Bull said. "It's not my fault Buck's not playing."

The biggest opening day ovation went to Buckner. "It was one of my biggest thrills," he said.

Ruthven makes it two straight the following day as the Cubs down the Mets and Tim Leary 5-2. Another well-pitched game coupled with some calculated hitting. The first inning for the Cubs is a bit bizarre.

After Dernier makes the first out, Sandberg, Matthews, Durham, Cey and Hall all reach safely only to run themselves out of the inning. The Cubs had five of six batters reach, they scored three times and were out of the inning.

The third-place Cubs, a game out and a game over .500 at 5-4 watch the rains fall. The finale against the Mets is rained out and rescheduled for August. The first game of the St. Louis series is lost to rain and replayed as part of a doubleheader the next day.

Joaquin Andujar takes it to the Cubs. Shuts them out 5-0 on only five hits. Is this the first crack or was this just a great pitching performance?

The second game proves the latter. Sanderson is superb through 8.2 and the Cubs use another big inning—a four-run sixth, to beat the Cards 6-1 in Game 2.

Trout puts together his second straight complete game in the last game of the series against St. Louis. It is hard to believe, but he is 2-1 with back-to-back complete games.

After the game Trout comes out with the incredible:

"We've got a chance to win this thing," he says. "I mean we could run away with it with the type of team we have."

It sounds crazy, but it also vocalizes the feeling throughout the clubhouse—the feeling Matthews and Dernier brought with them and added to the club. They are the fires that lit the fuse planted in Dallas' first two years. The Sarge said it all: "Everybody should know right up front that I take losing personally."

The Cubs close out their first homestand by splitting two games with the Pirates and losing another game to rain. Easter Sunday is washed out. Another doubleheader. Is this setting a bad precedent? Do the Cubs have the pitching to survive all these future make-up doubleheaders? What will this do to the attendance? With a new $1 million clubhouse and huge salaries to pay the club can't afford any missed dates. And they've already lost three on the first homestand.

The first game against Pittsburgh proves to be a character-builder. With the score tied after nine, Sandberg leads off the Cubs' 10th against Kent Tekulve, who is very tough on righthanded hitters. Sandberg triples. Two intentional walks later, Hall singles in the winning run.

Another highlight is Matthews who clubs a three-run homer. The fans are beginning to appreciate his style, his approach. He's what the club has been missing. He's no cure-all. But he sure was needed.

After the rain-out it's off to St. Louis. The second trip.

Busch Stadium. The old Bleacher Bums used to come to St. Louis and raise all kinds of hell. One of their favorite sayings was: "The beer is Busch, the Stadium's Busch, the fans are Busch and the team is Busch." When it's Cubs vs Cardinals, the fans are always there.

The Cubs come back with Sanderson and once again he is beautiful. He leaves after seven innings with a 3-2 lead after allowing only two hits. Two hits that produced two runs. Same old Cardinals.

It's a cool night and Frey removes Sanderson with the lead. It's not until the Cubs reach the Cardinal bullpen for three runs in the eighth that everyone rests easy. St. Louis has buried many Cub hopes here. But not tonight.

Frey continues to give Dernier some time off and plays Cotto again in center. He really likes Cotto. In fact, during spring training he was perhaps the only staff member who wanted to keep seeing more of Cotto. Dernier rides the bench.

After the game, a reporter is talking with Dernier for 20 minutes despite the fact that Dernier hadn't played. Hebner, who Dallas got almost as much for his humor and good cheer as his bat, walks by the reporter and Dernier and says, "What happened? Did his house burn down?"

It's a classic line.

The next night, Hebner delivers on the field. Trout hooks up with Danny Cox in a good pitching duel until the sixth. The Cards go ahead 2-1 and knock out Trout.

With a 2-1 lead in the eighth, Whitey Herzog goes to Sutter. Sandberg leads off with a double. Matthews and Durham follow with singles and the Cubs have tied it. After Hall is walked intentionally to fill the bases, it almost looks as if the Cubs have finally gotten Sutter's number after a couple of years of floundering. But Sutter survives when he gets Davis to ground into a rare 1-2-3 double play. The Cubs' hearts are almost broken.

The Cards threaten off Stoddard in their half of the eighth but don't score. In the Cubs' ninth lightning strikes.

Frey had sent up Hebner to pinch hit in the seventh. He singled. When Frey figured that Herzog would probably come in with Sutter with the lead, he decided to go against the grain and give Hebner another swing. He kept Hebner in the game playing right field.

In the ninth, the gamble paid nicely. With one out, Hebner lined a Sutter pitch into the right field seats. The Cubs had stunned the Cards, stunned Sutter and probably even stunned themselves a little. With Smith pitching, the Cubs held on for a 3-2 win.

"Who knows," Vukovich said. "There may come a time in this season when we look back on this game as something important."

The next day the Cubs and Cards go at it again. This time the Cards handle the Cubs and Ruthven easily, 7-5. The loss drops the Cubs out of first place by a game. They had enjoyed one day in first place for the first time in five years at this point in the season. It's not much to brag about just three weeks into the season, but it beats talking about fifth.

After an offday in Pittsburgh, the Cubs come out flat against Rick Rhoden who holds them to three hits and one run in six innings.

Rainey is in trouble from the outset but keeps escaping. The Pirates are a constant threat yet Rainey keeps the Cubs in the game. When he leaves after seven, the Pirates are clinging to a 2-1 lead.

Stoddard comes on to pitch in the eighth and gives up a one-out triple to Johnnie Ray. Ray comes around to score making it a 3-1 deficit. It's costly because the Cubs rally for a run in the ninth off Tekulve.

It's not enough. The Cubs fall to 10-8.

The next night it is Sanderson's turn again. Once again he is masterful. He throws a two-hitter, faces only 28 batters and gives the Cubs a lift.

"That," Pittsburgh manager Chuck Tanner admitted,

"was the best pitching we've seen all year. You can't do better than that. We've seen Fernando and Carlton and Denny and nobody was better than Sanderson."

The Cubs win easily 7-1. Cey hits his fourth homer.

Meanwhile, Matthews continues to be aggressive. He goes 1-for-2 but drives in three runs, steals one base and gets caught trying to swipe another.

The Sunday series wrapup puts Trout against Candelaria. Once again, it's a pitchers' duel. The Cubs have probably been involved in more great pitching matchups through April of 1984 than in all of last season.

The Cubs put together two scoring sessions in the first and sixth to give Trout a fragile 2-0 lead. After six, Frey has seen enough. Trout has given him a great six innings. It's time for the bullpen after Steve allows the first two hitters in the seventh to reach. Stoddard comes in and settles everyone down. The Pirates score on a sacrifice fly but no further damage is done. Smith finishes off Pittsburgh in the ninth giving the Cubs a 2-1 win. In the three-game series the Cubs allowed Pittsburgh a mere five runs. What a difference good pitching makes.

The Cubs come out of April with a 12-8 record. They head into New York for, believe it or not, a first-place series against the Mets.

New York is buzzing. Chicago is buzzing. The rest of the National League must be doubling over in laughter. The Cubs and Mets, yesterday's laughers, are battling for first at Shea even though the Cubs are barely over .500.

"What the hell," Matthews says. "We're playing good baseball. Let the people not take us serious. One day they'll have to."

The matchups are the same as opening day at Wrigley. Gooden against Ruthven. Gooden comes out in the New

York papers saying he has something to prove to the Cubs.

"They were showing me up last time, running on me with a big lead," he said. "That won't happen again."

For a brief moment it did happen again. Dernier led off with a walk and stole second. When Mike Fitzgerald's throw went into center field Dernier got up and went to third. With nobody out in the first the Cubs had a runner on third.

Then Gooden got tough. He threw nothing but heat to Sandberg who struck out, called. He threw nothing but heat to Matthews, who struck out, called. And then he got Buckner, making his first start since the San Diego series, to ground weakly back to the mound. The kid had made his point.

The game was scoreless through five when suddenly, the Mets scored seven times in the sixth. The game was over. Gooden lasted seven innings and fanned 10. The Mets took the first round of the first-place battle with an 8-1 victory.

The next night the Cubs break out to a 3-0 lead against Leary, but the Mets chip away at the lead. Little by little they come back against Rainey. They finally tie it in the seventh against Brusstar with a long homer by Foster.

It's over in the ninth when Danny Heep leads off with a triple. Heep has only been in the league a few years but he kills the Cubs, especially from the bench. He's like the second coming of Jerry Lynch.

Smith, who came on in the eighth, walks Wally Backman and the pinch-hitting Staub. Up comes Hernandez, who a couple of years ago as a Cardinal had seven game-winning hits against the Cubs alone. He gets his first of '84 against the Cubs with a sacrifice fly to Cotto in left. The Cubs fall two back of the Mets. New York is in ecstasy.

Why is it that whenever the Cubs appear to turn the corner the Mets are there waiting?

Bad planning?

The Cubs return to Wrigley Field. If anything, their two-day stay in New York left them leery of the Mets.

The Padres are in town for three games. The Cubs win the opener 7-6. Once again, it's a one-run game and once again, Monge walks in a run. This time it cost the Padres heavily. Monge walks Moreland in the ninth for the winner. The Cubs, who had only six hits, scored the winner without benefit of a hit. Moreland, Durham and Dernier all walked and Sandberg reached on an error.

The Cubs shake the New York experience and move to 13-10. It's not a bad start. But it it so, so early. Why even get excited?

The next day the Cubs and Padres do it one more time. This time Cey singles in the winner in the 10th breaking a 5-5 deadlock. The Cubs had taken a 5-2 lead on Durham's second homer in two days. The Cubs also led 4-0 at one point after Davis delivered a two-run homer off Whitson.

The Padres ruined it all with three runs in the ninth. They are tough. It's no wonder they are expected to win their first division title. They have great righty-lefty balance in the pitching department. They have experienced players in key positions, Garvey at first, Nettles at third and Gossage in the bullpen. They've got decent speed and fair power for a big ball park. Their starting pitching isn't bad, anchored by Show, although Dave Dravecky was on the block as was Lollar. They need a big year from Ed Whitson to fulfill the expectations.

It's Show time again. Ruthven, who hasn't won since early in the season, draws Show again. This game is different from the rest. First off, it's not a one-run decision. San Diego beats the Cubs 8-5 and is never really threatened. Secondly, Monge doesn't walk anyone.

Durham stays hot and homers again, giving him three in three games. It's great to see. Leon is one of the nicest guys in the game. He's got a big heart for the unfortunate. It goes beyond his donating $750 to Chicago Public High School athletic programs for every Wrigley Field homer he hits.

The fans have quieted from their early season booing. Leon was a victim of circumstance. There isn't a true fan out there that doesn't want Leon to have a great season. And after they get a look at the way Matthews plays they'll be glad to have them both.

The homestand continues against the Giants. Frank Robinson's club looked as if it might be pretty decent when they played the Cubs in the spring. But very quickly, the Giants have unravelled like a cheap pair of socks.

They come to Chicago with a weary pitching staff and it's only May 7. Once again, the Cubs see Mark Davis, who comes into the game 0-3.

With the wind blowing straight out, Davis doesn't have a chance. The Cubs score two in the first and seven in the second, all off Davis. Durham and Steve Lake both homer in the second.

Poor Davis. With the pitching depleted, Robinson makes him work five innings. By then he had allowed 14 hits and 10 earned runs.

But with the wind blowing out, no lead is ever safe in Wrigley.

The Giants come back with five runs in the seventh and single runs in the eighth and ninth, stranding two runners in each of the final three innings. They make it close, losing 10-7.

The win doesn't completely satisfy Frey. He's perturbed that Rainey can't prosper with a lead—a 10-run lead at that.

Chuck lasts into the seventh allowing eight hits and five earned runs.

"Once in awhile," Frey says, "it would be nice to see him pitch a complete game and work his way clear of trouble."

The next day is practically an instant replay. The Giants pitching isn't much better and rookie Scott Garrelts, a kid from downstate Illinois, is the sacrifical lamb. The Cubs put up a seven-spot in the third, thanks in part to Cey's sixth career grand slam. He absolutely kills the Giants.

Again a big lead isn't enough. This time Reuschel can't hold it. He leaves after six innings having allowed eight hits and five runs. The only performance more disheartening than Rick's was Noles' who followed. Dickie works only a third of an inning but he gives up five hits and four runs. The Giants aren't merely back in the game—they are in the lead after 6½ by a 9-8 margin.

Dickie's battle against alcoholism has been a bold one. The organization has backed him completely but his pitching performances have been unimpressive.

"He's always had great stuff," Bowa says. "He looks great. He's in the best shape of his life. But. . ."

But he can't get anyone out. Not yet anyway.

The Cubs need a rally. Losing this game could be disastrous even though they have come back into a first-place tie with the Mets. The Cubs add a run in the seventh to get even and then score two more in the eighth off Greg Minton, not an easy thing to do.

The first run that inning is a pinch homer by Hebner onto the right-field catwalk. It's the 200th homer of his career. "The Hacker" has done it again. What a key acquisition he has turned out to be.

The 11-9 lead falls apart in the ninth when the Giants tie it and leave the lead run on third.

The Cubs come back in the ninth when Hall singles leading off the inning and moves to third when Davis singles. After Bowa hits into a fielder's choice that catches Hall at the plate, Buckner, a forgotten player perhaps, hits into another fielder's choice.

That play does send Cotto, pinch running for Davis, to third. Frey substitutes Moreland for Dernier and Moreland comes through with a single to right off Gary Lavelle.

The Cubs win and the bench has again contributed.

Buckner has been as gracious as possible about his bench duty. He doesn't like it. He makes comments about it. He despises it. But the club is winning. Whatever he says against management flies right back in his face because the club is going well. For the time being he's stuck. But the fans still love him. For years he was all they had. If he's nothing else, he is a reminder as to how far the organization has come. Bill Buckner, one of the best hitters in the game, couldn't work his way back into the lineup.

Anyway the Cubs survived. They had taken two from the Giants by scores of 10-7 and 12-11.

"To say the least," Frey said. "We've had an interesting week around here. It's been a little too wild for me."

The Dodgers come back into town. Sanderson starts and is very tough. Once again the Cubs use a big inning—a four-run first—to grab the lead. In the fourth it's 7-0 and Sandberg, who was 6-for-10 against the Giants, has a triple and two walks that all produced runs.

But suddenly Sanderson has a problem. In the fifth inning, after Franklin Stubbs singles and Candy Maldonado flies out, Connors and Tony Garofalo visit the mound. Scott finishes the inning and gets the decision—a 7-0 shutout. But he is suffering with back spasms.

"I had them a few years ago," he says. "But I don't know when the last time was I really had them. I should be alright."

Bordi comes in and pitches great allowing only one hit in four innings. The Cubs are 17-11, but the concern now rests with Sanderson's back.

The Dodgers get a masterpiece from Bob Welch the next day and beat the Cubs 5-1. There isn't much a team can do when a pitcher is throwing as well as Welch did.

Sandberg doubles again. He finished off the previous day's game with a double to go along with his triple. He's having a great year thus far. But it's only mid-May.

It's back to the road. The Astrodome has long been the pits for the Cubs. Even Leo Durocher, who managed the best Cub teams in the last 40 years, couldn't win when he came to Houston. It was at the Dome that Leo ripped out the dugout phone and gave a vivid description of what he thought of the Astrodome.

To make matters worse, the Astros pitch Nolan Ryan in the first game. The Cubs historically have difficulty the first night on the road following a homestand. Going from daylight to artificial light isn't as easy as it might look. Against Ryan it's never easy.

The Cubs are held to one run again and Ruthven gets beat 3-1. Hall makes perhaps the best catch of the season (again it is early May) when he dives into foul territory down the right field line to snare a sinking liner hit by Phil Garner.

"That may be the best catch we see this season," Frey says.

"Was nothin' special," Hall counters. "Play me every day and I'll make plays like that."

NBC is on hand the next day as the Cubs and Astros play a rare afternoon game. Again it looks as if the Cubs are doomed. This time it's Joe Niekro. One night a guy throws 95 mph and the next day a guy throws 59. The Cubs gather two hits off Joe in the second and score and add another hit and another run in the third.

Houston comes back with its usual rally. A walk, sacrifice and single gives Houston a run in the third. The Astros use three singles to score in the sixth and then use one hit, a sacrifice and three walks to grab a 3-2 lead after seven.

Between the third and the ninth, Niekro allows two

measly walks. Two was obviously the limit because Bob Lillis pulled him with one out in the ninth when he walked Cey.

Cotto comes in to run for Cey and Frank DiPino, a tough lefty that the Astros stole from the Brewers in the Don Sutton deal late in 1982, comes in to face Buckner, who had already been announced as the pinch hitter.

Buck singles against the lefty. Moreland flies deep to right. With two outs and two on and the Cubs trailing by a run in the ninth, Davis pinch hits. DiPino goes to 3-0 on Jody. The next pitch is a belt-high fastball.

Davis sends a long drive to center field. Jerry Mumphrey goes back and keeps looking up. Amazingly the ball disappears just to the left field side of the driveway that runs to the deep center field wall. A three-run homer.

The place is quiet. The Cubs bench is exploding.

Nothing comes easy. The Astros get two runners on in the ninth off Smith. They score a run bringing the score to 5-4. Jose Cruz, who singled home Craig Reynolds, who doubled, steals second.

Smith faces Mumphrey, already two-for-three. He strikes him out. Enos Cabell then flies to Dernier in center. The Cubs survive.

It is a game that makes a team believe. Every team that has ever won anything in any sport has those games when somebody does the impossible. Davis homering on a 3-0 pitch, one out from a loss in the spacious, dead air of the Astrodome is as much talent as it is fate.

Maybe this year will be special.

In the Sunday game, Reuschel is outstanding. He's facing Mike Madden, another former Brewer. Madden beat Craig Lefferts last year at the Dome 1-0 when the Astros scored thanks to a passed ball and a 4-3 ground out.

On this particular night, the story line is the same. Madden is nowhere near as good as Reuschel, but Rick is nowhere near as lucky.

The Cubs leave six runners on in the first five innings and have six runners in scoring position, but they are helpless.

In the Houston fourth, Mumphrey hits a ball to the wall in right that Moreland just can't catch up with. It goes for a triple. It's a ball that Hall would have caught. On the other hand, Hall would have had no chance against Madden. Moreland singles twice.

With Mumphrey on third, Cabell flies to right scoring Jerry. That's the game. The Cubs get runners to first and third in the ninth with Buckner up but he grounds out to second.

"I started out tonight trying to get my game going," says Rick, whose comeback story is touching. "It's one of those things. We had chances. The thing I'm happiest about is the fact that I was able to bounce back from my last outing."

He has bounced back from more than that. After he went to the Yankees hours before the club was sold to the Tribune Company in June of 1981, Rick encountered shoulder problems. He pitched the rest of 1981 and appeared in postseason play. But 1982 was a washout. He never pitched and underwent surgery. 1983 was headed in the same direction until the Yankees released him and the Cubs invited him to give it a try in the minors. He commuted to Quad City, to A ball, to try again and in September the Cubs rewarded him with a ticket back to Wrigley. He was a great Cub pitcher. A master of control, a guy who could bust a hitter inside if the situation called for it. He was also a winner, an uncommon trait in the late 1970s and early 1980s at Wrigley.

He was glad to be back.

The next day is an offday on the schedule but the biggest day of the season in Des Moines. The Cubs and Iowa Cubs play an exhibition game at the Triple A site. It is nothing more than an eight-hour stop on the way to Cincinnati where the road trip continues Tuesday.

This exhibition will be remembered for two things; Buckner telling Frey to play him in left field and give him a chance to work his way into the lineup by playing the outfield. And also for Lake, who was diagnosed as having hepatitis that night.

Lake flew with the club to Cincinnati. The next day, weary, drawn and ill, he went back to Chicago. His season, at the least, is in doubt.

Buckner, meanwhile, tells the media he can help the club more than Matthews in left. It's frustrating more than anything for Buck. He's hot and it shows.

Frey asks him if he wants to come out after a couple of the exhibition game innings. He says no. He goes 5-for-5.

"I think I should be playing out there somewhere," he says. "I don't think Jim Frey knows what I can really do."

The trip to Cincy is uneventful except that Frey and Zimmer, two of the Cincinnati Western Hills High School alums who have made baseball their life, tell the bus driver to take a back route from the Cincinnati airport, which is actually in Kentucky.

They pull up at Skyline Chili and get off the bus. The players can't believe it. May 14th has slipped away to May 15th.

Buck is still frustrated as the series opens. It would have been easy for Frey to play him anywhere after he spoke out and then went 5-for-5. But Frey's not buying it. Buck decides to grow a beard in protest.

Matthews, meanwhile, obviously aware of Buckner's playing demands and finger pointing at the left fielder's job, goes 4-for-5 with a double, a run scored and a RBI.

But the big news is Sanderson again. He did not accompany the club to Houston or Des Moines, doctors feeling that any unnecessary movement would only do further damage. He comes into Cincy and starts the first inning with a one-run lead.

He fans Gary Redus leading off and walks Tom Foley. Then he's finished.

"I knew when I was warming up that it wasn't going to be there tonight," he said. "But I wanted to give it a try. It just hurts too much. Anyway by stopping as soon as I did I feel I haven't done it any more harm. I should be ready to go next time I'm up in the rotation."

The Cubs win 6-3 and Noles gets the win. Here he is back in Cincinnati. It's his first baseball appearance since he spent time in jail here during the offseason for his celebrated bar room fight with a police officer. Dickie works six innings allowing five hits and two runs. Stoddard closes with 2.2 hitless and shutout innings.

The concern is still for Sanderson.

The next night it is big-inning time again. The Cubs beat around Jeff Russell for three runs in the first and three in the second. Durham hits a three-run blast in the first and Davis adds a leadoff homer in the second. Cey makes it seven runs with a leadoff homer in the third.

The Cubs coast to a 10-4 win. They climb back into first by a half-game with a 20-14 record. Ever so slowly they are creeping away from the .500 mark, the record this team was supposed to be shooting for.

Suddenly Sandberg is catching everyone's eye. He was National League Player of the Week for his week against the West Coast teams at Wrigley. This week he is chasing Alan Trammell's 18-game hitting streak, and he matches it in the second game at Cincinnati. He is also being chased by the media. *Sports Illustrated* comes to talk with him. They

spend three days with him, watching every move, dissect-
ing every sentence and talking to everyone who has ever
had anything to do with Sandberg's career.

A Cub in *S.I.* Things are a little unusual.

Facing Mario Soto is no way to keep a streak going, Sandberg learns the next day. Soto is his usual self. He entered
the game with a 5-1 record and a 2.49 ERA with 57 strikeouts
in 61.1 innings. Typical Soto numbers.

He is also coming off a one-hitter that he threw against
the Cardinals on Saturday. Within moments after Davis beat
the Astros, St. Louis' George Hendrick stood at the plate
against Mario with two outs in the ninth, a no-hitter on the
board and a 1-2 count. Soto then chose to throw close to
Hendrick. Not a good idea. The next pitch Hendrick clubbed
over the left-center field fence. Soto still had a win, but he
no longer had a shutout or a no-hitter.

In this, his next start, he had a one-hitter until the seventh when the Cubs finally broke through for three runs,
two coming on a Davis homer.

The Reds had long since chased Ruthven with a four-run
fifth. The Reds won 5-3, Ruthven again was beaten (2-5).
Ruthven again went against somebody's ace. Meanwhile,
Buckner's beard grew thicker.

Two sidelights:

Tom Veryzer, who had a three-hit game in place of Bowa
in the second game of the series, breaks his left thumb making a play on Redus at second. Bowa, who had been ticked
off by his move to the bench by Frey, gets his job back by
default.

The other sidelight came in the eighth when Parker stole
second and Veryzer, unaware that the left thumb that hurt
was broken, thought that he had tagged Parker out. Veryzer
and umpire Bob Engel had a mild conversation. Frey came
out and had some words with Engel and also with Parker.

Frey is a foot shorter than Parker and probably 70 pounds to the light side of Dave. After the inning, Parker came chugging around third and said something to Frey. Frey came out like a man who'd been shot from a cannon—hoping that somebody would get in his way before Parker did.

Both parties were restrained.

"He said some things to me that I didn't like," Parker said. "I don't have to take that from anyone."

"I just told him to shut up," Frey said. "I was talking with the umpire and he keeps yapping. That's all."

"I'm glad somebody stopped us from going at it. I would have (note the twinkle in Frey's eyes) probably hurt him and I wouldn't want ruining his career on my conscience."

The Cubs head for home tied for first place at 20-15. Yes, this is getting interesting.

On the Johnny Carson show, NBC baseball announcer Joe Garagiola explains his recent meeting with a Cub fan.

"I'm on an elevator with some guy who starts talking about the Cubs. The guy says he can't remember the last time the Cubs had a lead this late into the season. I tell the guy it's only May."

Playing Houston outside the Dome is always a much different situation. In the Dome the Astros can play for one run and sit back and play good defense and win. On the road, especially at a park like Wrigley, they can be overwhelmed in a hurry.

The next series was a case in point. The Cubs score two in the first and add three in the third—coming on back-to-back homers by Hall and Durham. The Astros keep trying to come back adding a run here and a run there until they are finally even after six innings. They grab a lead in the ninth when Cabell hits a pinch homer off Stoddard. Suddenly, the punchless Astros have almost KO'd the Cubs in their own ballpark with their own weapon—the homer.

Not to be outdone, Matthews leads off the ninth with a single and Durham doubles him home. A sacrifice by Moreland puts Bull on third. Two intentional walks follow. Bowa pops up to third and it looks as if the Astros have at least a chance for extra innings. Woods, however, draws a walk from DiPino and the Cubs win 7-6. It's the fifth win in May alone that the Cubs have rung up in their final at-bat.

The rain nearly wipes out the Saturday game. NBC is back again. The Astros come out strong and cuff Reuschel around for four runs on ten hits in five innings. Now it's the Cubs who come back little-by-little.

Trailing 4-3 after six and a half, the Cubs put up two runs in the seventh. After two doubles to start the inning, the Cubs score the lead run on two sacrifice bunts and an error by Bill Dawley.

Revenge is sweet although not real pretty. Reuschel gets the win even though he allowed 11 hits in seven innings. His performance doesn't compare with the way he pitched in Houston when he lost 1-0. But the outcome was different—the ballpark different. He wins 5-4.

The Astros do make it somewhat exciting with a one-out double in the ninth off Smith. But he gets Kevin Bass to line out to Bowa and fans Garner pinch hitting, even though Phil is batting more than .500 off Smith for the last two seasons.

The Cubs maintain a one-game first-place lead. Finally they get a bona fide Cubs-Astros Wrigley Field game. They knock out seven extra-base hits including homers by Durham and Sandberg. It's Bull's ninth. He could be on the way to a great year if he can stay injury free.

The Cubs get a lift from Rich Bordi. Bordi goes five innings allowing only one run while his teammates have put seven on the board. It's his first major league win. At one point he was lucky to be here. Now with Sanderson hurting and Ruthven struggling and about to go on the DL, the Cubs are lucky he's here.

A year ago he was the last player cut in spring training. This year he was the last player kept in spring training.

Next up are the Braves. Now *they* can play a Wrigley type game. Power. Instead Trout and Craig McMurtry hook up in a great duel. Through 6½ innings, Trout has allowed no runs and three hits and McMurtry has allowed one run and two hits. One of those two hits was a Matthews homer that broke the no-hitter in the sixth.

Trout is relieved by Smith. Lee allows a run in the eighth that cuts the lead in half. The Cubs add one more in the eighth for a 3-1 win.

They are 24-15, nine games over .500 and lead the National League East by a game and a half.

Matthews continues to produce. He has five game-winning hits. A year ago as he sat and waited and pondered his future with the Phillies he didn't have any game-winners at this point. He had three last season, all down the stretch, all in September.

Ruthven's arm problems are getting serious. He has been going for tests. No one knows what exactly is going to happen to Rufus, but the consensus is he won't be pitching for a while.

The Cubs take off early again the next day against Pascual Perez in Game 1 of a doubleheader. He despises pitching at Wrigley Field. On the other hand, Durham loves hitting against him. He hits a pair of homers off Pascual—both gigantic three-run shots. The Cubs give Rainey a 9-0 lead. As usual, the Braves rally. The Cubs hold on for a 10-7 win.

Perez opened the season in a Dominican Republic jail. How could a pitcher who didn't have spring training come back so quickly and pitch so well? Would you believe that Perez threw every other day in prison? There happened to be a catcher who was also imprisoned. Perez is quite a character. When he won his first game of the season following his release, he dedicated the victory to all the inmates.

The news on Ruthven isn't good. He will undergo surgery to clear up an artery blockage in his right shoulder. The surgery will actually be to the neck area so his arm will not be touched. He had been complaining that when he pitched it felt as if the ball weighed 30 pounds. During the winter he went to the refrigerator to get a glass of milk. His arm began shaking. He feared he had deteriorated the muscles in his right arm. He was frightened.

For the last three years he thought something was wrong. Finally, during the tests the Cubs physicians were administering, his pulse was taken. The doctors were suspicious.

Surgery was the only answer. It may save his career, maybe even his life. From a team standpoint, Dallas has his back to the wall now. With Ruthven and Sanderson both out indefinitely, the pitching staff is dangerously close to collapsing. This season has the hallmarks of being a good one. But without pitching, it's foolish to believe the club will stay near the top.

The price to the Cubs for pitching has just skyrocketed. The strongest rumor has Buckner going to Boston. It began last winter but died when the Red Sox acquired Mike Easler from the Pirates. Cubs advance scout Charlie Fox has been with the Red Sox off and on for the last few days. The names mentioned about three weeks ago were Bruce Hurst and Bob Ojeda. Then both pitchers have excellent outings and the price goes up again.

But Boston is going nowhere. Its infield needs a stabilizer. The Red Sox would still love to get Buckner. For the right price.

Back to Game 2 of the doubleheader. Once again the Cubs power is evident. Davis homers in the second off Pete Falcone and Cey adds a three-run homer in the fifth. The Cubs hold a 7-4 lead after six and go on to sweep their first doubleheader in four years. Wrigley Field continues to be the Friendly Confines to the Cubs.

The Cubs are 16-4 at home, their best home start since 1907 when they were 18-4 and playing at the West Side Grounds. The Cubs may stay in the race because of their home record and because they have the potential to be a better team on the road with Dernier and Matthews in the outfield.

May 25. An era ends. After meeting with Dallas, Buckner agrees to go to Boston. He takes with him many fond memories as well as a nice buyout for relinquishing his no-trade clause. The Cubs gain Dennis Eckersley. While the hope was for a lefty starter, Eckersley may indeed be an answer.

Zimmer knows him from his Red Sox days and says he was the best of the lot. While Dennis hasn't pitched great the last couple years, his lack of success could be for any number of reasons. A change of scenery, especially to a team in the race, for a player who hasn't won a championship can usually rejuvenate whatever spirit was missing.

Historians like to point out that Dennis' best years were years ago. But he is still young. He's not 30 yet. He has been a quality pitcher. He's coming to a new league and he's coming to a team that isn't chasing the Tigers, who have opened up a lead that would take a month of losses to overcome.

"Last season," Dallas said, "the pitching staff was a complete disaster at the end. We don't want that happening again. For the first time we've got quality."

Buck comes in for the press conference. He's a little shaken. A year ago when his name came up he said he never wanted to leave Chicago and that for the first time since he came there in 1977 they had a chance to turn things around. He had become the Cubs' only shining light through a few dark years. Then he became the only true marketable player. He wanted to stay. The Cubs wanted Durham at first where he wouldn't be prone to hamstring problems and they wanted pitching. Finally it happened.

Even Dallas was taken aback by the emotion of the day.

"It is a very emotional day here," he said. "Bill Buckner has given the Cubs a lot in his career here. We'll miss him, but it's time to move on."

"I'm going to really miss Chicago," Buckner said. "I'm going to miss everybody. Play this game long enough and you'll have some tough moments. But all in all, my stay here has been great. I wish the Cubs all the luck in the world."

In the meantime, Eckersley was readying himself for the trip to Chicago.

"When will he pitch?" somebody asked Billy Connors. "When will he get here?" was Connors reply.

It's hard to believe that somebody is keeping track, but the magic number is 119.

Suddenly the hitting stops. The Reds pull Tom Hume out of the bullpen and he helps blank the Cubs 3-0.

The next day the Cubs hit and are holding a 6-5 lead in the ninth when suddenly the defense flattens. With Steve Trout working in a rare relief appearance—he was the fifth pitcher of the game for the Cubs—Eric Davis hits a grounder to Sandberg at second. Ryne can't come up with it. Cedeno hits a double play ball to Bowa that should end the game. He muffs it. After a ground out, Tony Perez hits a shot to right scoring two runs and giving the Reds a 7-6 lead.

The Cubs are shaken a little by the way that inning worked out. Sandberg and Bowa make very few errors and rarely when the game is on the line.

Still the Cubs have runners on first and second in the ninth but Davis and Bowa can't get the tying run across.

From a six-game winning streak to a two-game losing streak.

The Sunday game is one of the crazier games in a long time. Soto goes against Eckersley in his first National League appearance. In the second inning it seemed for a moment that Cey had given the Cubs a lead. He hit a long drive that appeared to most everybody to hook foul and crash against the fence beyond the lower left field boxes. But umpire Steve Rippley at third signaled home run. Everyone was surprised including Cey and Soto.

What followed was the longest argument in many years. It took 32 minutes to clear the confusion. By then Soto had charged the umpires and was intercepted by Zimmer. What was he doing trying to curtail Soto? He probably saved Mario a year's suspension. He was flying and fuming. It was an ugly scene. Frey was ejected, Soto ejected and Zimmer looked as if he were seconds away from a heart attack.

The game wasn't much prettier. Eck pitched very well. But in the eighth they tied the game at three on a Milner homer and in the ninth they won it on a double by Brad Gulden and a single by Wayne Krenchicki. A good performance by Eck went down the tubes and so did the Cubs for the third straight game.

The Mets and Phillies weren't doing much better. The Cubs only lost a game off their lead from two to one.

Rains washed out the Memorial Day game. It cost the

Cubs a great gate. But it didn't hurt to cool off the Reds and give the Cubs a day off. A major road trip was next.

Sanderson was going to start the next night in Atlanta. It was time to see again where the pitching staff stood.

Scotty can't get it going. He leaves after three innings. This could be a lingering problem; thank goodness, Dallas picked up Eckersley. The Cubs get off quickly with four runs off Perez, but after that he toughens up and the Braves win 7-4 with a three-run eighth off Brusstar.

It's not the best start to a road trip, but losing Sanderson, maybe indefinitely, is a hundred times worse than losing a game.

The next night, Trout is almost perfect. He has never pitched a better game. For 7.2 innings he has a no-hitter. Then with two out in the 8th, he walks Alex Trevino on a very close call that plate umpire Jim Quick thought was low. The next hitter, Jerry Royster, hits a grounder to Bowa. The ball handcuffs Larry and goes for an error. The inning should be over.

Albert Hall ruins the evening with a single to center. Rafael Ramirez takes advantage of a shaken Trout with another single. The Cubs 5-0 lead is down to 5-2. Frey goes to Smith, who retires the final four Braves.

The Cubs add a run in the ninth and come away with a 6-2 win.

"With any luck at all," Frey says, "Steve gets a no-hitter."

Trout is off to his best start at 6-3. Maybe he can pick up the slack.

Bowa starts talking about wearing glasses. He's having a difficult time adjusting to the ball coming off the bat. He's disappointed in his play. The toughest aspect of a player's career is when the sun starts setting whether it's after one year, 10 years or 20 years.

How about this headline: HOME ARE THE HEROES. A Chicago newspaper?

The *Philadelphia Inquirer* sends a writer to Atlanta. With the Cubs coming to Philly after the series with the Braves, the spotlight is turned to the former heroes of Philly. The only city where the Cubs are bigger news than Chicago is Philly. The combination of the Philly fan (tough on the home team), the lackluster performance of the Phillies and the sudden success of the Cubs has led to rave reviews for the Cubs from the Philly fans. While the social standing of Phils President Bill Giles has wavered in Philadelphia, respect for Dallas has multiplied. That is saying a lot. The man was one of the most revered in Philadelphia sports history even before he left to lead the Cubs.

Sports Illustrated continues its Cub coverage. First, the Sandberg article. Now the cover and Durham. Yes, things are heating up. Just keep that infamous *S.I.* jinx away. Put Schmidt on the cover, or Gooden, or Hernandez. The Cubs already have the goat to contend with.

The Philly series will be one to mark time with. Through the course of this season there will be many times when the mettle of the Cubs will be put to the test. This series is one of them. The artificial surface, the first time back for Sarge and Dernier, the pitching match-ups. They are all keys. The date is May 31.

Rainey opens for the Cubs in game one against Charles Hudson. The Cubs are horrendous. It's hard to remember a poorer 1984 showing. Philly has a 7-1 lead after two innings. The second inning is a nightmare, especially for Bowa. Larry makes two errors in the inning. Frey pulls him immediately. Bowa's confidence is waning. Of all places to have an off night, Philadelphia is the wrong one for Larry.

He was one of the players who pulled the Phillies through

in 1980. He went through a stretch that season—mid-August—when Dallas benched him, when he threw an obscene gesture the fans' way, when the Reading, PA drug case was surfacing, when he could have led the Philly collapse. Instead he helped carry Philly to its first World Championship. On this evening, the Phillies would once again look like champions and the Cubs would once again look like Cubs, old Cubs.

With Reuschel pitching the next game, one doesn't know what to think. Rick could get hammered like Rainey or he could throw like he did a month earlier in Houston.

If turnabout is fair play, never let it be said that the Phils don't play fair. On this night, it's the Phillies who can't get a handle on things. They commit five errors, one early and four late giving the Cubs the confidence they need. The Cubs behind Rick win 12-3. Sandberg adds to the destruction with two homers, one in the fifth, the other in the sixth. The second one was a line shot to deep center field. And Dernier makes a sensational catch. Later, he says "To me, that's baseball ecstasy."

One of the Philly errors was committed by DeJesus, the player Dallas sent the Phils for Ryno and Bowa in January of 1982. Another Philly error was committed by Juan Samuel, one of the players the Phillies had more confidence in than Sandberg. One solid bet this evening is that Paul Owens, Bill Giles and Hugh Alexander did not sleep real well.

The victory puts the Cubs a half-game in front of the Phillies. In terms of confidence, they are even further ahead. The Mets remain on the heels of both. The consensus is that they won't be there long. But after 1969 and 1973, one never knows about those Mets.

The talk in Philly is about Matthews, about leadership.

"You can talk leadership," Gary said. "But unless you back it up on the field it doesn't matter."

How true.

For the second straight game, Frey starts Dave Owen in place of Bowa. Larry's pride is hurting. But Frey can't do much about that. He's trying to win games, he says. He's not worried about stepping on egos. He believes the Cubs have a shot. It depends on how well the pitching holds up with Rufus and Sanderson both out and it also depends on how well the Cubs play defensively. Offensively, the questions are not as pressing.

The Saturday game is nationally televised and NBC gets to carry a beauty. Eckersley is outstanding. He seems to have found himself in this his second start. Unfortunately, the opponent for the day is Jerry Koosman, who has been doing this sort of thing for years. Cast off by the White Sox, Koos shows he still has it. Through seven innings, Koos and Eck are almost mirrored images. Koos allows one run on five hits and Eck allows one run on four hits.

The Phils call on Al Holland in the eighth and Moreland takes him deep. The Cubs lead 2-1 and the Phils are back on their heels. In the Philly eighth, Frey goes to Smith even though Eck has retired the last seven hitters. Two of the last three outs were hit fairly well to the outfield. Frey's thinking is clear. When you have a lead and Lee Smith, bring in the big guy.

Von Hayes reaches with a leadoff single bringing Schmidt to the plate. There are few hitters in the league that do well against Smitty and Mike is one of them. The figures don't lie. Schmidt hits one off the canvas backdrop beyond the left field fence. It is his 60th career homer against the Cubs. Philly regains the lead and the upperhand. They win 3-2. Frey is second guessed.

In his first start since the near no-hitter, Trout wins again. He only goes five innings but he leaves with a 3-2 lead. In comes Brusstar to throw four shutout innings of three-hit relief. Another former Philly does them in. Dernier, Sandberg and Matthews had one hit each and scored five runs. The Cubs romp 11-2 because of back-to-back four-run innings.

Sarge is still loved in Philly. His hustling play and leadership are missed already and it's only June, early June. Before one of the games he clowns around with Phillie Larry Andersen, who appears out of the Phillies' dugout wearing the face of Father Time. Andersen tells Matthews it's like Sarge is looking into a mirror. Sarge cracks up. A *SI* photographer captures it. It'll be national this week.

The Cubs are off to Montreal. Their confidence level is peaking. When all is said and done, this may be a series looked back upon as one that molded the psyche of the 1984 Cubs. They came into Philly a possible contender and left Philly believing they were real. "The Cubs belong," Frey says.

Bowa returns to shortstop against the Expos. Hebner is playing third again in place of Cey. When the Expos traded Sanderson to the Cubs by way of San Diego, one of the pitchers they had in mind to take Scott's place was Bryn Smith. Thus far, Smith has done fine.

The Cubs reach him for three runs in the second, taking advantage of two infield errors—one by Smith and the other by Brian Little. With Rainey pitching well the Cubs look as if they can maintain the one-game lead they brought into the game. Rainey lasts one out into the seventh.

With one out, a 3-1 lead and the tying run on first, Frey goes to Stoddard. He fans Mike Stenhouse, who is pinch hitting. Pete Rose follows with a pinch hit sending Terry Francona, who had singled and chased Rainey, to second.

It also scored Wallach cutting the Cub lead to 3-2. Stoddard pitches out of trouble by getting Miguel Dilone to pop out to Ryno.

Stoddard pitches a 1-2-3 eighth and leaves after walking Andre Dawson leading off the ninth. Smith follows and again is less than perfect.

He walks Tim Wallach. Derrel Thomas pinch runs. Francona lines out hard to Matthews. With runners on first and second, Speier grounds into a 1-4 fielder's choice. Two outs.

Jim Wohlford then hits a grounder to Durham at first. Leon comes up the line and tags the bag. The Cubs come off the field congratulating Smith. Suddenly, the ball is signalled foul by home plate umpire Lanny Harris, who two months earlier was involved in the call at the plate in San Diego that led to a 3-2 Cubs defeat.

Wohlford gets another chance and hits a shot to left center that Dernier outruns. Thank goodness for Bobby.

"What's with this umpiring crew?" Frey wonders.

The Cubs go two games up.

The rumors begin circulating that Dallas is about to make another deal for a pitcher. Believe it or not, the talk is of it being a multi-player deal. The name most often mentioned is Bert Blyleven of Cleveland. He's got some age, a questionable arm and a Brinks-delivered contract. But the guy pitched great in the five games he faced the Cubs in spring training.

There is also talk about Rick Sutcliffe, an All-Star the year before but a free agent candidate. If it's not Cleveland that Dallas deals with it could be Boston. There are more rumors that the Eckersley-Buckner deal may just be a prelude.

The Cubs are still sitting with one extra outfielder who could play fulltime—Moreland vs. Hall. Both have their pros and cons. Keith is more experienced and less prone to injury. Defensively he's not as flashy as Mel, but he's a little more stable. Mel has two bad knees and couldn't hit left-handed pitching if his career depended on it. Presently, it doesn't. Those are the prime candidates for a deal.

Reuschel is up next and he struggles. He's gone in the third and the game is all but over. The Expos are up 7-0 at that point. They win 8-1 behind Joliet's Bill Gullickson. How did he ever escape the Cubs?

If that's not bad enough, Charlie Lea is due in the series finale. Perhaps only San Diego's Eric Show handles the Cubs with more ease than Lea. Charlie just does it every time out. At least some of the Cubs can hit Steve Rogers, but Lea stops them all.

Eck pitches great again and once again doesn't come up with the win. The Cubs lose 2-1 when Eck gives up a two-out sixth-inning homer to Carter.

Bowa has ordered glasses. They should be in St. Louis for the weekend.

The loss costs the Cubs a half-game. They lead by 1½ games. St. Louis and a big weekend series is around the corner. The Cubs arrive in St. Louis in the wee hours of the morning and take the 30-minute bus ride to the country's liveliest weekend hotel—the Marriott across from the ballpark. It's hysteria. Especially with the Cubs on the rise. They are a very respectable 4-5 through the first three cities of this 12-game trip.

More than 40,000 show up for the Friday night opener. Trout is outstanding once again. He's on a real roll. Through five innings he has allowed nothing more than a double to Ozzie Smith. Then he comes down with a blister on his pitching hand. The Cubs fold like a cheap tent.

It's nightmare time again. Brusstar's magic disappears in a hurry. He's belted around for four hits and four runs in 1.1 innings. Stoddard isn't much better. Tim can't find the plate. The Cards bat 10 men in the seventh inning. Stoddard walks the first three batters he faces and four of the first five. A 4-0 Cub lead evaporates. St. Louis wins 5-4. The Cubs are tied for first.

The bar at the Marriott doesn't lack for business despite the sour Cub defeat. At 3 a.m. there are still people milling around the lobby.

It's time to take stock again. The Saturday night game is another fork in the road. Bordi gets a chance with Sanderson out. Scott is back in a Chicago hospital.

Give Bordi the ball and hope for the best. And the best is just what Connors and Frey get out of him. He hurls seven beautiful innings allowing just four hits. There's no comeback in sight for the Red Birds this night. Smitty closes them down with two scoreless innings. Bordi gets his second win of the season — a 5-0 masterpiece in front of more than 50,000. Bordi remarks, "I'm getting tired of walking through lobbies and people saying 'who's that?' " The Sunday game has the makings of a playoff atmosphere.

The sun beats down on the Busch Stadium carpet. It's Andujar against Rainey. A crowd of 44,453 looks on during a day perfect for baseball. Days like this make baseball the greatest game in creation.

The Cubs enter the game tied for first. The Cards are four games off the pace but they have one of the game's great pitchers working.

Through eight innings the game is scoreless. As usual, Rainey is in trouble for at least part of the way. In seven valiant innings Chuck allows five hits and leaves seven runners stranded.

In the sixth, Ken Oberkfell triples to left center. The shutout is in jeopardy. With Willie McGee hitting, anything is possible. The 90-degree field temperature has left Chuck

searching for whatever he has left. McGee pulls a long drive
to right center. Dernier, playing McGee to swing late, races
to the track, to the wall in right center. He grabs the ball
just as he hits the wall. A fan tosses a beer Dernier's way.
He looks up, ball in glove, and races back to the Cubs'
dugout. The shutout is safe.

In the top of the eighth, the Cubs load the bases on a
single by Davis, a crucial, clutch double by Bowa and an
intentional walk to the pinch hitter Johnstone. Dernier pops
up weakly to catcher Darrell Porter. With two outs, Sandberg steps in against Andujar. Ryno is hitting below .150
against Andujar for his career.

The tension is as thick as the humidity. Andujar throws
a fastball that cuffs Sandberg on the arm. The Cubs have
a run.

The Cubs bring in Smith. He sets the Cards down in order
in the eighth. The Cubs load the bases again in the ninth
after Durham leads off with a double. Two outs later, Leon
is on third. Herzog decides to walk Davis and Bowa intentionally. The move loads the bases and also forces Frey to
make a decision about Smith. He decides that he'll stick with
Lee. Lee has one career hit—a homer off the foul pole in
1982 against Atlanta's Phil Niekro at Fulton County Stadium. He should be no match for Andujar.

Zimmer coaching third, has other ideas. He notices that
Andujar isn't paying attention to Leon at third. Smith takes
the first pitch. Leon looks over at Zimmer. Zimmer gives
the sign to Davis and Bowa.

Triple steal! Leon slides home safely with the Cubs' second and the game's final run. The Cubs win 2-0. They take
the series two games to one and finish the crucial road trip
6-6 and a game in front.

A triple steal. Unbelievable. The press box's paid ob-
servers can't recall ever seeing a triple steal before. It was

an incredibly exciting series, washed in the sunlight of Sunday and the summer nights of Friday and Saturday. It was great baseball.

"After I got hit I saw Jody coming to the plate and he was so happy I didn't even feel my arm," Sandberg said.

"This win gives us a lot of spirit going home," Durham said. "And everyone knows how tough we can be at home."

Give a lot of credit to Zim. If he hadn't picked up Andujar's lack of interest in the runner, the game could have gone in the other direction. "I just told Durham that if Andujar was going to wind up we were going to steal on the second pitch," Don said. It almost sounded like there was nothing to it.

The Cubs returned to Wrigley Field. Trade rumors still abound. Dallas has only a couple of days left before the trading deadline—four to be exact. He's after Sutcliffe and he's curious as to Sutcliffe's success in pitching day games. That seems to be the only hangup. The contract he carries is huge and it's short—$900,000 and it only has 3½ months to run before it turns Rick into a free agent. "We'll worry about that later," Dallas says.

To satisfy Cleveland is the next step. The deal gets bigger and bigger. With Lake on the D.L. indefinitely and Jody working into the hot and humid months of July and August, the Cubs need another catcher. Ron Hassey is not only a lefthanded-hitting catcher, but he has been on the market since the spring. The Giants have shown a lot of interest in him.

Meanwhile, back on the field, the Cubs find themselves the victim of some heroics. The Expos ruin another great outing by Reuschel and beat the Cubs 2-1 with runs in the eighth and ninth off Smith.

Wallach's leadoff homer in the ninth comes off of Smith,

who continues to struggle. The Cubs reach Gullickson for only one run—that coming in the sixth when they manufactured a run on a hit. Dernier doubled and moved to third on an error by Gullickson. He scored on a 4-3 putout by Sandberg. The Cubs were coasting, but the Expos weren't finished. The lead was again down to a half game.

Always bouncing back, the Cubs beat Lea and Montreal 11-4 the next day. Hall, Matthews and Davis, who hit two, all homered as Eck was finally rewarded with some offensive support and his first Cub win.

On June 13, Trout went against Rogers. Trout was 5-1 and Rogers 2-5. Given past histories, anyone would have surmised that the records should have been reversed. The Cubs came up with three runs in the sixth inning to take a 7-4 lead.

Earlier, the game was delayed by rain for 1 hour and 40 minutes. Dallas spent the time well. He was on the phone to Indians G.M. Phil Seghi and Gabe Paul. The deal was complete pending the game being free of injury to Mel Hall.

The Indians were to receive Hall, Joe Carter, who was killing pitchers in the American Association, Iowa pitcher Don Schulze and Double A pitcher Darryl Banks. The Cubs would receive Sutcliffe, a two-time 17-game winner and a 1983 All-Star pitcher, George Frazier, an accomplished middle man and Hassey, the back-up catching insurance they needed.

The feeling Dallas had was this: He had built a team that was a contender and that could make a great move with the right additions. Pitching was scarce everywhere—that was a common fact. He could replace Hall with Moreland, who was dying to play every day and prove Dallas and Frey wrong. Carter, Schulze and Banks were playing in the minors. Carter may one day prove to be a very good player, Schulze is anyone's guess and Banks was struggling at Double A. There was no way Dallas couldn't make the deal even though the contracts of the three players he received were in the high-income bracket. It didn't matter. Winning the N.L. East, the pennant and the World Series—having that legitimate shot—meant more to Dallas and Tribune Company than anything.

The press conference took place immediately after the game. Dallas spoke highly of Hall, but pointed the media in the direction of the pitching and catching help he had pulled in. The media was apprehensive at first.

"I hate to give up the kids," Dallas said. "But you've got to take a chance at pitching when you get the opportunity."

Accenting the negative, the press countered that the Cubs were throwing away their best minor league every-day playing prospect—Carter—and their best minor league pitcher—Schulze. Dallas replied that he would have to live with that. Meanwhile, he had put together a solid team, a team even more well-rounded than the 1969 club. The pitching depth was there and would be even greater if and when Sanderson and Ruthven returned. Frazier would provide the bullpen with the middle man it lacked. And Hassey might prove to be invaluable. "Everybody else in Chicago may be worried about us pulling another Lou Brock, but not me," Green added.

Dallas was going for it. He has always been that type of individual. He looked at the Cubs and the near future and decided that great things were possible if he could just add a couple more pieces to the puzzle.

Moreland was ecstatic, "I don't know whether to laugh or cry," when told about the news that right field was his for the duration of the season. Keith was well liked by everyone. His contentment brought the club a little closer.

Meanwhile in Oakland, three former Indians were trying to figure a way to Chicago. They were scheduled to arrive during the next day's game against the Phillies. Instead they took the first flight out—a red eye.

"We couldn't get here fast enough," Sutcliffe said. "We've

just made up 20 games in the standings overnight. That is probably the greatest streak in the history of the game. It feels great to be on that side of it."

What followed continued to prove that nothing would come easy for the Cubs. All teams are required to have players pass through waivers. The Cubs failed to secure the necessary waivers. It is one of those technicalities that should never be overlooked. It could spell disaster, which it almost did in this case.

In the matter of a day, Dallas went from being lambasted for trading away the kids to being applauded for making a move that would definitely strengthen the club, and then back to being lambasted for the waiver situation.

He accepted the responsibility for the foul-up, the responsibility that comes with the general manager's position.

Dallas took the heat — and there was plenty of it. All that the Cubs, Dallas, the "traded" Cubs, the Indians and the baseball world could do was wait for five days and see if any of the general manager brotherhood was going to call the Cubs on the mistake.

In the five days it took to clear waivers, speculation was heavy. Philly certainly could have stepped in. The Phils were stung by Dallas in the Dernier deal when Dallas wouldn't allow the Phils to send Bobby back to the minors thus forcing the Phillies to either keep him on the roster or trade him. Philly also had a lot to lose. The Cubs were suddenly putting together a powerhouse built, in large part, with former Phillies.

But no one budged. The Cubs and Indians changed course slightly and made it a purchase deal for the three Indians who they acquired. Five days after the deal was supposed to have gone through Dallas got the all-clear from the waiver wire. All four players cleared.

When Hall was basically in limbo, the outfielder spoke

out. He complained that the Cubs were embarrassing him and hurting his former teammates. "I don't understand it," he said. "And who the heck is this Rick Sutcliffe anyway. I've never heard of him."

Sutcliffe's reply: "I see he says he never heard of me. Well all that tells me is that Mel Hall can't read the newspaper. I've been pitching in the big leagues for 6½ seasons.

"I'll get to face him next spring training. Maybe then he'll know who I am."

In the meantime, the Cubs, Dallas and his staff went through four days of incredible scrutiny and blasting from the media and also the Phillie bats. Philly came in and man-handled the Cubs.

The first game they won 11-2 behind Carlton. The Cubs did find a silver lining in the fact they had played 10 straight errorless games—a club record. But big deal.

Hudson beat Rainey 5-2 in the second game. The Phils routed Reuschel in the third game 8-2 and wrapped it up with a 9-7 win on Sunday. The Mets took the lead in the interim. The Phillies climbed into second, a half-game back and the Cubs were third, two games back. It wasn't until the finale that the Cubs got hot. They hit four homers that day including two by Moreland. Philly also hit four.

"We just got kicked," Dallas said. "No two ways about it. We got stomped on good. I hope this isn't a sign of where we are going."

The Cubs lost four straight for the second time this season. Coincidentally, both losing streaks followed the two big deals for Eckersley and Sutcliffe.

The Cubs take a day off to lick their wounds and also spend a night raising money for Cubs Care. It's a grand night at Wrigley Field. The camaraderie of this club is evident even at this function. Everyone makes the new players feel at home. Everyone realizes that this team, this year could be special and nobody is going to step out of line.

Sut goes out in his first Cub start. It's at Pittsburgh on June 19th. He had pitched well early in the season for the Indians before complications from root canal work sapped his strength. He lost 20 pounds and went from a 3-1 record to 4-5. In his first Cub start he looked just a little shaky but still went eight innings allowing only five hits with three walks and nine strikeouts.

"It's great to be here," he said after the Cubs held on for a 4-3 win.

Everything said and done, the Cubs were also glad he was here. Before Dallas acquired Ruthven in May of 1983, the Cubs were really without any proven starters who had anything left. Fergie was in the distant twilight of his brilliant career and the rest of the pitchers were number four pitchers at best. They were asked to fill roles they really weren't cut out for. Ruthven was not a number one starter. He had always been a No. 2 or No. 3 starter in Philly. At best he was always behind Carlton.

By going after Sanderson, Eckersley and Sut, Dallas had accomplished the most difficult feat facing general managers today. He put together a pitching staff in little more than a year. He had a bona fide number one in Sutcliffe, a number two and three and combo in Eckersley and Trout with Sanderson a legitimate third or fourth man and Ruthven in the fifth slot. Of all the great things he has done, that may be the best of Dallas.

Speaking of Ruthven, he's back to throwing on the sidelines. All seems well.

Highlighted in the 4-3 win over the Pirates was Moreland who continues to thrive in the everyday role. He doubles and triples. Smitty picks up a save but only after bringing the Cubs to the brink of defeat. The Pirates scored all three of their runs in the ninth before Smith eased into the final out by getting Bill Madlock to pop up to Sandberg.

Smitty is warranting some concern. Are his knees giving him problems? Is it his arm? His head? No one knows for sure. All anyone knows is that he has struggled more through three months of 1984 than he did all of last season.

The blues continue after the one night reprieve. The Pirates take the final two games of the series, winning 5-1 and 8-6. Eck gets bombed in the 8-6 game. He's 1-4 but this was really the only loss he deserved. Once again, Sandberg puts on a display. He goes 4-for-5 with four runs scored and an RBI. Frey has certainly transformed the approach of Ryno. He is showing signs of a tremendous season.

Thankfully, it's a short trip. After three days in Pittsburgh, it's back to play the Cardinals at Wrigley Field. It's another big series. NBC will be televising the Saturday game. It was a year ago, on the Cardinals' second trip in, that the Cubs and Jody put the country and NBC on notice that they could put on a show. That weekend in 1983 was the beginning of the "Joo-Dee Joo-Dee" chants that haven't stopped. That was the series that Jody jumped into the headlines with homers in all three games in front of sellout after sellout.

The Cubs come into the series 2½ games back while the Cardinals are in fourth place, five games behind. Obviously, a Cardinal sweep would put the Cubs in fourth place and in jeopardy of going into the tank.

It is time for the Cubs to get back to the business at hand. A baseball season is the equivalent of a marathon. It's a long, hard grind. There are days, as there are stretches of the marathon, that the participant wavers through. There are days when everyone is tired, everyone is down. It's then that champions are made. When a good team struggles, and they all do, all they can hope is that their struggle will be brief and their opponent won't be on a tear.

The Cubs are at a point where they can prove it to themselves again—just what place is rightfully theirs in the N.L. East. They have to rebound and in the meantime they have to hope that the Mets and Phillies continue to play rollercoaster ball—up one minute and down the next.

The Cubs are 35-31, dangerously close to the .500 level. In the desert sun of Mesa, the Cubs would have been happy with a record putting them four games over the break-even point 66 games into the schedule. But every day the perspective, the goals change. The team is looking higher and higher every day. Guys like Matthews, Cey, and Bowa refuse to accept anything else. Before long everyone feels that way. Losing is an upset. No one should ever accept losing at the pro level. Finally, there are no Cubs that do. They would rather walk over hot coals barefoot or eat broken glass than lose.

The Cardinal series. The Cubs could be in sixth 35 games out and the Cardinals in fifth 34½ games out and still this series would create tons of interest. There are enough brawls in dirt-floor bars in central and southern Illinois to convince any impartial observer that this rivalry is serious.

Reuschel and John Stuper get the call in the first game. More than 34,000 show up on a Friday afternoon. With the wind blowing from the right field pole across the diamond to the pole displaying the No. 14 of the great Ernie Banks, the Cubs jump out early. The power is back.

They score four runs in the first, three on another More-land homer. Sandberg doubles setting the stage for Moreland. Before Ryno came Dernier who singled. "The Daily Double" is what Harry Caray has tagged them. That they are. The Cards come back with three runs in the fourth off Rick. It's not enough. Davis and Cey hit two-run homers in the sixth and eighth putting the Cardinals away. One thing about St. Louis, they have a difficult time coming back from large deficits because they lack the power punch a three-run homer can give a team. Granted they have the speed team for the '80s, but they could use a few bashers, too.

Perhaps in an attempt to boost his confidence, Frey uses Smith again. This time Lee is better. He faces six hitters in 1.2 innings and fans four.

Ryno gets three hits, all in his first three at-bats. He has seven hits in eight at-bats through one stretch and three were for extra bases. He's found the stroke.

The win puts the Cubs 1½ back of the Mets. The date is June 23. Bob Costas and Tony Kubek from NBC are at the park. The wind is blowing straight in at 14 miles per hour. It will not help any ball hit to the outfield.

Trout is going for the Cubs. Herzog counters with a rookie, Ralph Citarella.

Before this game is over, the world will be aware of two very important Cub facts: 1) they are indeed for real and 2) Ryne Sandberg may be having the greatest year of his young career.

Before you could applaud the Cubs miraculous 12-11 comeback win, before you could praise the efforts of Willie McGee, who hit for the cycle, and before you thanked your lucky stars that Dallas acquired Dernier, who scored four runs, had a double, stolen base, three hits, two RBI and the most crucial walk to this point in the season, you had to shake your head and make sure that what you had witnessed really happened.

Years from now, nay decades and generations from now, the Cubs-Cardinals game of June 23, 1984 will be known as The Sandberg Game.

Ryno not only continued his marvelous streak, he surpassed what he had done in the first two games of the series and the first two years of his career. He did in one game what no player had ever done to the great reliever Bruce Sutter. Sandberg hit two homers—two game-tying homers in the waning stages of the game—off Sutter.

When rookie Dave Owen stroked a bases-loaded single to right center with nobody out in the 11th, the sellout crowd of 38,901 was delirious and emotionally worn from the afternoon.

In the beginning there was really no drama. The Cards scored in the first off Trout. The Cubs came back with a run off Citarella, who was a little jittery in his first start. If not for a great diving play by Ozzie Smith the Cubs might have gained enough early momentum to put the Cards away for the day.

Instead, Ozzie's play sparked St. Louis to a six-run second inning sending Trout to the showers and the NBC producers to the Excedrin bottle. After four innings the Cards led 7-1.

In the fifth the Cubs edged back with two runs cutting it to 7-3. Bordi, who replaced Trout, at least kept the Cards at bay. The Cards struck right back with two runs in the sixth, both coming on a McGee homer.

With one out and Moreland on first in the Cubs sixth, Citarella threw inside to Cey. It hit him on the left wrist. He immediately dropped the bat and headed for the dugout. By the look of disdain on his face, it looked as if his season was over. Cub trainer Garofalo came out and Cey stayed in. Herzog removed Citarella.

Neil Allen walked Bowa. Hebner, batting for Dickie Noles, who replaced Bordi during the two-run Cardinal sixth, singled to load bases. Moreland scored on Hebner's hit making it 9-4. Dernier followed with a low, line-hugging double to left scoring Cey and Bowa. It was 9-6.

Suddenly, NBC was mighty happy it had decided to televise this game. Especially when Sandberg singled to left scoring Hebner and Dernier. What the network had then was a 9-8 game. Stay tuned.

That is where the score remained until fates greater than Sutter's split-finger fastball came into play. Sutter came on with two outs in the seventh. The four batters he faced between his arrival and Sandberg's leadoff appearance in the ninth didn't get the ball out of the infield against him. Then came Sandberg. The crowd was ready. It was showdown time.

Sandberg took Sutter over the wall in left center. It was tied. Sandberg, who had only one hit in 10 lifetime at-bats against Sutter, made the second one count.

The Wrigley Field hysteria didn't last long. The Cards fought back with two runs off Smith in the 10th. The Cubs and Smitty were at their lowest point. No team likes to fight back from a deficit as large as the one the Cubs were faced with and then lose. They'd rather get beat 7-1.

The chances looked bleak. Especially after the first two Cubs in the 10th, Bowa and Hebner, grounded out weakly. Dernier was next. The count rose to 3-2. The next pitch was borderline low. Dernier never hesitated. He headed for first. The ball squirted from Porter's glove. Doug Harvey called ball four.

"Then," Herzog would say later, "up comes Babe Ruth."

By now, NBC had seen enough. They were awarding Willie McGee the Player of the Game award, an obvious choice on any normal day.

As soon as they finished, Ryno went to work. The count was 1-and-1 when time stood still.

The third Sutter pitch climbed into the heavens and landed

in nearly the same spot as his first homer. The game was again tied. Wrigley Field was up for grabs. Sutter was dying.

Costas looked across the booth and shook his head. "I don't believe it. This may be the greatest game I've seen."

It wasn't over yet.

With two outs in the Cardinals 11th, Andy Van Slyke walked and stole second off Smith. But Lee got Mike Ramsey to ground out to Sandberg. In this incredibly wild game, Ramsey would represent the last St. Louis batter.

Dave Rucker came on in the 11th for the Cards in place of Sutter. He walked Durham leading off the inning. Herzog went to Jeff Lahti. Durham took off for second with Moreland batting. He dove into second headfirst, ultimately jamming his shoulder. Porter's throw skipped into center field. Leon got up and went to third.

Herzog went to the mound. The decision was obvious. Lahti walked Moreland and Davis intentionally. Smith was due up in Cey's former spot. Frey went with Dave Owen, his last position player on the bench. Owen wrote the final chapter to the storybook ending. He singled to right center.

For the third time in less than three innings Wrigley Field rocked in ecstacy.

Sandberg was probably as shocked as Sutter who was definitely as shocked as Herzog.

"I think we kind of amazed ourselves," Sandberg said. "I'm in a state of shock. I don't even know what day it is. The last thing I was thinking both times was to hit the ball out. I guessed split-finger fastball both times and found them."

Said Sutter, "I made two bad pitches and both went out of the park." "Sandberg," Herzog said, "is the greatest player I've ever seen."

This game will last a lifetime. Anyone who was there will never forget it. Anyone who took part in it will always cherish the memory. If it had been a playoff game or a Series game it would have moved into a hallowed place next to the sixth game of the 1975 Red Sox-Reds World Series.

It was that good. Not merely as entertainment or exciting baseball, but for what it did for the Cubs, for Sandberg, for the city of Chicago. For three months, the Cubs had left a trail of explosives. On this day, Sandberg lit the fuse. The city would never be the same. Sandberg's life, his career may never be the same. He's on his way.

In his last 16 at-bats he had 12 hits. On this day he was 5 for 6 with two homers and seven RBI. The guy is phenomenal.

A victory like this has such beautiful ramifications. There won't be a game this season that the Cubs feel they can't win. It will make every obstacle beatable. It may make the Cubs unbeatable. It will certainly leave its impact on the team, the city, the baseball world.

Durham is hurting, the club decides to put him on the DL. Dallas recalls Bosley.

Sunday. The Day After. It's time to see Sutcliffe again. It's his first Wrigley Field appearance as a Cub. The place is still buzzing with 40,110 fans cramming into the oldest park in the league. Sutcliffe pitching in front of a home sellout and in a pennant race seizes the day and writes it his way. Through 4.2 innings he has a one-hitter along with eight strikeouts.

He also has a 3-0 lead with Sandberg tripling home Dernier with one of the runs and scoring another in the third inning. Davis finished off the Cards with a two-run homer in the eighth. The Red Birds are dead birds.

Sutcliffe strikes out 14, the most by a Cub pitcher since Fergie fanned 14 Phillies 13 years ago. It was a great welcome the fans gave Sutcliffe when he walked off the mound at the conclusion. It was a lovely first meeting. First impressions will hopefully be lasting impressions.

The Cubs win 5-0 and pull within a half-game of the Mets and Phils.

"This is the biggest game I've pitched in three years," Rick says.

Then comes another letdown with Pittsburgh in town. The Pirates shutout the Cubs 3-0 behind Jose DeLeon on Monday. How can any team be playing great for three days and then look this flat the next day?

"That's why I don't believe in momentum," Frey says. "Momentum is overrated. See what happened when a team with a lot of momentum played a team with no momentum. The other team's pitcher stuck it to us. Big deal, momentum."

Ditto for the next game. Pittsburgh 9, Cubs 0 in Game 1 of a double header. Jason Thompson homers twice. Jason homers twice again in Game 2 as does his teammate Doug Frobel but the Cubs manage to hang on after a six-run first inning that included Woods' second homer of the season, both off Larry McWilliams.

They come away with a split after a 9-8 win. Smith got his 15th save despite allowing two runs and four hits in 2.2 innings.

The Cubs stay close thanks to the Mets and Phils who continue to lose. The Cubs are still third but only a game back.

The last game before the big West Coast trip pegs Reuschel against Lee Tunnell. It's another crazy game. Sandberg belts a two-run homer in the first, his 10th of the season.

He goes 3-for-6 with three more RBIs, plus a double. But this game is one of those games when both teams score in bunches early and then sit back and play for a run here and a run there.

After five innings it's 6-5 Cubs. The Pirates end up tying the game in the ninth off, you guessed it, Smith.

In the 11th, Sandberg (who else?) starts the inning with a double off Rod Scurry. Cotto bats for Stoddard and singles Sandberg to third. Tanner orders Moreland walked. Hebner is next. With a chance to take out some aggression on his former teammates, Hebner fans as Tanner pulls right fielder Frobel into a second baseman's position and moves Ray behind the bag. He leaves the infield alignment intact for Davis but it goes for naught when Scurry can't find the plate and walks in Ryno with the winning run.

It wasn't pretty, but it got the job done. It's on to the West Coast and the final trip of the year to California. Unless, of course, the magic continues and San Diego is playing in October. San Diego in October. It must be gorgeous. But it is only June 27.

The Cubs leave, one game back.

The West Coast trip. Long the Waterloo of many a good team. The rotation is set. The Cubs open the series with Trout going against the Dodgers, who are in third, 5½ games back. The Cubs fall behind the Dodgers and Alejandro Pena 3-1 after five innings. Then grand things begin happening. Sandberg, who is trailing Steve Sax in the All-Star balloting by a hefty margin, leads off the sixth with a homer. A walk to Matthews, a Moreland single and a wild pitch tie the score.

Davis walks, Cey grounds into a fielder's choice and Johnstone pops out foul. The score is still tied with two outs. Tommy Lasorda walks Bowa intentionally forcing Frey's hand. Jim stays with Trout even though general strategy dictates a pinch hitter ("Every situation is different," Frey maintains. "Nobody knows as much about this game as they think. You make a decision based on the complete situation.")

Trout tops the ball down the third base line. Shortstop Dave Anderson charges in and throws to Mike Marshall.

The ball reaches Marshall the same time as Trout. The ball is loose. Two runs score. Cubs win 5-3.

Game 2 of the series. Sutcliffe, the boy wonder, returns to face the team, the manager, that left him confused and battered after the 1981 season. Much is made of the 1981 closing scene when Sutcliffe tore apart Lasorda's office after learning he had been left off the playoff roster.

Sutcliffe wants revenge. He is a great competitor. On this night, though, he wants more than he can possibly deliver. He only lasts four innings. The Dodgers cuff him around pretty good while Orel Hershiser, a bright light in a dark Dodger season, throws a complete game. The Cubs fall 7-1.

Connors isn't on hand. He is with Sanderson and Ruthven up the California coast. Both pitched in a Class A game for the Lodi club. Scott started and allowed a homer, but overall pitched well enough to satisfy Connors. Ruthven, way ahead of his scheduled return, also throws well.

Connors returns the next day and is about as happy as can be.

"They both threw well," he said. "Ruthven is amazing coming back this quick. We're not going to rush them though. It's a pair of delicate situations."

Scott and Rufus come back appreciating the big leagues. "It was so dark in the park I couldn't see the catcher's signs," Rufus said.

"The place was not one I'd like to return to," Sanderson says. "I guess this was major league appreciation day."

In the Saturday night game, Rainey struggles early. The Dodgers let Chuck off without doing much damage, but Frey has seen enough after 2.1 innings. By then the score is tied at three. The Cubs have a chance to win this game. But Frey isn't convinced they can outscore the Dodgers with Rainey struggling.

It's time to make a move to Frazier. George, who set a

World Series record by losing three games to the Dodgers in the 1981 Fall Classic, does a great job. He throws 3.2 innings allowing a run and a hit. The Cubs take a 7-4 lead into the ninth when they rip Carlos Diaz for seven runs and a 14-4 rout.

After the game, the Cubs' clubhouse is one big laughing box. The Dodgers are stunned. Lasorda sits in the Dodgers' dugout long after the game is over. The Cubs have regained a share of the division lead. The Dodgers may be finished. It isn't often the Dodgers are humiliated. It is even rarer that it should happen at Dodger Stadium in front of nearly 50,000. The only consolation is the Padres score. San Diego loses 4-1 to St. Louis farther down the Coast.

"This game doesn't mean anything if we don't win tomorrow," Frey says. A deal to send Dickie Noles to Texas is readied and will be announced following the Sunday wrapup in L.A. Dallas is about to begin stockpiling a few promises for the future. Dickie isn't pitching much and he has fallen back in the hierarchy of hurlers.

Sunday in L.A. is gorgeous. The Dodgers salute Pee Wee Reese and Don Drysdale before their regular game and after their Old-Timers Game.

Eckersley goes against Valenzuela. The Cubs take a 3-0 lead against Fernando on a two-run triple by Jody Davis and a double play by Cey that scored Moreland, who is still hitting cleanup and playing first with Durham sidelined. The Cubs add a very big run in the eighth on three consecutive hits by Dernier, Sandberg and Matthews, all with two out.

The Dodgers come back with one run in the fifth. In the ninth, Lee Smith comes on and gets Guerrero to fly out. Marshall singles and Frey comes out to talk with Smith. Mike Scioscia singles to right sending Marshall to second and bringing the tying run to the plate.

Greg Brock hits a grounder to Moreland who throws to

Owen at second for the force. Owen's return throw goes into the Cubs dugout scoring Marshall and sending Brock to second.

When Moreland comes over to retrieve the ball, Frey tells him to tell Smith not to worry about the baserunner and just concentrate on the hitter – pinch-hitter R.J. Reynolds.

Dodgers third base coach Joey Amalfitano catches on. The Dodgers protest on the grounds that Frey's talk with Moreland constituted a second trip to the mound. The rule book bears this out.

Smith has to be removed. Brusstar enters. Reynolds hits a shot to right scoring Brock and bringing the Dodgers within one run. Russell pinch hits and follows with another single putting Reynolds on second.

Brusstar can't find the plate. He walks Sax. This could be it.

Ken Landreaux is the next hitter. With the tying run on third, the winner on second, the lefthanded-hitting Landreaux is facing the struggling righthander Brusstar.

The count works its way to the limit. Brusstar throws a high fastball on 3-and-2. Landreaux swings and misses. The Cub dugout goes crazy.

"I said 'Thank the Lord,' " Frey says. "The Man was looking out for us today. I almost cost us the game but Landreaux saves us."

Three of four from the Dodgers in L.A. isn't bad. It moves the Cubs a game in front in the East. It's on to San Diego and the first-place Padres.

The Monday Night Game of the Week is the Cubs-Padres, the Eastern leader vs. the Western leader.

As the game unfolds, it appears that Dravecky will cause the Cubs problems.

It's a game they have little chance of winning. Dravecky holds the Cubs scoreless until the sixth when they finally inch a run across to tie the game at one.

The Padres come back with another run in the sixth thanks in part to a couple of Cub errors. McReynolds drives home the winner. The Padres add three runs in the seventh off Reuschel and Frazier making sure the Cubs don't harvest any comeback ideas. The Cubs drop a 5-1 decision. The loss puts the Cubs only .003 points ahead of the second-place Mets.

The Sandberg chase is on. The media hype heightens. Ryno has taken the country by storm. The All-Star balloting is coming to a close and Ryno has suddenly vaulted past Alan Wiggins and Sax. The L.A. fans were actually cheering Sandberg.

The second game of the series is a beauty. The Cubs win 3-2 but could easily have lost if it wasn't for a great throw from center by Dernier. The Cubs already led 3-2 when the Padres threatened in the fifth. With Wiggins on second and Gwynn on first, Garvey lined a single to center with one out. Wiggins wasn't about to stop. Dernier fielded the ball maybe 80 feet back of second. He came charging in and gloved the ball ankle-high on a bounce. In one fluid motion he threw to Davis at the plate. It wasn't even close. Wiggins was out by eight feet, Dernier's throw coming to Davis on the fly, about three inches off the ground. It was a perfect play.

"How about that throw?" crowed Frey afterward. "It was some kind of play. You've got to have that happen to be a contender."

"All I had to do was catch it," Davis said. "There was nothing else to do with something that perfect."

The Fourth of July. The Cubs come into the game tied for the lead. A festive holiday crowd comes out to Jack Murphy Stadium for the game. A total of 53,675,(52,134 paid) watch a classic from the old days—Sutcliffe vs. Show.

The crowd, the largest to attend a Padres game in San Diego, watched as Sut was in complete control. He allowed only four hits through 7.1 innings. He even contributed what turned out to be the game-winning hit when he doubled in the second scoring Ron Hassey. Hassey played first base allowing Moreland to shift to third. Talk about versatile. With Durham out the Cubs have used Moreland at first now and then. Tonight they gave Cey a night off to rest his wrist and moved Moreland to third.

Unfortunately, the versatility causes more problems. Hassey ends up tearing up his knee. He'll be going back to Chicago in the morning, probably for surgery. First Lake, then Durham, now Hassey. And that doesn't include Ruthven or Sanderson. This team is beginning to resemble a combat unit.

The Cubs doubled their lead in the fifth, 2-0. Just as quickly, the Padres cut it back to one at 2-1. It stayed that way but not because San Diego wasn't trying to do otherwise. With the tying run on third and the winner on first in the ninth, Frey went to Smith. He looked like a genius. Smith got Kennedy to ground into a rally-ending, game-ending double play.

The Cubs leave San Diego with their heads high. The two toughest stops on the West Coast are behind them. The last stop is San Francisco—a four-game series that will wrapup the regular season trips to California.

The Cubs have won five of seven on the trip. It's been successful to this point. It is not time to gloat. Rather, now is the time to accent the advantage the Cubs have—they are hot and the Giants are not. It's the last series before the All-Star Break. Even though the Giants are down and all but out, the Cubs remember very well that the last two seasons were turned upside down in San Francisco.

"The team came out here last year and got beat good,"

Frey said." I don't think anyone has forgotten that. Everyone is aware that history can repeat itself."

Trout comes down with a blister on his pitching hand and after he peels it, Frey is forced to scratch him from his final first half series rotation.

Hassey departs for Chicago. He'll undergo arthroscopic surgery on his knee. Just what he needed and just what the Cubs and Moreland needed. Once again Keith will become vital.

"I'll play anywhere they want," he says. "Anywhere that is except second base. I'll let Kid Natural (Sandberg) take care of that."

Sandberg and Davis will be held over in San Francisco for the All-Star Game. Ryno is starting, J.D. is the backup. Both are a few degrees above excited.

Cindy Sandberg is awake late at night with their baby. She learns that Ryno has made the All-Star team and promptly dials San Francisco to tell her husband the great news. Ryno is in the twilight zone – somewhere between 1 and 4 in the morning. Nevertheless, the moment is worth cherishing.

The first game of the series is highlighted by Sanderson's return. He works 5.1 innings allowing six hits and two runs earned. The Cubs beat up on Bill Laskey with four runs in five innings. Former Philly Randy Lerch is next. Lerch doesn't retire a hitter while the Cubs score three runs. They are on the way to a romp, 9-3.

Cey homers twice, giving him 36 lifetime against the Giants, the majority coming right at Candlestick.

He is still hurting. It's been three weeks since he last homered.

"My wrist isn't getting any better," he says. "I can't seem

to get any power in my swing." Don't tell Laskey that.

Dave Owen also hits the first homer of his career in the third inning.

The Cubs lead stays at a game.

Sanderson feels fine. The test will come in a day or two when the back muscles have a chance to react to tonight.

With Scott's return, it means someone has to be dropped from the rotation. That someone is Rainey. It's obvious, but it is also very telling of how far this club's pitching has come. Fergie is gone, Noles is gone, Bird is gone, Martz is gone and Ripley is gone. Rainey is out of the rotation. Only Trout and Ruthven remain from the group that has started the majority of the games the last two seasons.

The Cubs edge the Giants 5-4 on Friday night once again using the long ball to their advantage. Matthews homers and so does All-Star Davis. The Cubs break up a 3-3 deadlock with two runs in the seventh. Owen comes through for the second straight night with the game-winner in the seventh.

San Francisco adds a run in the seventh off Stoddard, who gets the win and is 6-1.

The rumor says the Giants would fire Frank Robinson if the All-Star Game wasn't in San Francisco. The story says that the Giants don't want to cast a shadow over the city in a proud moment. The Democratic Convention moves in after the baseball All-Star Break. That too is a proud moment for San Francisco so Frank will probably outlast July anyway.

Saturday is a big game. It's an NBC game. It's a start for Reuschel. With Sanderson back and Ruthven not far behind, the pitching staff will be undergoing a minor facelift. Will it be Reuschel? This start is key for Rick.

He lasts only 3.2 innings allowing six hits and three runs,

only one of which was earned. Two Cub errors don't help matters. The Giants knock the Cubs from first with a 7-2 win. When Frey is pressed about Reuschel's performance and the club's pitching plans he only says, "performance is the only criteria for judgment when you have more players than positions."

This must be the series for career firsts. Dan Rohn, up from Iowa in place of Hassey, hits his first homer, a pinch-hit one no less, off Krukow in the eighth. Rohn couldn't believe he hit it out. He stopped at second.

"I thought it bounced over," he says.

The Cubs enter the final game before the All-Star Break with a 47-36 record. They trail the Mets by a half-game. A year ago, the Cubs were on a tear following back-to-back weekend series against the Cardinals. They ended up losing a doubleheader to the Expos on the final day before the break. Sanderson won Game 2 and was injured in the process when he tripped over first base. The Cubs hit the break last year at 38-41 and were in fourth, four games back.

The Cubs, in reality, are much better than the 3½-game difference from one year to the next would indicate.

With the All-Star Game on deck, the national media converge on San Francisco beginning on Sunday. The top baseball story in the country is the Cubs. Jim Frey is the man of the hour. The most asked question is how is he doing it after that horrendous spring training?

"When we started the season we were looking for a fourth starter," he said. "Now we have five with a couple of others who could start if we needed them. That's an incredible change. Give Dallas the credit. He went out and got the pitching we needed.

"We said during the off-season that getting the rotation in order was our first priority. We're getting there now.

"I'll tell you right now that our pitching will be what carries us the second half.

"I don't know where we're going to finish. I have no idea. If I knew we were going to win it, I'd hop a plane to Vegas and throw all the money I could on the Cubs winning it. But I don't know, nobody knows. We are so far from the end of the season it's foolish to think in terms of winning a division or anything. All I want to do right now is win today."

He does his best by sending Sutcliffe out, a day early. Sut can handle it. He moves his record to 4-1 with a 6-3 win. He works 7.1 innings on three days of rest. He gives up only five hits and three runs (two earned). The Giants' pitcher is Mark Davis. He has struggled through a 3-8 first half after looking good in spring training.

Sandberg comes to the break with 118 hits, the most in the majors. He finishes up Sunday with a two-for-five day.

The Mets also win to maintain a half-game lead. The Cubs hit the break with a 48-36 record, a great improvement. There may be more to come.

"This is a great way to end the first half," Frey says. "It's marvelous to come out here and go home with an 8-3 record on the Coast."

The Cubs were 11-7 on the West Coast for the season. They have rarely been better.

"The key for us this half, the series that showed what we could do, was the one after Philly bombed us four straight and then we lost two of three in Pittsburgh," Frey said.

"After that we swept St. Louis. That was impressive."

"The Cubs," Herzog says," have great talent and they are putting it all together."

More than 2.1 million fans packed Wrigley Field in 1984.   (Photo by John Swart)

Yes, Cubs Fever brought the fans out early day after day.

(Photo by Stephen Green. Courtesy of the Chicago Cubs)

Dennis Eckersley was 8–3 during the second half of 1984. (Photo by John Swa

Keith Moreland was the first of Dallas' main acquisitions.   (Photo by John Swart)

Gary Matthews, "The Sarge," led the club on the field and in the clubhouse
(Photo by John Swa

The captain, Larry Bowa, brought leadership to the club and helped Sandberg develop into a Gold Glove infielder. (Photo by John Swart)

Cubs coach Don Zimmer greets Sandberg after Ryne's second homer against the Cardinals' Bruce Sutter on June 23, 1984.

(Photo by Phil Velasquez. Courtesy of the *Chicago Sun-Times*)

Ryne had an incredible season both in the field and at the plate in winning the eague's Most Valuable Player Award.

Cubs pitching coach Billy Connors always found a way to bring the best out of his staff.   (Photo by Stephen Green. Courtesy of the Chicago Cubs)

One of Connor's prize projects was Steve Trout who had his best season under Connors in 1984. (Photo by Stephen Green. Courtesy of the Chicago Cubs)

Coach Don Zimmer is like having a second manager. He waved the runners around third. (Photo by Stephen Green. Courtesy of the Chicago Cubs)

Jody Davis was one of three Cubs inherited by Dallas Green who starred for the division champions. (Photo by Stephen Green. Courtesy of the Chicago Cubs)

The most important position player acquired for the 1984 season was Bobby Dernier who led the club in steals.

(Photo by Stephen Green. Courtesy of the Chicago Cubs)

On August 23, 1983, Lee Elia addressed the media one day after he was replaced as the Cubs manager. (Photo by Stephen Green. Courtesy of the Chicago Cubs)

Dallas Green, left, and Jim Frey share a laugh during a rare lighter moment in the Cubs 1984 spring training camp.

(Photo by Stephen Green. Courtesy of the Chicago Cubs)

Pensive Jim Frey became the first manager to win a title with the Cubs since Charlie Grimm in 1945.   (Photo by Stephen Green. Courtesy of the Chicago Cubs)

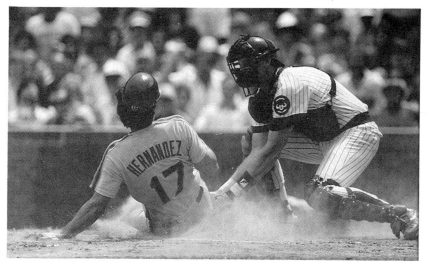

A key play in a key series. Jody Davis tags out New York's Keith Hernandez in a close play at the plate. (Photo by Stephen Green. Courtesy of the Chicago Cubs)

The celebration in Pittsburgh begins after Rick Sutcliffe struck out Joe Orsulak on September 24, 1984. (Photo by Stephen Green. Courtesy of the Chicago Cubs)

While the club celebrated in Pittsburgh, the Cubs faithful followed suit at Wrigley Field.   (Photo by Sandy Bertog)

The team returned to Chicago and was met by thousands of fans at O'Hare Airport following the clinching game in Pittsburgh.

(Photo by Stephen Green. Courtesy of the Chicago Cubs)

Following the final regular season game at Wrigley Field, the Cubs, led by Jim Frey, saluted the Cubs fans. (Photo by Stephen Green. Courtesy of the Chicago Cubs)

An agreement reached, Dallas shakes hands with Rick Sutcliffe. The Cubs signed Rick to a five-year contract in December, 1984.

(Photo by Stephen Green. Courtesy of the Chicago Cubs)

The Cubs returned from the All-Star Break to face the Dodgers and 34,615 fans on a Thursday afternoon at Wrigley Field. The city is captivated. The Cubs trail the Mets by a half-game but all in all the scene was reminiscent of 1969.

The crowds came early and stayed late. Their lives were filled with one thought and that was of winning a pennant for the first time in 39 years. In the previous six home dates, four weekday dates, the Cubs averaged more than 32,000 paid. It was incredible.

Trout began the Cubs' second half and pitched very well through eight-plus innings. Frey went to Stoddard who had been outstanding on the West Coast.

The game went into extra innings tied at two. The Cubs had trouble with Alejandro Pena but Lasorda pulled him after eight innings and came in with six-foot five-inch Tom Niedenfuer. Ryno had only one hit in eight at-bats against Niedenfuer, but as usual nothing that happened before seemed to matter. Faced with a 1-2 count, Sandberg drove the ball into the left-center field bleachers. It set off another incredible scene.

"I was down 1-2 and decided I had to choke up on the bat a little," Sandberg said. "As it turned out it helped me handle the high fastball which is just what he threw. I was just trying to get something started. I guess I got something finished instead."

It was still very, very early—only 85 games into the season. But the Chicago fans were being romanced again. For the first time in more than a few seasons the club was not only exciting but competitive and there were new heroes to idolize.

One of the problems inherent to the job of rebuilding is waiting for your players to become household names, waiting for them to be given a personality by the public.

Little by little, Davis, Durham and Sandberg began gaining that notoriety from the public. Jody's began in June of

1983 when he hit the three homers against the Cardinals. Sandberg's burst upon the world when he hit the two homers off Sutter on national television on June 23. From then on the bombardment came hurdling at him. Especially after the Whitey Herzog quote that set Sandberg above all others—Herzog called him the best player he'd ever seen. Then came the All-Star balloting and the late rally that pushed him far and away ahead of Sax and Wiggins.

"The last few days I've been asked a lot of questions by the media," Ryno said. "It doesn't bother me. Thus far, I've been able to concentrate totally on the game when it starts."

The 11-game homestand had begun and tickets were becoming a hot commodity. Was this all a mirage? The question was there. But at least there was that question to ask.

In the medicinal department, Trout came up with a new cure for a blister on the middle finger of his pitching hand. After peeling the skin off following his last start, he wasn't able to finish the pre-All-Star Break with a start. That didn't sit well with Frey.

Well he went eight-plus against the Dodgers and credited his longevity to a combination of rubbing pickle juice, crab meat and tobacco juice on the blister. So much for medical advancement.

Speaking of tobacco chewing. Frey quit cold turkey following Sunday's game in San Francisco. He quit smoking on New Year's Eve cold turkey. He's obviously a man of strong will.

Moreland is talking to some recording people in Los Angeles regarding a remake of the Cubs' theme song from 1969, "Hey-Hey, Holy Mackerel," Keith and Jody Davis are both interested and they'll spice it up into a country-western version. When reminded that when the '69 Cubs recorded it they finished behind the Mets, Keith said, "About the time it's ready to come out we'll decide if it's appropriate."

The Mets rally for five runs in the ninth in Atlanta to maintain their half-game lead. Somebody tells Frey that they can't believe the Mets are doing it. Frey's reply: "People are saying the same things about us. It doesn't make much difference."

The lead of Bernie Lincicome's July 13th column in the *Tribune* went like this:

"To be both shirtless and faithless is to be a Chicago Cub fan in July. The two naturally go together, as if everyone at Wrigley Field exposes his chest to make it easier for the Cubs to cut his heart out again. It is a bizarre devotion that passes for Cub tradition after the All-Star Break."

Leon is off the DL. Given the opportunity to leave the club while he was sidelined, Durham balked.

"They said I could go back to Cincinnati and I said no thanks," he said. "There is no way I don't want to be around these days. Any other year I may have gone but not this year."

On the subject of the rampaging Sandberg, Durham says, "You haven't seen the best of Ryne Sandberg yet."

Sandberg on Sandberg: "They told me I could hit 10-15 homers a year if I changed my hitting approach. But they didn't say it would be this year."

The next day the Cubs play before yet another SRO crowd. When it's your year things happen that turn heads. The Cubs led 3-0 before the Dodgers rallied to tie the score. L.A. had the momentum, but the Cubs came charging back again behind Moreland.

Moreland has been playing very well since the Hall trade.

He has 23 RBIs and is batting close to .300. Plus, any ball he can get to he catches. Make no mistake, Roberto Clemente and Keith Moreland won't ever be confused as outfielders, but Moreland is getting the job done.

He had four RBI in the 7-5 win on a two-run double and a two-run homer that put the Cubs back in front.

The key to this win beyond the obvious was the defensive play and defensive adjustments made by Frey in the ninth inning. Terry Whitfield leads off for the Dodgers and hits a soft fly to left. Henry Cotto, just in the game defensively after pinch-hitting in the eighth, makes a shoestring diving catch. The next hitter is Sax. He tops a ball down the line at third. Owen, in the game defensively, races in and throws off balance to get Sax, who is one of the quickest down the line.

"In a normal year," Lasorda says. "Nobody makes that play."

Who said this is normal?

Landreaux is next. With two outs he hits a rope off Smith to left center. The ball hangs just enough so Dernier gets to it.

A year ago, none of the three were on the club. At the beginning of spring training two of the three didn't figure to make the team, especially Cotto.

He came out of nowhere. It was one of those situations where a young player suddenly gets a chance to play a few games in the late innings. He makes a good running catch one day, a diving catch the next day. He gets two or three hits while everyone else is taking it easy, and pretty soon management is looking seriously at the guy. Cotto played more and more as the spring wore on and as long as he played he was impressive. He led the club in hitting and played flawlessly in the field. The kid was a definite bonus.

Owen came up when Veryzer went down in Cincinnati with the broken left thumb. Owen has a great arm, better-than-average range and good speed on the bases. He reminds a lot of people of Don Kessinger, same kind of player, same kind of build—tall and lanky.

And of course there's Dernier. He's been the biggest addition to the club as far as everyday players are concerned. There is no telling where we'd be without him and no telling where he'd be without us. Philly had just about written him off.

The Saturday crowd is circling Wrigley Field. The scalpers are making more than ends meet. For every scalper there must be ten buyers.

It's not only where the Cubs are in the standings, it's the way they are playing. It is exciting to watch the Cubs play. Except today. Orel Hershiser crushed the Cubs for the second straight time. He beat them in L.A. with a superb complete-game effort with nine strikeouts. The guys can't believe that Lasorda's had him working from the pen. He drops the Cubs again in front of more than 40,000. The Cubs get only two runners into scoring position all day. Another complete game for Orel—a two-hitter.

It's time to bring on Fernando.

And, of course, watch those Mets in Atlanta.

Preparation begins for the possibility of playing in October. The word is that player appearances should be cut down, especially for the everyday players. What's another $300 when a guy is making $500,000 a year or just under $10,000 a week. Isn't a shot at the division title worth more?

Unfortunately, nobody thought about that in 1969. Leo's boys were out almost every night pulling in a few extra dollars. In their defense the salary structure was much tighter.

It's another drawback to not having lights. No other team in baseball has to worry about its players staying out late at night making personal appearances.

NBC is adding two more Cubs games to the schedule. The Cubs are the hottest item on the network schedule, or so it seems.

The finale against L.A. and what a finish. Fernando and Eckersley are both perfect through four innings. L.A. scores in the sixth and for a short time it looks as if Fernando may stick it to the Cubs.

But just as was the case on the West Coast, whenever the possibility appears to exist for a crack to develop, the Cubs rally. Sandberg leads off the bottom of the seventh with a homer and Matthews follows with a double. After Moreland fans, Jody is walked intentionally. Fernando gets himself in bigger trouble by throwing a wild pitch putting runners on second and third with Cey batting.

Cey lines one to center field. Rookie Franklin Stubbs comes in and puts his glove up. It's one of those bizarre plays that people may remember for years to come. Stubbs goes to throw the ball an instant before he catches it. The ball glances off his glove and rolls past him practically to the warning track.

Matthews scores easily from third and Davis from second. Cey makes it to third. He scores a moment later when Woods flies again to Stubbs. From then on it's academic, the Cubs pull within a half-game of the Mets again, after Atlanta finally wins one of the four.

The crowd totals 146,014 for the four-day series, the second largest in the history of Wrigley Field.

In the first inning Frey asks the umpires if there is a rule prohibiting a pitcher from pitching with a white flap hanging over his shoe, which Fernando has.

The umpires confer and say yes there is such a rule. They tell Fernando to change shoes. Lasorda can't believe it and protests on the grounds that he never saw the bulletin from the league claiming that a pitcher couldn't wear shoes with a white tongue.

If it upset Fernando it was difficult to tell. He set down the next 10 Cubs, four by strikeouts. He had a one-hitter going for six innings before Sandberg reached him for the second hit—a long homer to right center.

"If somebody thinks it was a psychological ploy to get at Fernando they're wrong," Frey says. "It obviously had a big effect on him didn't it? We couldn't get the ball out of the infield for six innings."

Eckersley was equally tough. He went into the eighth inning having allowed only four hits and no walks while fanning seven. He was tough and has been in two of his last three starts. He's up to 3-5 and the pitchers Dallas has obtained since the end of last season are 21-9. That's a main difference from a year ago.

With Ruthven coming off the DL tomorrow, the Cubs are forced to make a move. They send Rainey to Oakland for the infamous player to be named later. Dallas is stockpiling for the future. You never know who Texas may come up with for Noles and who Oakland may yield for Chuck once those teams are out of the race. It's a slight gamble but one definitely worth taking. With Rufus coming back there isn't a place for Rainey except in long relief. With the way Bordi and Frazier have been pitching and with Reuschel available it was a good idea to secure some futures with a Rainey deal.

Chuck will be missed as a person. He's one of the most down-to-earth players in the game. He turned 30 only a day before.

Once again, it's a battle of powerhouses. Monday the Padres come in for three games. They're leading the West by a week of losses. But the Cubs are still rolling.

What do they say about good pitching and good hitting? Well, the Cubs were stopped Monday 4-0. It was their second shutout in three days. The Cubs seem to go through this once a month.

They've gotten 16 hits in the last four games and have scored in one inning of their last 27, the four-run seventh against Fernando.

This is no time to panic even though Mark Thurmond is a household name only in his own household.

Thurmond was tough and the Cubs weren't.

Rufus comes back to work eight good innings. Even in defeat, the possibilities of a healthy Ruthven are a big plus. Just think, the Cubs with five solid starters, with Rufus as the fifth.

"The true test was not today but the rest of the season. And I honestly believe it will be there," he says.

He had struggled practically every outing before the operation on May 23.

"The hitters were looking for what I'd thrown them the previous nine or 10 years and by the second or third time around, they were sure I didn't have it anymore. It was killing me.

"I wanted to retire. I wanted to give them their money back. I felt terrible because I knew how much I meant to the team and I knew my own ability.

"The doctors could have said that my arm was dead because of age or that it was all in my mind. But they didn't. I've got them to thank for giving me my career back."

"He demonstrated his ability today," Frey said. "For a guy to miss 60 days and then throw the stuff he did and get it over, that was a strong performance.

"Our starting pitching can be the high point of the second half."

It would be a good time to rest Jody or Ryno or Dernier before the Philadelphia–New York trip.

Currently, Moreland is the lone backup catcher. By September, Frey will have Hassey, Lake and Moreland behind Jody. That's not too bad. Let's hope it's not too late.

For the first time in 19 games the Cubs suffer two straight defeats. It appears as if everyone is a little mentally winded. Show beats the Cubs and Trout, 6-5.

Moreland hits a pair of homers including one—a two-run shot—off Gossage. The Cubs rally but can't get the job done.

A play that hurts occurs in the third inning. Dave Owen leads off with a triple. But Trout grounds out and Dernier hits a tapper back to the mound. Frey's got a contact play on, which means as soon as the bat meets the ball the runner takes off for the plate. Unfortunately, the worst place on the field for the ball to go is the pitchers' mound and that's what happens. Show throws to Kennedy who runs Owen back to third. As Show moves along and gathers a 6-1 lead, the potential run doesn't seem to matter. But as the rally begins it looms bigger.

But there are about 20 plays a game that people can point to. It's just the obvious ones that earn the second guess.

The Cubs draw 29,499 paid fans, bringing them to within 3,000 of the million mark at home. The Cubs have never reached a million paid fans at home this quickly into a season. Then again, the Cubs haven't had too many teams as exciting as this year's.

The Cubs reach a million on Wednesday. They burst through that mark without question as 27,471 came to watch Sutcliffe and Whitson. Does Sut disappoint his new-found following? Not a chance.

The guy has been masterful. For the first time in quite some time, it looks as if the Cubs have a legitimate stopper. He beat the Padres 4-1. Just when it looked as if the club could take a spin downwards, Rick comes through. He is 6-1 as a Cub and three of the wins have followed losses.

The Mets keep winning but that doesn't concern the club as much as the Phillies winning. The Phils are two games behind the Cubs and the Cubs trail the Mets by a game and a half.

"Everyone is concerned about the Mets," Rick said. "I'm not really that worried about them. We'll have our chance to do something about them the rest of the season. We've got a few games remaining."

Dave Anderson from *The New York Times* calls on July 19. He's doing a column on Dallas and all the trades and the reversal of the franchise. It's utterly amazing how far the club has come in terms of the national exposure and the belief in what can be done.

Hebner goes on the DL. He's the 10th Cub to be DLed this season—the Cubs have totaled 323 DL days through July 18th. A full season is 180 days so they have already missed the equivalent of practically two full seasons.

Bowa's continued distress over not playing reached a new level on July 17. Bowa told Dallas that if the club didn't plan on playing him they should release him. The next day, Frey says Bowa will be in the lineup most of the way from now on.

Since all the turmoil over the trade for Dernier and Matthews, everything has been fairly quiet in the locker room—not overly quiet but not bad. Bowa has really been the only item and it looks as if that will be resolved.

Presto. The Sarge does it again. He drives in four runs and the Cubs beat the Giants 6-4. Matthews belts a three-run homer in the seventh to break a 3-3 deadlock. It's his

12th game-winning hit—a sometimes misleading stat. But not in this case. The Mets lose, bringing the Cubs to within a half-game.

Matthews has developed a great relationship with the left field bleacherites. It is really no surprise. He's a very energetic player, a high-powered type that fans can't see enough of. The fans love a guy like that.

It's like 1969 when Billy Williams and Willie Smith would hold running conversations with the fans. Sarge has picked it right up.

Sanderson works only four innings against the Giants. Something says he isn't 100 percent. He looked like he did in spring training—throwing a lot of soft stuff and getting beat on pitches he wouldn't ordinarily throw in game situations. If he isn't healthy, does it mean that the Cubs traded Rainey too soon?

Dernier and Sandberg once again begin working wonders. Ryno has another three-hit game giving him four for the season. Dernier steals his 32nd base of the season tying Adolfo Phillips' club record for steals by a center fielder.

On Friday, the Cubs fall just short. They lose 3-2 although Eckersley allows only three hits. Unfortunately, all three come in one inning. The Cubs have a couple of opportunities to rescue this one, but a strong wind keeps long drives by Matthews and Davis in the park.

Saturday is a classic day with a pair of classic games— one that counts and one that doesn't. In the one that counted, Bosley delivers a 11th-inning RBI single giving the Cubs a 4-3 win.

Thad was leading Iowa and the American Association in hitting when Durham was hurt on June 23. Two days later, Thad was back in the big leagues.

At one time he was considered an outstanding outfield

prospect by both the White Sox and Angels. Whatever happened in the interim is anyone's guess, but he ended up
playing in the Mexican League, the last stop before retire-
ment. The Cubs signed him last season.

He didn't receive a great opportunity in the spring,
especially after the deal with Philly. Bosley may have been
ready to cash it in. It wasn't until he came up in June that
his next chance came.

"There were a couple of teams that said they'd like to
get me if the Cubs couldn't use me," he said. "I was ready
to give anyone a try."

The win was the Cubs 12th in their last at-bat and it improved their extra inning record to 7-0.

The Cubs are 54-40. A year ago the Cubs won their 54th
game on August 8th when they were 54-66 and had played
120 games. They are 25 games ahead of that pace when they
finished 20 games out. Does that mean anything?

Not really. The Mets have improved even more.

The Giants look dismal. Nobody runs hard. It looks as
if they are playing to get Frank Robby fired. It's a distinct
possibility.

The crowds have been staggering. A Cub ticket has become a rarity. The people who stand in line all night aren't
even irate about it. They just keep smiling and standing in
line. In the last 16 Wrigley Field dates the Cubs have drawn
more than a half-million paid fans and 12 of those dates
have been weekdays.

The city has always loved the Cubs, but this season it
has grown to a passion.

Before Bosley's heroics, it was a time to remember, a time
when the crowds also circled Wrigley Field early and stayed
late. The pre-game was an Old-Timers Game between the

1969 Cubs and the 1969 Orioles. These clubs had one major thing in common—both were stunned by the Mets that season.

Nearly all the former Cubs return. Williams, Fergie, Jim Hickman and Al Spangler were among the missing as was Durocher.

The reunion is priceless. No team in the last 50 years of Chicago baseball captured the hearts of the city like the 1969 Cubs. They were everyone's heroes. Every kid on the block had his or her favorite. Today's middle-age business men were the kids of that day—the Bleacher Bums turned season-ticket holders. It was a beautiful year except for the last six weeks when the Mets caught fire.

"Nobody gives the Mets enough credit," says Randy Hundley, the Cubs catcher that season. They won 37 of their last 49 games. Plus, the Cubs were helpless. From early August, when the Cubs led by 8½ games, until the Mets clinched the division, the two teams played each other twice.

"Today everyone says the Cubs can't win because of playing all day games," Hundley said. "I never believed that. In 1969 that was never mentioned. If you have the players who can win day or night it doesn't matter. We had the players but we didn't have the bench. And Leo wore out Phil Regan (the Cubs' bullpen ace).

"On August 1, Spangler tells me, 'if we play .500 ball, the Mets have to win 35 of 45.' For them it was a miracle."

"It won't happen this time," Willie Smith said. "This team has better depth. It's a good team that has players on it who have won something.

"I remember opening day that year. I helped get us started with that homer against the Phillies (an 11th-inning game winner). What I remember is I got four or five spike wounds in the celebration at home plate."

A no-show was Leo, who hadn't been feeling well lately.

"Where's Leo?" one player asks. "He's up at camp to-day," someone chips in. The place busts up. Laughter comes flowing out of the Cubs' dugout. There was no laughter 15 years ago when Leo disappeared for a weekend to visit his stepson at camp in Wisconsin.

Sitting there together for perhaps the first time as a unit in 15 years, these men had opened their talents to a city that engulfed them as all-time favorites even though the city was left with a bittersweet memory to last a lifetime.

Saturday night the reunion continued at the Hyatt Regency on Wacker Drive. Dick Selma's career was established in that season—his memory engraved in every fan's heart. He led the Bums in the bleachers. He was one of the most cheerful and good-natured people on the club.

It was more unusual not to find Dick at Ray's Bleachers after a game than it was to find him there. He was the only player with a gold card membership from the Bums.

It was a very big part of his life.

"I still get a letter a week from some kid who is doing a school paper or a thesis on what happened," says Selma, who coaches a junior college team in Fresno, CA.

"I've got a letter at home from a mother, a letter that the Cubs had engraved for all the players. It says that while people say we blew the pennant, we really didn't. Because for the summer of 1969, her son wasn't out running the streets or getting into drugs. He was going to the ball park to see his heroes.

"The letter is priceless. It ends by saying that her boy fell off the bottom step of the bus the other day and came in crying that the Cubs lost the pennant. But she says that we really won it. It was just signed, Mom. We've tried to find that woman, but with no luck."

"Every time I read the letter," say Dick's wife Sherry, "it breaks me up."

"We wanted to win it for Chicago," Selma continued.

"Sure we'd like to have been a champion and get the ring and the extra money. But we sincerely wanted to do it for the people of the city. The people of Chicago are like no other. A lot of people say that about a lot of different cities, but I sincerely mean it. It broke our hearts not to be able to do it."

Sunday the Cubs find they can't do it either. The Giants crush them 11-5 and pound out 17 hits.

"We beat the Giants in nine of 11 games and then in the last game they come out and get us," Frey says. "Figure that out."

It is on to Philadelphia and New York.

"We sure didn't play well today," Dallas says. He says no more but his expression keeps on talking. He is far from carefree. He knows, as well as anyone, what this race entails.

So this is it. The first of what could be many crucial segments of the season. After a 6-5 homestand that was less-than-convincing, the Cubs headed for three games at Philadelphia and four against the incredible Mets.

It is only the end of July but the chase is beginning. Can the Cubs sustain the first-half consistency and drive that has brought them this far? Can the Mets? This trip will not, in all probability, determine the final outcome, but it could very well set everything up for the two months ahead.

"This is a big trip," Frey says. "But the first team that gets hot in August will set the pace. Myself, I'd like to see us win five or six in a row starting now."

Before the opening game on Monday Night Baseball, Frey tells the club that the second-half swoon theory is a bunch of garbage. He recites the club's final two months of 1982 when it was hopelessly out of the race on August 1 and still came back to play nine games over .500 for the last two months (33-24). Only the Giants had a better record in the league and only three American League teams bettered what the Cubs did down the stretch.

Now is the time to see what happens and exactly how far and how good this club is.

In the trip opener, Sutcliffe goes against lefty Shane Rawley. Most of the Cubs have never seen Rawley pitch. Most of the Phillies haven't seen Sutcliffe for a few years. Rick struggles early but this guy is turning into one of the great competitors of his time.

He keeps battling. The Phils get five doubles in their first five hits but all it costs Rick is one run.

Cey finally busts loose after the Phils fail to turn an inning-ending double play. Samuel overthrows first base allowing Moreland to reach safely after Matthews had been rubbed out on the front end. With two outs, Davis singles and up comes Cey.

The Penguin has struggled a little physically. Ever since he was hit by a pitch on his right wrist on June 23, he feels he hasn't been the same. He feels the power is gone from his swing.

Power or no power he jacks a Rawley pitch up against the black canvas above the left field wall. Suddenly Sutcliffe is holding a 3-1 lead going into the bottom of the sixth.

The Phils always have looked to come back quickly. The first two hitters reach and Ozzie Virgil, having an outstanding year, works the count to 2-2. Rick's next pitch is an inside fast ball that comes in tight on Virgil.

With a 3-2 count, Sutcliffe is one pitch from deep trouble ("If he doesn't come in with a strike there, we are really in deep," Frey says).

The pitch drops out of the strike zone. Virgil catches his swing in time and takes a step toward first. But Jim Quick, the same umpire who ejected Cey last week in Chicago, calls Virgil out.

Rick gets the next two hitters and the Cubs enter the seventh with a 3-1 lead. Once again the Cubs have been practically unbeatable when leading in the seventh. They are 39-4.

But in the bottom of the inning, Rick hangs a slider that his former Cleveland teammate Von Hayes rips off the right field foul pole. It's now a 3-2 game.

That's the way it ends. Smith, who hasn't had a lot of success against the Phils, gets the side out in order in the ninth.

"This is the type of game we're going to need to win this year," Frey says. "There's no way we can keep scoring six or seven runs every time. We've got to come up with a couple of 2-1, 3-2 games. The big red head (Sutcliffe) was really something again tonight. When he came out after the eighth inning, I told him that was it and he looked at me like he wanted to hit me. The guy loves to pitch and win.

"He's been beautiful."

Meanwhile, up the turnpike, the Mets hold on to beat the Cards 4-3 in 12 innings. It's the Mets' 11th one-run win in their last 12 victories. Are they living on borrowed time? Then again, wasn't that the early prognosis in 1969?

The second game of the Philly series turns just the opposite. The Cubs have no problem getting base runners, but they can't beat Jerry Koosman and Al Holland. It's one of those games that one pennant contender loses and another one wins.

The winning run is a pinch homer off Tim Stoddard by Len Matuszek, the man who took over for Pete Rose at first base this season. Matuszek belted a hanging slider on the inside of the plate.

The maniac Mets did it again. They rallied to beat the Cardinals in 10 innings. Keith Hernandez beats his old manager and verbal combatant Whitey Herzog. In fact, he beat Neil Allen, the player Keith was traded for. Keith wasn't too happy about the deal two years ago when it was made but a $5 million dollar deal and a contender help his attitude some.

It was his 13th game-winning hit.

In the wrapup in Philly the Cubs climb all over Charlie Hudson for a 9-4 win. Finally the Cubs begin hitting again. Sandberg gets his 14th triple. The last Cub to have more was Phil Cavarretta in 1944. Phil had 15. Ryno has 49 extra base hits this season and is leading the league in total bases. He's been incredible and he enjoys every minute of it.

What a year.

After an off day at Atlantic City, it's on to the Apple. The last big Cubs-Mets series was 1983 when they battled for fifth place. It's been a long time since the two clubs were competitive. This is like a flashback. When the Cubs became good in the late 1960s-early 1970s, the Mets came around. Now the same thing is happening.

It will be Gooden and 50,000 crazies packed into Shea on Friday. What a wonderful series this could be. Being in a pennant race is the best feeling there is in the game.

There may be no place in America as depressing as New York City when it rains. That is what greets the Cubs on Friday.

A majority of the players had left for Shea Stadium earlier in the day, beating the rush hour traffic the team bus would have to negotiate. The New York media machine was in full force. The field was littered with wires and microphones and notepad carriers.

This indeed was the beginning of the serious segment of the pennant race. The Cubs came into the game and the series 3½ back of the Mets. The Phils were left 5½ back and eight down in the loss column.

Opening night featured Gooden who didn't have his usual control but did have his usual pop on the fastball.

He walks seven, but fans eight. He allows only four hits, though, and that forces the Cubs into making a calculated move in sending Sandberg from third on a short fly ball in the fifth. Mookie Wilson gets a great spring into the throw and it skids toward Mike Fitzgerald, the catcher. He holds on and Sandberg slides into him. The Mets, faced with a 1-1 game and Cub runners on first and third with no out, weathered the storm.

They find Rufus not as fast, better controlled and allowing nothing more than a couple threats. Until the seventh.

A walk to the No. 8 hitter, Rafael Santana, opens the inning. Gooden sacrifices him to second. Wally Backman, who has developed into a good ball player, rips a shot to center field. Dernier charges, Santana doesn't get the good jump.

Dernier gambles that he can come up with the ball on the run, on the wet grass, and in one motion throw to the plate. The ball caroms off his glove. The gamble has failed and the Mets have scored. A crowd of 52,610 goes wild. The last six Cubs go peacefully. Met fans have been building their "Wave" all season and use it repeatedly throughout the night.

"It wasn't that bad an effort on our part," Frey says. "We had some good chances. There's no way we can't send Sandberg on that play. They've got Gooden pitching. How many chances are we going to get that are that good?

"This is only one game in July. There are no pennants won or lost in July.

I'm waiting for those guys over there to pop off," Frey says of the Mets. "Tell me about their character. Tell me what they've done so far? Have they won anything yet?"

Saturday's game may be the biggest of the year. If the Cubs lose they fall 5½ games back going into the Sunday doubleheader. Anything can happen at that point, but the chances of sweeping the rampaging Mets at home aren't real good.

The fans await the Cubs bus outside Shea. "Four-game sweep . . . Four-game sweep . . . Four-game sweep," they chant.

What a brutal thought.

The next day's papers are full of the Mets. "The pressure is on the Cubs," Backman claims. "We won't fold, but I don't know about them."

The excitement in the Mets' clubhouse is obvious. The mood in the Cubs' clubhouse is far from subdued but it certainly isn't overflowing past the bounds of the rational.

Bill Murray of *Saturday Night Live* fame recently named his newborn son, Homer Banks Murray. Is there something special about the Cubs and their fans or what?

A Mets fan dressed in a white sheet paraded around Shea Stadium Friday night carrying a sign that read: "The Spirit of '69."

The New York fans have been calling the Cubs' players at all hours of the night. There have been death threats, there have been nuisance calls. So what finally happens on Saturday? The team bus leaves for Shea Stadium. What should be an easy non-congested ride through a slumbering Manhattan and Queens turns into a tour.

The driver can't find Shea Stadium. He asks a cabbie, stops in a laundromat and at the Flushing Plumbing Co., Inc. for directions. He finally gets the team to Shea but can't maneuver the bus to the players' gate. The players walk from the edge of the parking lot to the players' gate through the Mets' fans who are out tailgating.

Survival. It's all part of the great pennant race.

A crowd of 41,170 shows up at Shea on Saturday to watch Ron Darling and Sutcliffe. Rick's been moved up a day in the rotation. He has pitched a day early before and won. There isn't much he hasn't done including win four games following Cub losses. Once again, NBC is on hand.

For six innings, it's a great pitchers' duel with Sutcliffe in trouble only once – in the sixth when the Mets had three hits from the bottom of the order and scored twice cutting a Cub lead to 3-2.

In the Mets seventh, the impossible seemed to happen. With one on and one out, Fitzgerald hits a fly ball to center field. Dernier moves in and is in short center when he suddenly loses touch with the play. The ball glances off his glove and rolls behind him. The runner on first, Hubie Brooks, comes all the way around to tie the game. Fitzgerald makes it to second.

Suddenly it's 1969 all over again. Don Young. A July game in New York. An error in center field. Momentum rushing toward the Mets.

Just as quickly it's 1984.

The Cubs shake off the error and tie the score cutting through the maddening racket exuding from 40,000 plus.

In the eighth they pull off their biggest inning of the season – an eight-run burst highlighted by two-run singles by Sandberg, Cotto and Cey.

The Cubs pull within 3½ again with an 11-4 win.

"I was ashamed of myself at first because Rick had pitched such a great game," Dernier said. "It was a knuckle ball and I had trouble figuring out which way to turn my glove.

"Sometimes human errors come into play. My teammates picked me up though."

How desperately did the Cubs need the win? Frey was asked. "Like oxygen.

"I've been one of these guys saying these games aren't that important, but it's getting a little late to be saying that now, isn't it?

"It looked like things were slipping away from us for a while, then all of a sudden everything turned around."

The turnaround didn't begin with the Cubs' eighth. Rather it started in the Mets' seventh when, with runners on first and second and one out, Rusty Staub, one of the all-time Cub killers, comes out to pinch hit against Lee Smith. Staub hit a soft, sinking liner between Sandberg and Durham at first. The runners are moving. It is almost like the play in which Billy Martin robbed Jackie Robinson in the seventh game of the 1956 World Series—it's just an infield play, but with everyone running there is no telling what could happen if the ball isn't caught.

Durham dives and comes up with it on the fly. He turns to Bowa and doubles off Fitzgerald.

Joe Garagiola before the NBC Game of the Week with the Cubs-Mets: "This match up is a dream. Every time I turn around I run into a Cubs fan. I wonder where they were when I was playing."

"The fans in this place get the adrenaline flowing," Gary Matthews says. "Even for the opposition. These fans are wild."

Friday night, Matthews dodged a bottle in the outfield.

"When we came to town," Frey said, "all we heard was the way the Mets were winning. When Bobby dropped that ball, I thought I was about to see it for myself. But we have the kind of team that responds, too."

Meanwhile, in Chicago a radio station hears that Mets fans are calling the Cubs at all hours of the night. The station gives the Mets' road hotels and the phone numbers for their next trip out over the air with the instructions to call the Mets all night long and let them know "you're behind the Cubs."

The doubleheader. Two more games against the Mets. A chance to be 3½ back . . . to be 1½ back . . . to be 5½ back. It's pivotal.

It's a time for a team of character to show it. There are still more than 60 games to play but it is about time for teams to start compiling some intimidation against each other.

It's time for a sweep. The Cubs pull it off with two great performances— one by Trout and one by Sanderson. Trout threw his best game in a couple of months and Sanderson quieted the skeptics who questioned his arm and his back.

Trout beat Walt Terrell 3-0 in the opener. It was his first shutout in more than four years. The Cubs scored twice in the fifth and again in the ninth. They only managed seven hits off the Mets, but put together two scoring innings. The Mets looked flat. Good pitching can do that.

In Game 2, Sanderson was equal to Trout. For 7.2 innings he had a shutout. The Mets finally scored in the eighth but by then the Cubs were leading 5-1 following a three-run homer by Davis and Sandberg's 14th.

After the inning in which Davis homered, Berenyi and Hernandez, the Mets' leader, return to the dugout—heads down. The Cubs may finally be getting to the Mets.

On the bus on the way out of New York, the fans still wait. "Chicago Sucks," is the chant.

"Where's that bleepin' wave," Moreland yells out.

"We're not hearing anything about that four-game sweep now, are we?" Bowa adds.

"I'm telling you," Moreland adds. "You get the feeling with this ballclub that we can win any game we play."

The plane ride home is uneventful. There is a quiet confidence building.

Gary Matthews sums up his role perfectly when he says, "I didn't come here to lose. I've never lost anywhere."

It echoes what Johnny Oates had said months earlier. "I've only been on one losing club in my career and I didn't like that a bit."

"We didn't lose any momentum," Mookie Wilson says. "We did lose some ground but we have to play the Cubs a lot more (10 times) and that's the bottom line. If there are any skeptics that wonder what kind of club they are, it's too late to say they're a fortunate club."

The Cubs are welcomed by a couple of hundred fans at the airport. It's a beautiful sight. Who would have thought it possible after watching 1982 and 1983 slip by in silence and defeat?

Philly is next, followed by four with the Expos and four with the Mets.

"We will have our 10th man out there at Wrigley," Bowa says in reference to the fans. "The Mets will be coming to our playpen now."

The Mets leave for St. Louis where they'll play three games before going to Pittsburgh and Chicago. The Mets play 20 of their next 24 on the road including their final West Coast trip. It's beginning to become a very telling period for them. They've been great on the road thus far. But so have the 30-24 Cubs.

It's Eckersley against the Phils and Charlie Hudson. Another 30,000-plus crowd shows up at Wrigley Field.

Both teams score in the first. It's another great duel. In the sixth the Cubs negotiate a run off Hudson with Davis doubling in Durham, who walked. Walks that score, what a crucial statistic. It's a killer.

In the seventh, Ryno adds his 16th triple, scoring Thad Bosley, who singled pinch-hitting for Eck.

The Phils come back with one more run but Lee closes them out in the ninth.

Jerry Holtzman of the *Chicago Tribune* writes, "Two months to go and anything can happen. But after seeing the enemy this past week—in three games at Philadelphia and four in New York—my instincts are beginning to tell me that the Cubs will win the National League East."

Jerome has been covering baseball for decades. He was here in 1969. That club, he contends, didn't know how to lose. They didn't realize that there are 162 games and one game, unless it's the do-or-die final game, doesn't make or break a season. It's more important to rebound after a loss.

The Cubs have been able to do that well. Even after the loss to the Mets in the series opener, nobody was looking for the Brooklyn Bridge as a jumping-off point.

The Cubs are 60-43, 17 over for the first time since 1977. The city is buzzing. It's too early too tell, but the Mets may be about to have their bluff called. And the Phils are searching for something positive to hang some momentum on. Everyone else has begun thinking about 1985.

What a grand conglomeration of talent Dallas has put together. This may or may not be the best team in the East, or in the league, but it is, as Frey put it in spring training, one that fits like a perfect puzzle.

On the day Eck shuts down the Phils, the Cubs get a clubhouse visitor—Bill Buckner. He's doing well in Boston. He'll probably lead the league in hitting and doubles one season.

His trade seems like it happened years ago.

The Cards come up with two runs in the 10th to beat the Mets in St. Louis. The Mets lead is down to a half-game after being 4½ just four days earlier.

It's the first one-run loss for the Mets in ages. Keith Hernandez' quote, "we've got to beat the second-division clubs," didn't hit his former teammates too well.

Tuesday is a heartbreaker for the Cubs. Rich Bordi in a rare start handles the Phillies flawlessly. All the Phils have to show for 8.2 innings is a single by Garry Maddox. The Cubs don't have much more to show off of John Denny, who is coming back from an arm problem. The Cubs do have a homer by Cey that puts Bordi one out away from a 1-0 one-hit shutout.

Then Juan Samuel drills Bordi's first pitch barely over the basket in left center. The 35,000-plus at Wrigley Field were on their feet awaiting the third out. Samuel killed them. Killed them all with his homer.

It took until the 12th for the Phils to edge out a 2-1 win. The Cubs had a couple of other opportunities against reliever Holland but they just couldn't get the job done.

Once again, the next few days will tell another story about the 1984 Cubs.

For the third time in 39 years, they raised the Cubs' flag to the top of the center field scoreboard in August. The Mets falter again, losing 11-2 to Andujar and the Cards. Gooden gets crushed.

While the Mets-Cards game is progressing in St. Louis, the Cubs set out to erase the memory of yesterday and Bordi's near one-hit shutout that blew up.

No one thought it would be easy to beat Carlton. Lefty had been pitching very well of late. Rufus, still looking for his first win since early April, allowed a pair of homers and Philly grabbed a 3-0 lead.

But then the Cubs came back. Ryno homered to right to lead off the fourth. Cey, who appears to be gradually coming back to life, hit one onto Waveland Avenue opening the fifth. And Moreland tied the score leading off the sixth with another Waveland shot.

Suddenly, Lefty wasn't baffling. Rufus helped himself out with a run-scoring single in the sixth giving the Cubs a 4-3 lead.

Again, disaster appeared to be awaiting the Cubs. In the ninth, Tim Corcoran struck out as a pinch hitter for the first out. Then George Frazier, who had come on and pitched strongly from the middle of the seventh, walked Lezcano.

Frey went right to Smith. There would be no chance to second guess this one. Samuel, yesterday's ninth-inning terror, slashed a ball to right field sending Lezcano to third.

Then came a play that could have killed the club. Samuel takes off for second. Davis' throw hits in front of the bag, glances off Bowa's chest and hops into Sandberg's glove in short center.

Lezcano comes in to score and tie the game. With Samuel still in scoring position, the trouble isn't over. Smith gets Gross to ground out sending Samuel to third. With two out, Hayes also grounds out.

Tied at four, the Cubs open the ninth with Cotto doubling off Holland. Cotto has been superb—"just outstanding," says Frey—in replacing Dernier. The Phils walk Ryno intentionally.

Then Matthews attempts to move both runners along with a bunt. The bunt pops over Holland's head. He retrieves it but finds Kiko Garcia in his line of vision blocking third. Holland tries to go to second but nobody is covering since Garcia is standing closer to third than second. Everyone's safe. Holland's hot. The bases are loaded.

The Phils bring in Hayes to play behind Holland. They go with a five-man infield. Moreland strikes out swinging and then Davis lines a sacrifice fly to Maddox, who had shifted over to left center. Cotto scores the winner. Holland claims he left third too early.

"But the umpires aren't listening," he says later. "If they call him out the crowd comes out of the stands and kills them. There's no way we're going to get that call. We don't even get the appeal."

It's the 13th time the Cubs have won in their final at-bat this season. As incredible as it seems, the team is gaining more and more momentum. After losing Tuesday's heartbreaker, it was definitely a time for the meek to doubt.

Was this win as big as the win against the Cardinals in April when Hebner homered off Sutter? . . . bigger than Jody Davis' three-run homer in Houston that came in the ninth inning in a nationally televised game? . . . what about Sandberg's two-homer game against Sutter in the wild 12-11 win? (will there every be a more dramatic finish?) . . . or the 8-3 West Coast trip? . . . or the 5-2 East Coast trip?. . . or coming back from a tough, tough loss against the Phils?

It has been that type of season already. And it's only August 1.

"This was an important game because the Phillies won last year," Frey said, "Everybody knows that. They had a guy out there throwing who is going into the Hall of Fame, no doubt. When you come back from 3-0 against a guy like that, that to me is important."

"The Cubs are in a situation where they have so many positive vibes coming to this club from this city that they've got to feel like they're on top of the world. They must feel like they're unbeatable here," says Matuszek.

The Expos end up seconding that notion.

You're living right when . . . your center fielder, your backup center fielder makes not one but two great catches and drives in the winning run on a fielder's choice—one of two RBI fielder's choices in a 3-2 victory.

You're also living right when, with a tying run on third base and the lead run on first with one out in the ninth and

Pete Rose batting, you survive. Especially when Rose hits a bullet up the middle that glances off the pitcher (Lee Smith) and caroms on the fly to the shortstop (Dave Owen) who catches it and doubles up the runner on first (Mike Stenhouse) ending the game and preserving a 3-2 win.

"I wonder how they work on that play in spring training," Rose says. "Must be a lot of sore shoulders."

"Everybody says you need luck in this game and sometimes people don't like to admit it," Frey acknowledged. "But I'll tell you there was no dismissing luck's role today."

It's the third one-run victory in four one-run games for the Cubs. The White Sox were winning ugly last year and the Cubs have suddenly been winning lucky—but as Harry Caray says, Lady Luck is a beautiful lady.

Sutcliffe wins his sixth straight in beating the Expos. The Cubs find their 1-0 lead isn't enough after Andre Dawson's two-run fifth-inning homer. The Cubs tie it in the sixth as Moreland hits another homer—his 12th and his second in two days. In the seventh, Cey doubles and moves to third. After Sutcliffe walks, Cotto hits into a fielder's choice scoring Penguin with the winner.

Smitty closes the Expos out for his 23rd save although he needed a bit of luck to pull it off. The Expos left the field shaking their heads.

"It happened so fast," Lee said, "that I didn't realize there were three outs. I yelled over to Bull that it was only two outs and he said, 'get off the mound brother, the game's over.'

"So I strolled off the field and tried to act like everything was cool."

The next day the Cubs nearly pull off a miracle. Down 5-0 to the Expos and Bill Gullickson, they rally for five runs and stand tied in the eighth. The Cubs load the bases with nobody out. But they don't score.

Talk about frustrating. With the bases loaded, Steve Lake, back in his first major league game since May 12, grounds into a force play at the plate.

Bowa is next. Jeff Reardon throws the first pitch outside. With a 1-0 count, Frey puts on the suicide squeeze play. Reardon's next pitch is a fastball deeper than the inside corner and lower than Bowa's knees. Bowa can't get the bat down ("I want to meet the player who could hit that ball," he says later).

Moreland is a dead duck. Catcher Bobby Ramos runs him back to third where Wallach tags him out for the second out. Bowa taps weakly to first to end the inning.

And that's not the worst.

In the ninth, the Expos load the bases with one out. Stoddard gets Driessen—a man with a bad hamstring no less—to ground to Sandberg on two quick hops. Sandberg goes to second for the force but Bowa triple clutches and can't get the ball to Durham in time to double up Driessen. The lead run scores and the Cubs lose 6-5.

Another heartbreaker. The last five games have come down to the final inning. The Cubs are 3-2 in the five, but could very easily have been 5-0.

The Mets start breathing again. Terrell pitches New York past woebegone Pittsburgh and brings the Mets back to within a half-game. The Phils lose staying 5½ back.

The Cubs are in first place and it's August 4.

Since the 1945 glory year, only the 1969 Cubs have been in first place as late as August 4.

Only two in the last 39 years.

Only two.

39 years.

Eckersley beats the Expos 4-1 giving him a 4-1 record since the break. He's been a different pitcher since then. He kept the Expos off balance all afternoon.

Jody hits another homer—his 16th and another sellout crowd fills Wrigley. In the last 23 home dates the Cubs have averaged more than 31,000 paid fans. If it wasn't for the early-season rainouts the Cubs would have a shot at two million—the first club in the history of the game to draw two million playing day baseball.

The bullpen has been better this season, probably because it hasn't worked as much. Through 108 games it is 66 relief appearances shy of last season's total. That's an incredible figure related to arm-weary pitchers.

Moreland continues to play well. In the second inning, he's on first and Bull hits a check-swing dribbler down the third base line. Wallach charges but can't throw out Durham. Moreland, who isn't known for his speed, keeps on coming to the unguarded third base. Dan Driessen throws hurriedly across the field to shortstop Derrel Thomas, who is trying to cover more ground than Moreland. Thomas, who once played eight positions in a game, can't play two at a time. The throw goes into left field and Moreland scores.

It's a great heads-up play by a guy who doesn't have the speed to pull it off—just the guts and desire.

That's the type of play that wins pennants and Eckersley's pitching is the type of pitching that makes general managers look like genuises.

It shouldn't be forgotten that Dallas traded for Dennis when Ruthven went down and the price of a starting pitcher heading to Chicago should have gone up.

Since last October, Dallas has acquired five pitchers; Eckersley (6-6), Sanderson (6-2), Stoddard (7-4), Frazier (2-0) and Sutcliffe (8-1). They have combined for a 29-13 record. Frazier, Sutcliffe and Eck all came after May 25 and are 16-7 overall. Not a bad parlay considering the scarcity of good pitchers.

The Mets keep pace by beating Pittsburgh. The Cubs still lead by a half-game. But the Cubs gain some ground on the Phils who lose and drop 5½ games back.

On the day before another crucial Mets series, the Cubs use the Earl Weaver Theory of managing for a 4-3 win over the Expos.

The Cubs used one swing of the bat—a grand slam homer by Moreland off Dick Grapenthin to beat the Expos.

Bordi lasted four innings before Frey went to Reuschel, the forgotten man of the staff. Rick pitched well through three innings and picked up a win—his first since June 22. It seems imperative that the Cubs hold on to Rick in the event that Scott's back acts up on him and DLs him once again.

Rick is the only holdover from the previous semi-glory days of 1977 when the Cubs were in contention for four-fifths of the year.

The Mets beat the Pirates thanks to a Dale Berra 10th-inning error. They come into town a half-game back. The Phillies also beat the Cardinals in a come-from-behind decision. They remain 5½ back.

The Cubs went into Shea Stadium last Friday 3½ games out and left 1½ back. It will be interesting to see what develops. The Mets are coming off a week in which they dropped three of four to the Cubs and also lost seven straight. Yet, they find themselves only a half-game back and the Cubs have won eight of 10. It's indeed a strange division.

"That last series with the Mets meant something," Reuschel says, "but I'm not convinced it meant all that much."

When asked about the degree of importance the Mets series should have, Frey responded, "A crucial series is one in which they'll put you in front of the firing squad if you lose it. I don't think we're ready for that yet."

"We can't feel that way anymore," Frey later admits.

"These are big games. The Cubs will be jacked up, the fans will be jacked up and I know the Mets will be jacked up. It's a big game, we can't tell that lie anymore."

It's official. This is August and this is the pennant race and yes, these are the Cubs. It really is happening. The crowds are descending on Wrigley Field like the old days—actually the days of 15 years ago. The magic is back.

The lines for bleacher seats begin forming before the sun pokes out of Lake Michigan. It's everything baseball is supposed to be, as well as everything that has been lacking for the last decade.

It's Gooden and Ruthven in a rematch. The wind is blowing out. The temperature is in the 90s and the humidity is matching it percent for degree. It's incredibly hot and so are the Cubs.

They strike early off Gooden reaching the Mets' rookie for two runs in the first inning. Davis' two-out RBI double produces the second run after Moreland, on an absolute white-hot tear, drills a single into left, scoring Sandberg.

In the third, Davis catches a 2-0 curve ball and rides it out into the vacated center field bleachers—the ball lands in the top row. There have been few balls hit that far in the last 10 years.

In 1969, it was a weak-hitting second baseman named Al Weis who killed the Cubs in the identical series—Mets second trip in, mid-week, pennant race conditions. Weis hit two homers in three games that time. He had hit four in his previous big league career that had already spanned six seasons. He would hit a career total of seven. But two came in three days.

This time it was the Cubs' Owen. Owen tripled off Gooden in the third scoring another run. Owen came around on a passed ball. It was 6-0 Cubs and would soon rise to the 9-3 final.

The first round belonged to the Cubs. They improved

their lead over the Mets to 1½ games. Wrigley Field, as Harry Caray has said once or twice, was going bananas.

And so were the Mets in the locker room afterward. Keith Hernandez, who had been ejected by third base umpire Charlie Williams for a sign language demonstration following Williams' call on an alleged checked swing, took to task a Chicago radio reporter. Nothing came of it and Hernandez eventually settled down. But the hissing in the visitors locker room was more than the showers letting off steam.

"We're a young club," Hernandez said. "Our time may come in the future. Right now the Cubs are the team to beat. They are the team that's got the right blend. There's no doubt that they are the best in the division."

"I'm not sure today is going to have an affect whatsoever on tomorrow's two games," said ever diplomatic Frey. "What I'm concerned with is tomorrow's games."

"All I know," Backman says, "is that club is good enough that Ron Cey bats seventh."

The bleacher crowd camps out again. Sleeping bags, radios, walkmen, beer and Coppertone. It's flashback time to '69.

The doubleheader—Sutcliffe vs. Darling in game one.
The Mets strike early for two. A Durham homer and single by Owen driving home Davis ties the score. The Mets come back with two more. Sutcliffe, who is shooting for his seventh straight, isn't as sharp as usual. However, he is as tough as ever.
It takes the Cubs until the fifth. Then they explode for six runs off Darling. Moreland hits his third homer in the

last six games—a three-run shot off a Darling fastball that rode in on him and met his bat at the perfect spot. After a walk to Davis, Cey hits a towering homer onto the catwalk. The next hitter is Owen—Darling drills him.

It's the prelude to game two.

The Cubs hold off a minor Met uprising in the seventh and come away with an 8-6 victory in game one.

In the second game, Frey replaces Dernier with Cotto and takes out Matthews and inserts Bosley. The man looks like a genius. Cotto goes 4-for-5 with two runs scored and Bosley goes 3-for-3 with two runs batted in and a run scored. Cotto also makes his daily outstanding catch in the vines in left center.

The Cubs take the second game also, winning 8-4 but not before some more dramatic occurrences.

The Cubs rip Ed Lynch for five runs in the fourth inning. After Cey doubles in two runs, Lynch hits Moreland. In Keith's typical Texas style he charges Lynch, throws a cross body block at the pitcher and both benches clear. There's nothing like pennant fever at fever's pitch.

"I just went out there to get my point across," Moreland said. "It's part of the game of baseball. I have no hard feelings against anyone."

"I was just trying to set the tone for the at-bat," Lynch said." I wasn't aware of what went on in game one. I was upstairs getting dressed," he said in reference to Moreland's three-run homer. "I guess I can't blame him for coming out."

The outburst does end up costing Scott Sanderson a win. With the 5-0 lead and both benches warned, Scott hit Kelvin Chapman with a pitch with one on and no out in the 5th. Fred Brocklander ejected Scott and Frey immediately.

"I know he wasn't trying to throw at me," Chapman said.

"But Brocklander did what he had to do," Frey said.

"Otherwise we may be out there wrestling all night long."

Following the game Frey is as calm as possible. "So what if we won twice today," he says. "What if we lose tomorrow. A loss tomorrow isn't going to make me happy.

"You think I'm having fun? Fun to me is having a couple of beers and playing golf. This is work. We've got to go out there everyday and start over. This team can't afford to get too high or too low. That's the key. We've got to keep at an even keel."

The Mets, meanwhile, were still reeling.

"We got the shit kicked out of us," Chapman admitted.

"The Cubs have to feel that they can beat any team," Backman said. "They must feel like every time they play us they can beat us. We have to win Wednesday because it's in the back of our minds, too. We haven't been getting beat by one or two runs. We've been getting crushed."

"I think there will be bad blood between us from now on," Hernandez said.

"We've got a great sense of confidence," Cey said. "We know we can win. Talking about it is one thing, but doing it is another. I think today was a perfect example of how to use 25 guys effectively."

Penguin had five RBIs in the doubleheader and has 996 for his career. He also has 17 homers, tying him with Jody for the team lead. He has really come on lately. At this point he'll have his typical power season—25 homers and 85 RBI.

Everything isn't beautiful for everyone. Bowa gets booed as Owen's replacement, mostly leftover catcalls from the other day. Larry continues to be as diplomatic as possible.

"I'd rather they boo me than a younger player," he says. "I'm on a team that doesn't need me to hit in order to win."

"My biggest problem now," Frey says, "is trying to get home and get something to eat."

The Mets need the fourth game desperately. The Cubs have won six straight from the Mets and have changed a 4½-game Mets lead into a 3½-game Cub lead in the space of 13 games.

"The way I figure it the percentages are in our favor coming back to win tomorrow," Dave Johnson says. Percentages or not, the Cubs made it a sweep, their first four-game sweep over the Mets in 18 years.

This time it's a comeback win as the Mets take a 5-3 lead when Steve Trout can't work his way out of a jam and Brusstar throws fuel on the fire. The rally begins with Johnstone sending a pinch triple to right center. Dernier is next. Walt Terrell has a high fast ball get away from him, hitting Dernier on the helmet. Once again, the fuse is lit. Dernier is alright, but Terrell is ejected by Charlie Williams.

Both clubs had been warned in the pre-game that nothing would be tolerated—not even a brush back, as Lee Smith discovered an inning later when he was ejected for throwing close to George Foster.

But first Moreland delivers again. Since the All-Star Break he has 28 RBI—most in the majors. He also has seven homers, the most in the league.

He had what could have been a game-winning hit on three different occasions during the finale on Wednesday. Finally, in the seventh he got the clincher after Dave Johnson decided against walking him in a crucial situation.

It was Keith's fourth game-winning hit in the last four days and five games.

After the game, Frey is as happy as anyone has seen him. Make no mistake, Frey is not a sullen individual. What he is is a man of perspective, if anything a guarded perspective.

The sweep of the Mets, the 4½-game lead, the nine-game swing his club has pulled on the Mets in two weeks leaves him in a good mood.

Moreland, meanwhile, has destroyed the Mets.

"I'd like to take him out looking for wallets right now," Terrell says. "He's always a tough hitter but right now he is awesome."

On the team bus to the airport, Matthews examines the series and Moreland's play.

"They are not going to intimidate us with knock-down pitches. We're a good team and a close team. I'd do anything for my teammates. We're in this together. I think they found out how good we are. And we're not going to be moving off the dish very often.

"Moreland's been super. He gives the team everything he has. He's a tough clutch player."

The team plane departs O'Hare after spending two hours on the runway awaiting clearance due to weather problems in the south. The extra time keeps the conversations going.

"Has there ever been a more crucial, bigger series than this one?" Steve Stone asks. "Being a first-place team which is playing the second-place team, a team that has taken the heart out of Chicago in the past, playing games in front of sellout after sellout. And then winning, winning four in a row. It is unquestionably one of the biggest series in the history of the club."

"What a series this was," Harry Caray said. "It had everything."

The Mets return to New York for four games against the Pirates. After that they have a nine-game road trip to the West Coast—perhaps the final stage of their drive. In the New York papers following the sweep the talk among the Mets is of regrouping, holding their heads high, that it's not too late yet. The typical rebounding conversations.

The Cubs land in Montreal after midnight. The airport is deserted except for the customs people and another large traveling party—the Phillies. The Phillies are waiting for the Cubs' plane to take them out of town. Hours earlier the Phils were beaten by the Expos and fell 7½ games off the pace. They are struggling to get hot and make a run. No one knows it better than they do. The clock is running.

The Mets are a different story. Terrell is quoted as saying, "They [the Cubs] are not that good. Anybody who says they are doesn't know much about baseball."

Who would have thought that a big series like this would be played and the Mets' ace reliever Jesse Orosco wouldn't even get into a game?

"It was a severe series for us," Johnson said. "But we're not through yet."

"I've never seen a champion that couldn't get off the canvas," Coach Bobby Valentine said. "We'll find out if we are champions now because right now we are on the canvas."

Jack Lang of the *New York Daily News* writes in the Thursday paper: "The Mets left Chicago, bloodied, beaten and bowed."

It doesn't take long for reality to come back at the Cubs. The opener of the road trip is a pitching masterpiece between Eck and Schatzeder, the lefty from the Chicago area.

Schatz is making only his sixth start of the season but still manages to go the distance, which on this night is 10 innings. He blanks the Cubs on four hits while Eck lasts nine allowing four hits. Frazier works the 10th for the Cubs and Montreal reaches him for the game's only run.

The Cubs have a couple of chances to score off Schatzeder but nothing really major. On the other hand, the Expos leave the bases loaded in the seventh and again in the ninth. It looked as if the game was over in the ninth when they loaded them with nobody out. Somehow, Eck got Tim Wallach to pop up to Davis right at the screen. Stenhouse pinch hit for Flynn and grounded to first. Moreland threw to the plate for the force. With two out, Rose pinch hits. Pete lashes a drive a couple of feet foul down the right field line. Eck works the count to 2-2 and then gets Pete swinging. The bench goes crazy.

With two outs in the 10th and a runner on first Bowa reaches on an error by Tim Raines, who had gone in at second to open the inning. With runners on first and second, Frey puts Durham up to pinch hit. Leon, who has missed the last 2½ games with a slightly strained left hamstring, is called out on strikes.

With one out in the Expos' half of the inning, Raines singles and steals second. Frazier doesn't keep him close and he steals third. Max Venable fouls out to Bowa. With two out, Dawson reaches out and hits a soft pop just over Moreland's head at first and in front of Sandberg. It goes for a hit and a great pitching duel ends in Montreal's favor.

The silence is deafening. The Mets were getting blitzed again in New York against the Pirates. The Phillies—watch those Phillies is the clubhouse byword—tie the Cardinals and send the game into extra innings.

Once again, it's time to rebound. That is what makes the baseball pennant race the greatest of them all. There are so many games, so many trials, triumphs and tribulations that only a true champion can survive.

"You didn't think we'd win the 50 games we have left, did you?" Frey asks. "We've been in worse positions than this."

The Friday game doesn't prove to be any better. The Expos break a 2-2 tie in the eighth and win 4-2 behind a rookie, Joe Hesketh. Reuschel starts for the Cubs and does an admirable job working seven innings allowing eight hits and two runs. The loss goes to Stoddard who gives up a Gary Carter homer in the eighth.

A two-game losing streak. Only the club's third since June 22. Saturday, it ends with Ruthven tap dancing through 13 stranded Expos and 14 baserunners through 7.1 innings.

Smith keeps the Expos at bay while the Cubs go to work on Charlie Lea in the ninth. Sandberg singles to open the inning, steals second and moves to third on a right field fly by Matthews. Who notices that Matthews has given himself up and moved the runner within a sacrifice fly of scoring? — just the entire bench. After Expo manager Bill Virdon — for some unexplainable reason — walks Durham intentionally, Moreland singles home Sandberg with the winning run. It's his fifth game-winner of the week.

It marks the 14th time the Cubs win in their final at-bat. It was a very trying, emotional game, a momentum swinger — another NBC special.

"What a great relaxing way to earn a living," Frey says. "You know when I knew we had it won? When Cotto makes the catch with two out in the ninth."

The next day Sutcliffe is outstanding again as the Cubs even the series with a 7-3 win. The Expos are all but done. Rogers doesn't pitch badly although it's obvious this is not a typical Steve Rogers season. He takes the loss making him 3-12. The most surprising statistic is his strikeout-to-walk ratio. Career-wise he's been better than 2-to-1. This season he has walked 53 and struck out only 41.

It's no wonder the Expos are faltering and Bill Virdon is on the way out.

Cey hits his 18th homer and four Cubs hit doubles, including Ryno, who has been struggling for extra-base production recently. Veryzer, who is playing in place of Bowa, also doubles.

Moreland doubles. He is still hot. When the season is going in the right direction somebody else always picks up someone else and that's what is happening. Moreland is carrying the club.

He may be the best player Dallas never traded.

The great plane ride debacle follows. It's normally a four hour flight from Montreal to Houston. The itinerary claims the flight leaves at five and arrives in Houston around eight.

No such story.

The United charter never leaves Allentown, PA—mechanical problems. Finally, after the Allentown mechanics decide the plane is hopeless, the crew is shuttled to New York's Kennedy airport. From there they take a limo to LaGuardia and board a plane. The plane takes off for Montreal. It is now in the early evening.

The final event of the L.A. Olympics—the marathon—is in full force. It was quite appropriate that the Cubs too would be putting in a marathon evening-morning.

United sends the club back past through customs on to a bus to the airport Hilton for dinner. Dinner gets loud, loud and louder. Gatherings like this always seem like riots waiting to happen.

Finally at 11:30—5½ hours after the scheduled departure, the club gets back on a bus to the terminal. The plane arrives and everything is loaded. Finally, the team is on its way. But to where?

First to Chicago so the crew can be changed. They had had a long day. At least their union realizes that. The Cubs land in Chicago past 1 a.m. A new crew comes on. They take off for Houston, arriving at 4:04 a.m.

As the team boarded the plane in Montreal, Frey says, "Good, we're boarding. For a minute there I thought it was going to be a long delay." Always the twinkle in his eye.

The ride to the Greenway Plaza in Houston is not a short one. Houston is one of the great planning nightmares in American city management history. Have land, will build — anywhere, anything. In the wide world of malls and express-- ways, Houston ranks at the top.

Hotel arrival is at 5 a.m. and the bags follow shortly. It has been an incredible journey, highlighted by an O'Hare visit from the fine folks from Kelly Mondelli's restaurant. Frey, Connors and Vuk eat there all the time.

The scheduled four-hour trip took 13 hours. Batting prac- tice begins in less than 12 hours. Who ever said traveling was glamorous?

The phones begin ringing four hours later. Everybody loves the Cubs. They are the media event of '84. People are coming from everywhere. Sandberg gets a call at 10 in the morning regarding a 30-second interview for a 6 o'clock news show. Some people aren't real sensible. The person who called happened to be on the Cubs charter.

The game at the Dome. The Cubs historically haven't done well here. The Cubs live by the long ball and the big inning, surrounded by capable starters that for the first time in years keep the club in the ballgame nightly.

Sanderson is pitching great but the story back in Chicago is the first inning collision between Ryno and first baseman Enos Cabell. Ryno goes down in a heap after Cabell's knee crunches him just below the ribs. For five minutes the Cubs heart of '84 stopped beating. He suffered a bad bruise to the left hip. Veryzer replaces him at second the next inning.

Sanderson and Mike LaCoss duel for eight innings with two sacrifice flies accounting for all the offensive produc- tion. The game is tied at one. A key play resulted in the Houston run. Bill Doran led off the Astros' sixth with a sink- ing liner to left center. Bosley came over and had a chance to make a backhanded grab of the ball. It wasn't any easy catch, but it was catchable. It glances off the heel of his glove and goes for three bases. Doran ties it when he scores on a sacrifice fly by Craig Reynolds.

In the ninth, the Astros score on a one-out single by Jerry Mumphrey. Mumphrey, who beat Reuschel at the Dome in May, 1-0 with a triple, singles home Cruz who had singled and stole second. It was a typical Astrodome game.

After the game Sanderson is prone on the training table. He's halfway devastated. In seclusion is Bosley, tears in his eyes. He's hurting inside. This is no Don Young incident. But Bos has fought long and hard to make it back to the big leagues, to play on a winner. The chance is his and tonight he just missed the ball. It shows that the pressure is there. It's always there. It's part of what makes a long season a test of every skill—both physical and mental.

The Mets, meanwhile, have done nothing to strike fear in the Cubs. They lose to the Dodgers 9-2 in the opening game of their crucial West Coast excursion.

The Cubs have been getting great pitching. They have lost seven games since July 22—23 days ago. Six of the seven have been by one run and the other by two runs. The ERA in the defeats is 2.57. The pitching has been superb.

Sanderson has been very good at times. He probably didn't think the 1984 season was going to be so fulfilling when he was traded.

"One thing that you don't have to be a genius to figure out, is the way Dallas went out and got guys with playoff and World Series experience, players who have been on winning teams," he said.

"Take that kind of experience and add the talented guys

who were already here and suddenly you've got a team that doesn't give up. It's great to be a part of it."

The second game of the Houston series finds the Cubs hitting better but Trout's pitching goes south. The Astros and Cubs hand the lead back and forth five times before Houston survives for a 7-6 victory.

Matthews has four hits. Cotto extends his hitting streak to 14 games. Veryzer plays again in place of Ryno and goes hitless in six at-bats. Ryno will probably be out for a couple more days. He may play Friday in Cincinnati. This may be a blessing in disguise. He needed some time off. So does Dernier. He has two hits in his last 25 at-bats. He's pressing. Now isn't the time to get excited.

The good news is the Phillies also lost to stay 6½ games back. The bad news is the Mets blanked the Dodgers 4-0 in L.A. They've come to within 3½ games.

In the Houston finale, the club is listless. The Cubs haven't had a letdown in a long time but Wednesday night's game sure shows the signs. The Cubs lose 6-2 and commit three errors—two at second base where Veryzer and Owen are trying to replace Ryno.

The third error was charged to Eckersley in probably the worst call of the season. The official scorer gave the error to Eck for throwing the ball "too hard" to first base where Owen was covering on a sacrifice. Owen just plain missed the ball.

By then it really didn't matter. Eck pitched great again but the Astros scored once in the seventh to break a 2-2 deadlock and then added three more in the eighth thanks to the error.

The sweep is complete. The Cubs came within one swing— Davis' three-run homer back in May—of losing all six games in the Dome.

Teams have lost three straight in mid-August and still won the division. But once again, the Cubs rest at the cross-roads. Does the team pick itself up once again or does it finally crack. The winners get down, but the winners never crack.

The Mets are back to within 2½ games, the Phillies can't make up much ground. They remain six games back going into the weekend. Philly came back on Wednesday night with three runs in the ninth at San Diego to tie the game only to lose it in the bottom of the ninth, 4-3.

On the morning of August 16, the team arrives in Cincinnati at 4 a.m. Thank goodness Thursday is an off day. The club collectively sleeps past noon. The last three plane flights have given new meaning to the reality of jet lag.

In Cincinnati, Pete Rose is named the player-manager. Vuk had word of this a week earlier in Montreal. It is great for Pete, great for Cincinnati and great for baseball. Time will tell if Pete can manage. There are days that only a manager can tell you about.

Jim Frey is feeling it right now. "It's easy," he says, "to manage when you win and it's different when you lose. Not too many guys want to be sitting in my seat right now (after losing three straight). But when we win a few then everybody will be happy again."

Riverfront Stadium will have new life Friday night. Pete will have Soto pitching—not a bad way to break in. Instead of a club being 19 games under with nothing to play for and nobody to play in front of, the Reds will be rejuvenated for at least this series.

"I don't know if we can win the division next year," Rose says at his press conference. "But you look at the Cubs and the Mets and see what great progress they have made in just a year. They were fifth and sixth last year and they're one and two this year. It can be done when players dedicate themselves to winning like the Cubs and Mets have for the first 4½ months of the season."

The losing streak reaches four. The Mets win on the Coast as Gooden fans 12 and Wally Backman breaks up a double shutout with a two-run 10th inning homer to beat the Giants 2-0. The lead is down to 1½ games. The Phillies keep losing.

Almost lost in the shuffle is the losing streak. Pete Rose came home Friday night. Came home to the largest crowd at Riverfront since opening day. Came home and did what everyone always remembered him for. Two hits, two RBIs. Two head-first slides, one into third, the other second.

"There are some guys who were made for this game and for the glory," Frey says. "They turn the spotlight on and they can't help but do well. They live for those moments. He's one of the greats. He always manages to do something right."

The fans went crazy. Rose turned the light back on and restarted the hearts of baseball fans in Cincy. Fans showered Pete with roses at the outset of the game, tossing them near the on deck circle. Their man, their all-time player, all-time homegrown hero was back.

This is no time for panic. "It's nothing big," Gary Woods says. "We've lost four games. We'll start hitting and everyone will forget about it."

Cey dives for a ball Brad Gulden slices foul down the line. He can't reach it and ends up landing on his left wrist. Now he has two sore wrists. Say what they will about Cey, he's given the Cubs everything he has all season, both seasons.

The Bowa-Frey story heats up. The Chicago papers run stories on the offday regarding the shortstop situation. Bowa says that he's not playing because of a personality problem with Frey. "He doesn't like me and I don't like him."

Frey refuses to get involved in a verbal war. "Let's drop it," he says. "I'm trying to win games and get production out of that position. Whoever produces will play but right now nobody is producing."

Bowa is batting .216 with no RBIs since the end of June and no extra base hits since the middle of June. Owen is batting .205. Veryzer, .195.

It seems like the wrong time to be going to war internally. Dallas is quoted as saying that Bowa should be given a chance and the fans and media should get off his back and let him play. For the record, during the 1980 August stretch run, Phillies manager Dallas Green sat down shortstop Larry Bowa amid Bowa's cries. Once back in the lineup, Bowa helped make the Phils champions.

Has anything changed?

The Cincinnati bars are full of Cub fans. This has turned into another St. Louis. The hotel bar is SRO. The home-grown Cincy band is playing Sinatra's "Chicago." The city is fast becoming Dallas' and Frey's.

To be in the throes of a four-game losing streak is nothing to get crazy about. Certainly, Frey isn't crazy about it. But neither is he panicking. Nobody is panicking. This club is loose and confident and dedicated.

The major concern is the hitting. The Dome does that to a team and so does Soto.

Saturday night is different. The club comes out behind Sutcliffe and scores seven runs in the first inning thanks to a comedy of errors by the Reds. Fundamentally sound Pete Rose stood and watched his fundamentally poor Reds make four first-inning errors.

Sutcliffe pitching on five day's rest for the first time as a Cub needs all the support he can get. He leaves in the fifth with an 8-5 lead.

"I can't pitch on five day's rest," he says.

The Cubs survive anyway as the Reds keep coming back and turn a 7-0 deficit into an 13-11 loss. Valiant, but not enough. The Mets lose on the Coast and the Cubs' lead swells to 2½. The Phils stay six games back. They're not budging.

Rumors abound that Philly is about to make a deal.

The road trip finale features Sanderson and Jeff Russell. Sanderson has never lost to the Reds. Another big first inning for the Cubs. Cey homers in the Cubs' four-run first. Ron has been exceptional the last couple of weeks. Who would have believed that at this point after his start, his wrist injury and everything else, that he'd be carrying the club at the most crucial point? Maybe no one. But certainly he did.

"Sometimes you just have to play through things," he said. "The wrist was one thing. But you learn something in this game and about yourself at all times."

Cey hits a three-run first inning blast and the Cubs take a 4-0 lead. But the Reds come flying back against Sanderson and knock him out in the fourth. Frey is livid and everyone in the dugout knows it. He is hot.

The Cubs rescue the decision in the fifth with five runs, the big shot a three-run homer by Thad Bosley. Bos comes through in the pinch partially erasing the dropped fly in Houston.

It may have been the first strategic move by Rose that backfired. He figured that if he changed to Bob Owchinko, a lefty in the bullpen, the Cubs would counter with Woods. Rose thought he'd rather face Bos than Woods.

He figured wrong. Anyway, that's what happens sometimes. The Cubs escape Cincy with a 9-6 victory and a 4-6 road trip that could have been disastrous.

It's back to Wrigley and the beginning of the home stretch.

One final observation: Sales are running close to the same on two items: Pete Rose T-shirts; Cubs hats. This *is* Cincinnati. Isn't it?

The Cubs are a different team at home. They never figure they're beaten at home. They have a 38-21 record at the Friendly Confines, the best record in the league at home.

Dallas has built a club that functions well both at home and on the road, on natural grass and artificial surfaces. The great teams of the past that have graced Wrigley Field were always one-dimensional power-packed teams without speed. No more. Dallas has found the right blend.

Trout struggles through the first five innings against the Astros, then suddenly settles into a groove. The Astros can't touch him and he wins a 6-1 decision. It's his 11th victory, tying his previous best.

Once again Cey and Moreland come through. Moreland knocks in the game-winner early and Cey powers another three-run homer onto the catwalk. It's Cey's 21st of the season and his third in three games. He's caught fire.

"My career responsibilities have always been the same," he said. "Run production. And my run production numbers are right in line."

Frey has a relative staying with him in his Sheridan Road apartment. Frey lets the guest use his bedroom while he sleeps on the couch. Great host. Frey can't sleep. Finally it's three in the morning and he's dying to find out the Mets score. He dials Sportsphone and finds out that they lost. In the calm of the evening, with the stillness of Lake Michigan within eyeshot, Frey is feverishly pacing the floors concerned about a game on the West Coast. The excitement inside the skipper is also building. On the outside, he's as calm and as one-day-at-a-time oriented as ever.

The second game against the Astros is a typical Wrigley Field win for the Cubs. They beat the Astros 11-5 behind Eck. They carry an 8-1 lead most of the day before both teams put up matching three spots in the eighth.

Matthews and Davis homer for the Cubs.

"Everybody here is picking everyone else up," Matthews says. "It's no pressure once you get to the LCS or the World Series. The pressure is getting there."

"The Cubs come to this ballpark with one thing in mind," Terry Puhl figures. "They just try to get the ball in the air. They just don't try and beat you, they blow you out. They punish you."

Frey on Davis: "There are so many good qualities that you don't worry about stats with Davis."

Jody's average has slipped 40 points since the Break. Fatigue is a factor although Jody seems to be holding on. At least better than Hundley did in 1969 when Leo played him into submission.

The 11-5 win gives the Cubs a five-game lead over the Mets, who lose in San Diego. It's the biggest lead in the N.L. East this season, but by no means insurmountable. It's easy to recall that the Mets led the Cubs by 4½ games one Saturday morning and 13 days later were 4½ games out. The Phillies with Schmitty are still out there. It's about time to keep an eye on Mike. He's carried them before and it appears as if he's ready to give it another go.

Nolan Ryan sticks it to the Cubs in the series finale. Ryan fans 12 and the Astros win one of six games at Wrigley by an 8-3 score.

There isn't much you're going to be able to do against a guy as good as Ryan when he's on.

Dernier is having a dream season but he's having nothing of premature dreams.

"There is no such term as 'I' on this team," he said. "We're all here together. My season doesn't mean anything to me right now. Our season does. We're taking every day one at a time just like we did in April, May, June and July. Now isn't the time to think any differently because things change quickly."

Dale Murphy of the Braves endorses the Cubs: "The Cubs should win it. They are my pick to win the East. Easily."

Keith Hernandez of the Mets: "The Cubs are a very good team. If we don't win it they should because they are a very good club."

Al Oliver goes from the Giants to the Phillies. It's a deal that may make the Phillies a little tougher. He could help carry them. But he may also be finished. He still hasn't homered. Not that Oliver has ever been judged by his power. It is obvious that he is not the player he once was, otherwise he wouldn't be putting on his third uniform in the last eight months.

Dernier reaches safely leading off the game for the fifth straight day. He appears to be coming back strong, as does Ryno.

"Early in the year," Frey recalled, "we said the front two guys and Bull were doing a big job along with Matthews. Then it swung around with just Dernier and Sandberg carrying the load for us and Jody had a big month. All of a sudden Moreland comes up and gets hot and Cey and Matthews get hot. We've had people all year who have contributed."

"There have always been two or three guys hitting," Davis says. "But our pitching staff has gone through a three-week period where we were winning 2-1, 3-2 or 4-3 everyday."

Through it all, Matthews has been the consistent guiding force. The man's enthusiasm is catching. It hasn't wavered.

The bleacher fans have gone crazy over him. He's giving them all "sarge" hats one day. Ryno, Jody, Dernier, Moreland and Durham are also giving out 3,000 T-shirts to the bleacher fans. There may never be another incredible fan-reaction season like 1969. But 15 years from now people will most likely be saying that there will never be another year like '84.

Matthews has provided the missing ingredient. Is he the Most Valuable Player? Probably not. But could the Cubs have been in this position without him? Probably not.

"I've been called a leader before," he says, "but that's not for me to say. I'm a pretty hard critic, but I play unselfishly. The main thing is we are winning. Today I homered, but there are heroes throughout this room. I wasn't the only one that did something today."

Sandberg and Davis make an appearance at a Chicago car showroom. The place is mobbed. An elderly woman says she wanted to see them but was afraid that a riot might break out.

"There were people lined up around the block and when they finally said that no one else would be let inside, I was frightened. But where can I find out where they'll be next?"

"These people are going wacko," Moreland says. "Just get a hit to give us a lead and you get a standing ovation."

The contract negotiations between Sutcliffe and the Cubs begin. "Dallas said he'd sit down and talk with my agent (Barry Axelrod) after I made 10 starts and that's exactly what he did."

Axelrod says he's looking to better the contract Gossage got ($1.5 million per year) because Sutcliffe is younger and is having a better season. Sut could bring in a bundle.

Hank Borowy was 11-2 for the 1945 pennant-winning Cubs after being acquired from the Yankees. He was 10-5 with the Yanks. Sutcliffe is having a similar season. Maybe the Cubs will, too.

Frey isn't big on meetings, but he calls one anyway.

"We held a one-minute meeting before today's game and all I told these guys is that I was proud of the way they have played this season. Every day they have gone about their work the right way. We've played every day like we played every game in April and May," he said.

"Now is the time to grind it out day by day by day. It's just time to take it to them."

Sutcliffe wins his 10th straight and is masterful. He blanks the Braves 3-0 on five hits. There is talk about him being the first pitcher to win the Cy Young Award after beginning the season in another league.

Andujar has won 16 and Lea 15, but overall Sutcliffe has also won 16. His overall record is far and away better than either one.

There is also talk about Sutcliffe's upcoming contract and his free agent potential.

"I told Dallas let's just win this thing and everything else will take care of itself," he said. "I'm not concerned. It's because of this team that I'm 12-1. All my record means is that it's helped this team be where it is."

Sandberg's first homer since August 1st is enough for Rick in the 3-0 victory. Ryno has hit 16 and nine have either tied the game or given the Cubs the lead. MVP he is.

There is a growing feeling. The city is definitely getting more turned on day by day. The electricity is heightened almost to the point of frenzy.

The bleacher lines form early. The games are sellouts. The players get standing ovations when they park their cars in the lot. The fans have tried to remain cool and calm as long

as possible. But it is slowly getting beyond the usual limits.
Officially, this is pennant fever.

As Sutcliffe left the mound Friday, Davis threw his arms
around him. The camaraderie that has developed within
a team put together quickly is awesome.

The Cubs of 1984 have officially passed the Cubs of 1969.
On August 25, 1984 the Cubs led the Mets by 5½ games.
Exactly 15 years earlier, the Cubs led the Mets by 4½ games
on August 25.

The 1984 Cubs and the 1969 Cubs are like two ships pass-
ing in the night. The current is still sailing along in the right
direction this time.

The lead is 5½ because the Mets lost a doubleheader to
the Giants after holding leads in both games. They are all
but finished.

"We've got to beat the second-division clubs," Hernandez
says of the Giants, who have the worst record in the league.
"Otherwise we can't expect to contend."

"I can't believe we lost to those guys," Mookie Wilson
says.

The Phillies win in 10 innings. They are six games back
and could be ready to change places with the Mets.

Charlie Fox returned from Pittsburgh with a deal cooking
for a southpaw pitcher. Candelaria, Tudor or McWilliams
are the names mentioned. The Pirates are looking toward
the future and players to be named later. Perhaps an outfielder with power, perhaps a pitcher.

After the Mets drop a pair to the Giants, Fox spends the
evening and the early morning hours on the phone with
the Pirates.

"At four in the morning I was on the phone trying to find a lefthander," he says.

On Saturday, the Cubs fall behind the Braves 1-0 before tying it on Bowa's first RBI since June 30. Sanderson is working on a solid game but so is Rick Mahler. Sanderson gives up a two-out homer to Brad Komminsk in the sixth. The Cubs fall behind 3-1. In the seventh they come back with a run, cutting it to 3-2. Mahler appears to be on the ropes. Durham almost gets the game-tying run in the ninth when he sends a long, towering drive to right field. The ball appears to be headed out of the park, but the wind, blowing in strongly off the lake, holds the ball up and brings it down into the glove of Claudell Washington. Bull can't believe it. But you live by the wind and die by the wind at Wrigley.

"Sanderson pitched a great game by any standards," Frey says. "He just made one bad pitch."

Meanwhile, in Philadelphia the Dodgers drop the Phillies, who continue to spin their wheels. In New York, the Giants and Bob Brenly do it to the Mets again—the third straight loss for the Mets to the Giants by a run.

They remain 5½ games back and the Phillies are still six back.

In 1969, the Cubs were sliding through their nightmare by now. They led the Mets by three games on August 26.

At 11:10 p.m. Saturday, August 25, three lonely figures sit in lawn chairs outside the center field gate. The long wait into night has been going on for a couple of weeks now. For the trio, game time is only 14 hours and 10 minutes away.

Everywhere you look on the Chicago streets there are Cub hats. Everywhere.

Monday is an off day. The last one for 20 days and only two remain after that.

"We've got a big three weeks coming up," Dallas says.

The Sunday papers are full of Dallas stories. It has taken three years and the media still aren't completely behind him. They still look for the cracks in the character. But for now, they can do nothing but shake his hand.

Fox is off to Philadelphia and then to New York. After that he heads west to San Diego. Advance scouting is one of Charlie's greatest attributes. He is as psyched as anyone. After all those years in baseball, Charlie still can smell success and can't get enough.

Trout gives the Cubs their 13th series victory in their last 18. They have lost only two of the 18 with three splits. The Cubs send the Braves back to Atlanta 5-0 losers.

Trout throws his second shutout and his fifth complete game. But the bigger story is Durham.

The Bull takes Perez deep twice for two homers and four RBIs. It's his second two-homer game of the season and both have come off Perez. Over the last two seasons, Leon has hit six homers and driven in 19 runs off Perez, who some consider among the best in the league.

It's great to see Leon come on now. He's been struggling. He had been 0-for-12 and 1-for-21 in the last week. His main concern is not a hamstring, but his wife, Angela.

Angela is 9½ months pregnant. Thursday doctors will induce labor in Cincinnati. Bull will be there. And Perez will be pitching against the Cubs on Friday.

Besides Bull's power, Cey also homers. The Cubs have out-homered the Braves 31-5 in their last 20 meetings. That is incredible considering that both teams contain some pretty good power hitters.

Attendance-wise the Cubs are 6,000 away from breaking their home record of 1,674,993. Is the city going Cubs crazy?

Consider that the Cubs have drawn 98.5 percent of capacity in their last 11 home dates.

In the East, the Phillies were down 7-1 to the Dodgers at home before they came back with a couple of big innings to pull out a 10-8 win. The Mets do likewise. The Giants broke out to a 5-1 lead and it looked like the Mets may have been close to collapse. But they avoided the sweep and rallied for an 11-6 win.

When someone suggests that the Phillies may be rejuvenated after the comeback, Vuk says, "Oh yeah, well, think of it this way. They pull out a game they could have lost and what does it mean in the standings? It means another day has gone by and they still haven't picked up a game."

Monday, August 27. The Cubs lose a half-game to both the Mets and the Phillies who win. It's an off day for the Cubs. Time to take a deep breath. The next off day is September 17. There are miles to go. In the next 20 days the Cubs will play 11 games on the road, finish up against the Western Division teams and make their last trip east to play the Phillies, Expos and Mets. It's a road trip that will tell a story.

Meanwhile, the Phillie fans are having doubts about their club. The Phillies are a bit battered. Schmitty is hurt but playing, as is Virgil. Joe Lefebrve is out, Samuel is hurt and not playing and Maddox is on the DL. Holland hasn't been effective.

They are talking to the Giants about Lavelle, as are the Cubs. Huey Alexander goes on Philly radio and says that in the next couple of days the front office will get together and decide if the club can win it. If they can, they are going to make a major deal. Probably for Lavelle. You can tell September is getting close.

The day off doesn't hurt any. The Cubs win their third straight doubleheader sweeping the Reds twice by 5-2 scores. Moreland uses three days off to come back strong. Sandberg hits No. 17 and all is well.

Ruthven and Eckersley earn the wins. The club is getting methodical in winning.

"We're not doing anything sensational," Bowa says. "But every day we make all the plays, get the right kind of hits at the right time and get the job done.

"It's nice and consistent. Nothing flashy. We're just working and winning."

Moreland gets six RBIs for the game. He's got to be in the running for the August Player of the Month award. He has been awesome in August.

He's also the player rep and one guy who is well liked by just about everybody on the club.

"We really got going in June when we made that big deal," he says. "Everybody who came aboard in the last year wanted to play and wanted to win.

"The fans in this place are great. I've never had so much fun playing ball. Every day you come out here and the place is loaded. It sure beats playing in front of 4,000.

"The cable TV also helps. We go into cities where there are as many Cub fans as fans for the opposition. It's really something."

Another 30,000-plus crowd fills Wrigley. Today the Cubs surpassed the franchise attendance mark. The Cubs have passed 1.7 million, with 2 million a distinct possibility.

The lights issue continues to simmer. Nobody is saying much but everyone is interested. The word travesty comes into many conversations when lights at Wrigley Field for post-season play are brought up.

A vote for the Cubs comes from Rose. Pete says between games of the double-header that he doesn't see how the Cubs can lose in the division race.

"There isn't anyone as strong. They've got too many positives," he says. "For a team that has been to the World Series once in 39 years they field a team that is loaded with players with World Series experience. They've probably got more starters who have been in the World Series than any team.

"I don't think they'll lose enough games the rest of the season to let anybody get hot and beat them."

Still, the road trip through Atlanta, Philly, Montreal and New York awaits.

"I think that will tell the story," Bowa says. "If we win that we'll win this thing. If we come back four games up, it's over."

Rose likes what he sees of the Cubs. He likes their depth and their talent, but mainly he likes the experience.

"They've got Cey, Bowa, Matthews, Moreland, Dernier. That's five regulars who have been in the World Series plus the manager.

"For those who think that team is going to get nervous they better think again. The team that beats them is going to have to beat them because they won't beat themselves.

"They're getting into a situation where the Phillies and Mets are going to have to beat them every time they play.

"Probably the biggest thing being in the playoffs and World Series does for you is the next time you're in a pennant race you realize what's ahead of you if you play good.

"The pressure is getting to the playoffs. The rest is fun."

The fans show up with brooms as the Cubs sweep the Reds 7-2. Wrigley Field continues to be a godsend for the ballclub. The 7-2 homestand gives the Cubs a 45-23 record at home, the best home record in baseball.

The win is the Cubs' fourth straight. Since June 26 when the Cubs split a doubleheader against the Pirates they are playing .672 baseball (41-20).

Wednesday it's a typical Cub victory. Sandberg has a double and a triple. Dernier hits a rare homer but it goes for the game-winning hit—the fifth win in a row that was provided by a game-winning homer.

Matthews makes a great catch in left. Durham, who left for Cincy after the game to be with Angela during the birth of their first child, had two hits and three RBIs along with his 20th homer of the season.

Last, but far, far, far from least, is Sutcliffe who won his 11th straight and is 13-1. Only three pitchers have won 20 games in a season in which they were traded from one league to the other. The last time it happened may be more than a mere coincidence. It occurred in 1945 when the Yankees sent Borowy to the Cubs.

Ryno improves his chances of achieving baseball's first 20-double, 20-triple, 20-homer, 20-stolen bases and 200-hit season. He needs 24 hits including three triples and three homers.

"He is having one of the greatest years ever," Harry Caray says.

"It's hard to believe that a guy can play as consistent as he has all year with his composure and skill," Frey says. "You just don't see players do things like that every single day from April through August."

The Mets, however, continue to keep up with the Cubs' pace. They drop the Dodgers 3-2 to stay 5½ back. The Phillies, however, are just about finished. They are seven games back after losing to the Padres 2-0.

The psychological effect on the Cubs playing and winning in the daytime has to have an effect on the Mets and Phils.

"When we win in the afternoon and they show up at the ballpark that night they know before they start there cannot be any errors," Matthews said. "The pressure starts right then."

Before the Wednesday game, Matthews, Dernier, Moreland, Durham and Sandberg distribute T-shirts and offer thanks to the bleacherites for their season-long support.

One of the season's great, subtle scenes: Matthews makes a fine running catch off Milner in the seventh. Sutcliffe gets the ball back and waits on the edge of the mound to catch Gary's attention. Once he does, he salutes the Sarge ever so subtly. It's quite a gesture from two guys who never knew each other until two months ago.

The inner feeling that everyone on this club has for one another is beautiful. It's hard to imagine a better blend of talent and emotion. Respect is overflowing.

In this crazy, wild season of "can you top this" the Cubs prove that they can write scripts with the best of them.

Atlanta's Perez pitches the opener of the road trip against the Cubs and Sanderson. Scott has one bad inning when he allows four straight hits and three runs. Unfortunately, Perez is on tonight.

Through six innings he has eight strikeouts and has allowed a measly three hits. Then in the seventh the Cubs start coming back. An error by Randy Johnson opens the inning. Bosley singles. He's playing for the expecting father Durham. Davis walks. Bases loaded, nobody out. Johnstone hits a looper into left field that Komminsk just can't reach. The runners had to play it safe and Davis gets forced at second with a run scoring.

Rohn pinch hits and flies out in foul territory in right. Bosley tags and scores. It is 3-2. That's where the rally ends.

Perez tires after eight and Garber comes in. Bosley hits a one-out homer in the ninth to tie the score. Your basic unbelievable ending.

But wait, there's much more.

In the Cubs 10th, the first seven hitters reach with Moreland and Cey producing back-to-back two-run hits.. The Cubs score five runs and beat the Braves 8-3.

Meanwhile, up the East Coast, the Mets are taking an off day before meeting San Diego in back-to-back doubleheaders on Friday and Saturday. In Philly, the Giants and Brenly do in the Phils in the first game of a doubleheader. Brenly hits a homer to beat Holland in game one.

Hugh Alexander, the Phillies chief scout, can't stand it any longer. After watching most of the Cubs-Braves game he leaves his seat and heads for cover. The scoreboard watchers in Philly must have fallen over. They went from picking up a game to losing one in a matter of minutes. The cable TV watchers in New York must have damaged a few sets.

When Bosley went to the plate, Bowa told him to look for a change or a palm ball from Garber. He got it and rode it out.

"This team works great together," Frey said. "We've got veterans who help the kids and kids who look up to and respect the veterans."

While Frey is bubbling over the win, he's fuming over baseball's decision on the light issue at Wrigley.

If the Cubs win the division, they will still host the first two games of the LCS in daylight. The World Series, however, will be changed. The Cubs would have hosted Games 1,2,6 & 7 and gained the home field advantage. Games 3-4-5 would have been played on the weekend. To keep the Cubs playing day ball baseball changed the sites giving the American League team the advantage but letting the Cubs play in daylight on the weekend.

Frey and Dallas were not happy.

"I guess baseball got what it wanted," Dallas snapped. "Other than that I've got nothing to say."

Frey was as adamant as could be.

"I can't believe that baseball would mess with the schedule. This is the year for the National League to have an advantage. Why punish us? Four games in daylight at Wrigley Field would be in our favor. But I don't see why it shouldn't be in our favor. That's the way it's set up. When baseball and TV signed the contract didn't they know the Cubs were in baseball and that this might happen? Did they just find out in the last week that we're in the league?

"Anything but four day games at Wrigley Field in the World Series is a disadvantage for the Cubs and I don't like it one bit. Why should I?"

The wheels keep turning. It is August 31. The day that post-season rosters are pretty much firmed up. There are a few questions regarding the Cubs. Do they collect on their players to be named later deals of the mid-summer before the deadline? What do they do about the guys on the DL— Hebner, Hassey and Reuschel? Who do they move off the roster that is currently on it.

The coaches meet long into the night. It's a decision that for the first time in 15 years the Cubs have to be concerned with.

"After this game tonight I hope I locked myself in," Bosley says. "I know in my heart that I have."

Time will tell for many of them.

The long-awaited deal for Davey Lopes comes through
at the deadline. Lopes comes from Oakland to complete the
Chuck Rainey deal of July 15th. It seems like Rainey left
last season.

Lopes will probably play third, second and the outfield
and may even play some at shortstop. He can still play at
38. Plus he's been in the race many, many times.

The sad news is that Jay is being reassigned, which means
that he's finished as a Cub. Jay was with the Cubs for more
than two seasons—for this club that's a long time.

Leaving the game is nothing any player looks forward
to. Johnstone is a bit stunned, a little hurt. He may stay with
the club in some capacity to finish out the season.

Lopes has to be in Atlanta before midnight on August
31. He arrives by private Lear jet at 11:40. The Lear was the
only way to get him from Oakland to Atlanta before the
deadline.

At the ballpark, the Braves score in the ninth to beat the
Cubs 3-2. The Phillies lose again, staying 7½ games back
and the Mets split with the Padres to gain the half-game
they lost the night before. They are 5½ games back.

Sandberg and Cey both homer in the first two innings
and it looks as if the Cubs may turn the game into a rout.
But the Braves settle down and match the Cubs with single
runs in the first and second.

The best Cubs opportunity came late when with the bases
loaded and one out Matthews lined into a double play.

A loss isn't wanted, but it's no disaster. Not at this point.

The Cubs exhibit more rebounding power. After losing
the tough 3-2 game on Friday they come back behind Eck

and beat the Braves 4-1. Durham returns from Cincy. Angela and new daughter Loren are doing fine.

Matthews continues to show the way. He gets the equivalent of two game-winners in this one. He gives the Cubs a 1-0 lead. Then when the game is tied in the ninth, he drives in Sandberg with a clutch double.

He's got 14 game-winners this season.

It marks the 16th time this season the Cubs have won in their final at-bat.

Every day turns up more confidence. The club has become more and more methodical.

Sandberg is featured at length on the NBC pre-game show. The building of an MVP starts on the field, but it ends with the media.

Ryno scored his 100th run today. He also played in his 57th straight game at second without an error, equalling the league high this season. He's just incredible. Day in, day out what more could anyone want from a player?

Sunday wraps up the Cubs' regular season competition against the West. Philly awaits . . . and then New York after Montreal.

"Their season is coming up real soon," one player says.

Eck doesn't get the win but he allows just one run in seven innings knocking his post-break ERA under 2.00.

He, too, will become a free agent.

"Well, Rick and Dallas are talking now," he said. "I'll have to wait and see how much money is left."

Lopes makes his clubhouse debut. Matthews sees Lopes and Cey standing next to each other and wonders aloud who is shorter. Penguin is always catching grief because of his size. "Take a bleepin' picture," Ron tells Matthews. "I'm taller."

Getting back to Eck, when someone asked him about his evaluation of the club he responded: "This is no Cinderella team. This is one awesome ballclub. We've got a great collection of baseball talent."

The final game in Atlanta is not only a big game for the Cubs but it's a bigger game for Ruthven. He's been struggling all season and lately he's moved dangerously close to falling from the rotation.

He knows it. He shows it. And Sunday he went out and did something about it.

He held the Braves to four hits through six innings. The Cubs weren't sending balls flying all over Fulton County but they did manage to get two from a Durham homer in the fourth. The Braves countered with a Washington homer in the seventh. It was their first round-tripper at home against the Cubs in two seasons. The Cubs had outhomered Atlanta 35-5 overall.

Frey gets seven outstanding innings from Ruthven. He goes to Smith for the fifth time in five days after the Cubs add two more runs in the eighth taking advantage of a walk, an error and a two-run single by Matthews. The Sarge has been hot.

"It seems like Matthews has been hot for six weeks," Frey says. "Sarge always contributes something."

Defensively, Bowa looks like 1974 instead of 1984. He makes at least four great defensive plays. In September you go with the veteran.

Smith doesn't have much problem nailing down his 28th save.

But the Mets stay hot. After sweeping the Padres on Saturday they come back and knock them off again in 12 on a hit by Foster.

The lead is up to five games over the Mets and 8½ over the Phillies. The Cubs have a chance to put the Phillies away with the next two games at the Vet.

Joe Torre leaves his stamp of approval as the Cubs pull out of Atlanta.

"Nobody will catch the Cubs now," he said. "They're too deep and they play with great confidence. You can see it. At one time I thought the Phillies would catch them but not any longer. They're the best in the division and maybe the league."

There are rumors in Chicago that Dallas may be leaving for Philly at the end of the season even though he has two years left on his contract. Bob Verdi writes a Sunday column on it in the *Tribune*. Granted, Dallas has had his moments with the press and with the fans. But he has always honored his contracts, he says. And he's got to be happy with what has transpired lately.

One writer recently labeled Dallas as the Baseball Executive of the Century for turning the Cubs around.

"What Dallas has done in three years is awesome," Bowa says. "Nobody in their right mind would have believed it. But he's done it."

On to Philly. Denny, the 1983 Cy Young Winner vs. Sutcliffe, the 1984 candidate.

"This should be a great game," Frey says. "We've got two Cy Young Award winning type pitchers going. If Denny isn't sharp with his curve ball we've got a chance. Otherwise it's going to be very tough.

"We've got some big games coming up. We'll take it a day at a time. There is no game as important as this one. But we've got a chance to put some distance between ourselves and the Mets and Phils."

The game is indeed a pitchers duel. Sutcliffe is awesome. He strikes out 15, equalling the Cubs record. He allows three hits in eight innings but he won't get the win. It takes 12 innings and of course, two Philly errors, before the Cubs can beat the Phils 4-3.

"Philly should be finished now," Bowa says. "Nine and a half games is a long way to go. They're done."

Cey homers off Denny in the second, his 24th. And in the third, Denny allows a single to Sutcliffe and walks Sandberg and Matthews (his curve ball isn't working to perfection). Durham grounds out scoring Sutcliffe. In the fifth, Matthews homers.

As he rounds the bases the crowd is practically on its feet with cheers. If there were five bases instead of four, The Sarge would have had a standing ovation in an enemy ballpark.

"I told the Phillies that they'd have trouble replacing me in left. Every team has. I just asked them to trade me to the East and I thank them for it."

The 3-0 lead wilts in the Labor Day heat. It's 90-plus degrees on the field and Sutcliffe feels it as the day heads into dusk.

Schmidt homers leading off the fifth. It's the first hit off Rick. Philly gets two hits and two runs in the seventh, set up by a two-out double by Al Oliver.

Jody suspects Oliver of using an illegal bat. Bruce Froemming, who is behind the plate, throws the bat out of the game. It takes 10 minutes to straighten everything out.

Ozzie Virgil greets Sutcliffe, who had been waiting out the conversations, with a two-run single. The game is tied.

The Cubs win in the 12th when Hebner leads off with a grounder to Samuel. He muffs it for his 30th error. By comparison, Sandberg has four.

Dernier sacrifices Hebner to second. Sandberg then hits a grounder to Kiko Garcia at short. Hebner breaks and is thrown out. Sandberg is on at first with two outs. With John Wockenfuss catching, Sandberg is running. He steals second and suddenly, a bad baserunning play by Hebner turns into a Cub advantage. Instead of two outs and Hebner at second, it's Sandberg. Matthews grounds one toward Kiko. It bounces off his arm and into short left field, scoring Sandberg.

Smitty comes in to start the bottom of the 12th and retires the side.

The Phillies may, indeed, be finished.

"Catch the Cubs?" Phils manager Paul Owens says. "How about us catching the Mets first?"

But are the Phillies dead? The Cubs won't admit it.

A sign hung over the leftfield wall at the Vet. It read: Phillies Win or Die.

The Phillies died.

The Cubs took it to Steve Carlton in the first inning. Matthews singled home Lopes who had doubled in his first Cub at-bat. Cey followed with his 25th homer.

Carlton was gone midway through the fifth when the Cubs came up with four more runs. There was no debating the scene. Sanderson was breezing along. Every time he got in trouble, he got tougher.

He had a shutout into the ninth even though he had allowed a dozen hits. He didn't get the shutout but he got the victory, a 7-2 decision.

The Phillies were beaten. They were finished. They left for St. Louis 10½ games behind the Cubs. The Mets were also staggering. They had won eight of 10 including four of five against San Diego in what they considered the must series of the season. But what did they gain for all their victories? Nothing, only a bigger lead over the third-place Phillies. The Cubs matched them win for win and did it on the road.

The Mets have played St. Louis the last two days and haven't been able to get it together. "You've got to believe that it took some of the wind from them when they beat San Diego and pick up zero ground," Steve Stone said.

At about the time the Cubs score and victory was posted in St. Louis, the Cards blitzed the Mets with a nine-run inning. While the Cubs traveled to Montreal as loose as can be, the Mets prepared for a series against the Cubs at Shea this weekend. A series they must sweep.

The league has given the Cubs permission to print playoff tickets. It is happening. It is really and truly happening. The monkey is coming off the Cubs' back. The years, the jokes, the ridicule is being smitten away. Brushed away like dirt on the carpet. The Cubs are not only good but they are becoming a truly great team. No one knows what's ahead. All anyone knows is what's gone on before and before this season it wasn't all good. This year, however, has been magical.

Absolutely magical. This is the kind of year that everyone connected with the game dreams of. But wait, there are still division playoffs and then the Series. First there is a division to be won.

The magic number is 18. And it is truly magical.

It's into Mirabel Airport in Montreal. Actually it's closer to the North Pole than it is to Montreal. The city has an ordinance prohibiting air traffic into the main airport—Dorval—after midnight. The Cubs touch down at Mirabel, a ghost town of an airport and then bus into the city, a 40-minute ride through the hinterlands.

Montreal's weather has turned to fall. A windy, cool-to-cold day turns into a worse situation at night. Following the hot and humid days at Wrigley Field and Atlanta and even Philly, the change in temperature is a shock.

The club isn't sharp. A letdown may have been natural following the big wins in Philly. Trout doesn't have it and lasts only 3.1 innings. The Expos replace Schatzeder in the second after Dan comes down with an inflamed elbow. Considering the way he handled the Cubs a month ago in Montreal it could have been a blessing. But it's not. David Palmer comes in and three-hits the Cubs for six innings.

Brusstar, Frazier and Stoddard work scoreless innings for the Cubs but it's too late. The club isn't hitting and one bad inning costs them. They lose 3-1.

The seven-game lead is cut to six. No big deal.

The final day in Montreal this season. Eck works against Lea. Two outstanding pitchers who have both struggled for support. Lea has an ERA of 2.84 for the season but hasn't won in his last nine starts. Eck has an ERA under 2.00 since the All-Star Break and he's only had a handful of wins.

After a shaky first inning, Eck settles down and stops Montreal on seven hits, 4-1. Frazier, however, gets the win. He's been awesome during the last month.

A key play develops in the fourth when Matthews guns down Wallach at the plate with a perfect throw. It was still 1-0 Montreal at the time. Who knows what another run would have meant?

The Cubs come alive in the seventh on a Durham double and a Moreland single. Dernier triples leading off the eighth and Sandberg scores him with a sacrifice. Two unearned runs in the ninth give Smitty some breathing room for his 30th save.

The clubhouse is jumping. Frey says, "How many big games are there? Maybe I've said we've had five. Well, tonight we've got six. This was a big game and I'm as happy as can be.

"Eckersley pitched a great game. After what happened to him in the first he was great. A lesser pitcher and a lesser man doesn't come out of that."

A quote in the *New York Daily News:* "The Cubs have five guys with great RBI seasons. Sutcliffe is having his greatest year for them. They're overachieving," says Mets manager Davey Johnson on the eve of the Cubs-Mets New York series.

The Cubs respond. Especially after Johnson and the Mets drop a 2-0 decision to the Pirates in front of 3,000 at Three Rivers. Johnson moved Gooden back in the rotation in order to use him in the opener against the Cubs.

Johnson was trying to do a little Cubs Busting of his own.

While Johnson is trying to light a fire for his club, the Mets are facing the finale and they realize it. The Mets must win.

"We're living by the skin of our teeth," Hernandez says. "And it's been that way for the last few weeks. There really is no tomorrow."

The Cubs must face Gooden in the opener. The series begins with the Cubs seven games ahead of the Mets and a bulging 11½ ahead of the Phillies.

Ruthven once again draws Gooden. It's the fourth time this season Rufus has gone against the kid.

On this night, Gooden is just overpowering. He fans 11 and walks four in a 10-0 crushing of the Cubs. While all those numbers are impressive, the most impressive number is this—one hit. Moreland's slow roller in the fifth was all that kept the rookie from throwing a no-hitter.

It was a play that will be talked about for a very long time.

Moreland topped the ball and had a little trouble getting out of the box. The ball rolled toward the bag at third. Ray Knight came charging in and was forced to glove the ball almost on his backhand, but not quite. He had a quick notion to throw and then decided against it. Almost immediately, the official scorer, Maury Allen of the *New York Post*, flashed base hit.

There is no way Allen could rule an error on a ball Knight didn't misplay. Yet, the feeling was that if Knight would have at least tried to throw Moreland out there would never be any questions. Had Knight thrown to first would Moreland have been out and would Dwight have thrown the no-hitter?

The Mets blew the game open in the third with five runs. Sandberg committed his first error in 62 games during the inning. This was definitely a night to forget.

With 21 games remaining, the Cubs lead is six games. Following the Friday night game Davis pulls Sutcliffe to one side and tells him that the Saturday game is so very important. Sut can't get Jody's words out of his mind.

"I took those words back with me to the hotel," he said. "This was the biggest game I've had to pitch."

He allowed four hits but didn't walk a batter and fanned 12, giving the Cubs the win they needed in the series. They beat Terrell 6-0. This was a great game.

The Cubs scored a single run in the second on a Cey single and then added another run in the sixth. With Sutcliffe throwing as well as he was, that could have been enough. For good measure, the Cubs added two runs in the seventh and the ninth.

Besides Sut's masterful pitching, Matthews contributed three hits, a walk and three RBIs. One of the hits was his 11th homer.

During the game, plate umpire Doug Harvey went to the

Mets dugout for a drink of water. He spotted Johnson and said, "This guy (Sutcliffe) has the best stuff I've seen all season."

Sut's record is 14-1. He has won a dozen decisions in a row without a loss.

"This," Frey said," was one of the biggest games of the season. And remember, I don't usually get excited."

The wrap-up in the Apple. The Cubs won the game they needed to win. Getting at least one win out of New York meant that the Cubs could only lose one game while knocking three off the schedule. That's acceptable.

In the first inning, the Mets try to change their fate. The Black Cat returns. In the first inning a Met fan drops a black cat into the Cubs dugout.

"I thought it was a rat," Richie Hebner says.

"Can you believe it?" Gary Woods asks. "We all scattered. But to tell you the truth the cat was more scared than we were."

You cannot adjust the fates. Even so, Ron Darling is sensational. Not as good as Gooden and not as good as Sutcliffe but good enough to beat the Cubs 5-1.

He doesn't finish, yielding to Orosco. It's the first time in the last 10 meetings that the Cubs have met up with the Mets' closer—Orosco. That is a definite statement about the way the series has been going. The Cubs have won eight of 10 since the race heated up.

For the trip the Cubs are 7-4. Frey would have been happy with 5-6, very happy with 6-5. So what is he with 7-4? "Pleased, I guess. What do all these numbers mean anyway? Let's win tomorrow."

Before tomorrow comes there is a plane ride to O'Hare.

Close to a thousand fans line the gate area and the corridor. Sandberg nearly is drowned in a sea of loving humanity and ballpoint pens.

It will get crazier. These are moments to savor.

Radio stations everywhere are talking Cubs. News shows begin with the Cubs' score and stories. Fans are celebrities. Apartment owners on Sheffield and Waveland are suddenly finding their roof tops worth a lot more than the apartments.

Atop the building across from the left field catwalk, the people have set up a giant Rusty Jones balloon.

"That's really Rick Sutcliffe," Stoddard says.

People are coming from all over. There have been buses coming from Nebraska for a one-game weekend jaunt. There are people who have flown in from Hawaii for a weekend series.

This country isn't nuts about the Cubs?

Three blocks from Shea Stadium is the Louis Armstrong Tennis Center. The U.S. Open finished there Sunday night. Allen, the New York writer who was the official scorer during Gooden's one-hitter, posed a question at Open champion John McEnroe. McEnroe said, "Let me ask you a question? How could you give Moreland a hit Friday night?"

Everyone has at least a corner of their eyes on the Cubs . . . and the Mets.

Back to Wrigley with a magic number of 13. The Mets series is behind them. The black cat. The Met faithful. The media madness.

It will take a major, major disaster to keep the Cubs from the division title. Even 1969 would pale if this one slipped away. But it won't. It can't. There is just too much going the Cubs' way. The balls they hit stay fair. The pitches they take are just off the black. And it's just the opposite for the other guy.

Lord knows, every Cub fan has seen it happen the other way for what seems like forever.

On September 10, 1969 the Cubs were in second place. Fifteen years later, they are up by six games. But . . . but the day they return to meet the Phils is eerie.

For some reason there were bad vibes in the opener against the Phils. Somehow the Mets picked up a game on the Cubs over the weekend when the Cubs could have put them away. What would a Cub loss mean on September 10, the date in 1969 when they fell from first? What would a loss mean coupled with a Met win against the Cards? It would mean a five-game lead. Not nearly as invincible as six.

For six innings the Cubs looked listless. The Phils scored two runs in the fifth when Hayes singled on a 3-2 pitch with the bases loaded. Connors was ejected seconds later by Joe West. West was squeezing Trout and suddenly Connors lost it.

In the seventh, the fates smile again through the dark clouds. With one out, Davis walks. Bowa singles just up the middle. Woods pinch hits and lifts a broken-bat fly to right that drops. The bases are loaded.

Dernier works the count from 1-2 to 2-2, 3-2 and finally takes ball four, forcing in the first run. Sandberg is next. He has been struggling.

Owens goes to Andersen, pulling Koosman. Ryno is 0-for-10 career vs. Andersen. He grounds to Steve Jeltz at short who throws to Samuel at second forcing Dernier. Bobby comes in hard and quick on Juan. Samuel's throw goes into the crowd. Two runs score. The Cubs lead 3-2.

It's the third time this season that a Samuel throwing error has helped the Cubs to victory. It's, to borrow a Mets word, amazing.

Smitty closes the Phils down in the eighth and ninth. The magic number is 12. The Mets are home to play the Cards.

And then it is 11. The Cards are playing great. Thank

goodness they took most of the midsummer off. Otherwise, the Cubs could be in trouble.

The next day, it is the Cubs' turn to give one away. It's a typical 1984 Cub game at Wrigley. There is electricity in the air. The crowd is back to a decent noise level. New heroes arise. Old heroes check in again.

After trailing 2-0 through most of the afternoon, the Cubs come up with a run in the fifth. In the eighth they come up with two runs keyed by a pinch hit by Ron Hassey worth an RBI, and a run-scoring single by Ryno. The Cubs enter the ninth with a 3-2 lead and Lee Smith pitching.

Suddenly, it's over in a hurry. The Phils score four times off Lee.

It's the first time in 2½ seasons that a team hits Lee for four earned runs in one game. The Phils hand the Cubs a little of their own medicine.

Philly wins 6-3.

"We've won a few like that," Ryno says. "It's no big deal."

"It's good we won yesterday," Matthews said. "Yesterday was a game that could have changed some things. Then again, we're not going to let any one game change us. If we do lose this thing people will rank us with the 1969 club in a hurry. But believe me, it won't happen."

In New York, Orosco walks in two runs with the bases loaded and gives up a three-run triple in the eighth. The Cards do it again. The Cubs lose a game and the Mets lose a number. It's down to 10.

The firehouse across from Wrigley Field's leftfield foul area proclaims itself as the Official 1984 World Series Firehouse.

The ticket plan is announced. Seven thousand tickets will

be sold to the public not counting the 12,000 eaten up by season ticket holders. It is a massive undertaking.

The media crunch continues. *Good Morning America*, the *Today* show, *CBS Morning News*. You name it, they want the Cubs.

Steve Daley of the *Tribune* gets a phone call from Calgary, Alberta about the Cubs and this player named Sandberg. Everyone is a Cub fan.

A writer from *Sports Illustrated* visits. He's doing a piece on the city, the ball park, the area, the team, the happening, the phenomena.

"This," Bill Nack says, "is one sports story I cannot compare to anything that has happened before. This is totally unique.

"I was talking to someone in a bar across from the park today. He told me he didn't know whether to laugh or cry if they won. He told me he's always told people 'wait 'til next year.' And now he doesn't know what he's going to tell people. What is left?"

The hitting slump isn't officially over. But for a day there is hope that the Cubs have weathered the breakdown. They trounce Montreal—one of the great wait-'til-next-year clubs, 11-5. The teams out of the race begin each game as gung-ho as the teams in the race. But as the game moves along and it gets down to the tough times, the pennant contender has that little extra. Always has, always will.

The Cubs break open a 2-1 Expo advantage in the sixth with five runs. They had three in the seventh and two in the eighth. More old heroes—Sandberg's 19th homer, a three-run shot in the sixth. More new heroes—Hassey again comes through with his first 1984 homer, an opposite-field shot to left center. It's the fifth pinch homer of the season for the Cubs.

Ryno gets a standing ovation. So does Hassey. All Cubs are created equal.

"This still doesn't mean you're getting a full share," Sutcliffe kids his former teammate and batterymate.

All Cubs are created equal. Up to a point.

Sandberg's public continues to clamor for him. He has taken home the fourth box full of letters. Not a shoe box, but a moving box. He has become a hero, a steadfast hero, the kind that comes around once or maybe twice a generation. Fans continue to send him rhinoceroses. It's kind of touching.

Speaking of rhinoceroses. On the subject of the Cubs grassy infield—especially on the left side, Mark Whicker of the *Philadelphia Daily News* had this to say: "When people in Chicago refer to Ryno do they mean Sandberg or the rhinoceros that's wandering around in the heavy brush to the left of the pitcher's mound? Is it true that Rudyard Kipling wrote 'The Jungle Book' from inside the Wrigley Field infield?"

With the final game against the Expos rained out, the Cubs have a day of rest before playing the Mets in the season series finale. The Mets aren't catching any breaks. Sutcliffe was slated to work against the Expos but the rainout moved him back to the opener against the Mets. When it's your year, things work out that way. The Mets can't draw a break.

September 14. The weather is overcast, the temperature is barely into the 60s and the wind is blowing right in the hitter's face. Still, 36,334 fans show up. It's the Cubs against the Mets; Sutcliffe against Darling.

Through the first two innings neither team can get

anything started. Then in the Cubs third, Bowa starts the Cubs off with a one-out single to left center. Darling commits a pitcher's sin by walking Sutcliffe. Dernier, who had only four hits in his last 20 at-bats, puts the Cubs ahead with an RBI double to left, scoring Bowa. Sut comes in on Ryno's sacrifice fly to right. The Cubs have a 2-0 lead and Sutcliffe throwing at home. The Mets can't afford to fall 8½ back.

Sut isn't yielding. Through six Met innings, he has allowed just four hits, all singles, and no walks. It's now the Cubs sixth. Dernier and Sandberg start it off by reaching base—Dernier on a single and Sandberg on a walk off reliever Brent Gaff.

Matthews fans, but Dernier and Sandberg move up to second and third on a wild pitch. Durham is walked intentionally to fill the bases. Moreland grounds out on a deflected ground ball scoring Dernier and leaving first base open again. Davey Johnson doesn't want Gaff pitching to Cey. He walks Cey intentionally.

That brings up Davis. On the first pitch, Davis buries the Mets, buries the past, buries the memory of Al Weis' two homers in a mid-July, 1969 visit by the Mets. Davis hits a grand slam to deep left center. The Mets are finished.

Sut allows a consolation run in the eighth. It only means that he won't get a shutout. The complete game is his, the 7-1 win belongs to the Cubs. The Mets trail by 8½ games. The Cubs have only 14 remaining. It may finally be over.

"We haven't won anything yet," Frey rants in the Cubs' clubhouse. "I've been around long enough to know that this doesn't mean anything. Sure it puts us closer but what if we lose tomorrow? It brings them that much closer. Forget about it. We haven't won anything yet.

"Do you know what the most important game of the year

is?" he asks the assembled media. "Well, it's tomorrow's game. That's the only game I'm concerned with. The only one that means anything to me."

But the Davis slam sapped the last breath from the Mets. The Mets had an incredible run. There was no way anyone could have predicted that after spring training the Mets would ride with the best of the N.L. East all season. The Cubs had strengthened themselves with the Stoddard and Matthews-Dernier deals coming out of camp. The Mets were going with kid pitchers and a team that was questionable in the middle infield. But they had hung in the race to mid-September, long after the favored Phillies and Cardinals and Expos had fallen by the wayside.

For all the good the Mets accomplished, they could not do what they had to do and that was beat the Cubs. From June on, the Cubs and Mets went head-to-head a dozen times and the Cubs were 9-3. The Mets had to beat the Cubs to stand a chance of pulling it off. With only two games remaining between the clubs it didn't seem possible.

"We needed to sweep here," Johnson said. "But until you're mathematically eliminated anything can happen."

"The Cubs are a good team," Hubie Brooks added. "You can't feel sorry for us. We figured we had to win three games here to have a chance. The odds are really stacked against us.

"It's not that we haven't played well this season. We win 10 of 13 but the Cubs win 10 of 13. We can't gain ground playing that well?"

Throughout the season the Mets had looked to Keith Hernandez for leadership. Along with Sandberg, Hernandez had to be considered a candidate for MVP honors. With a young team, the Mets looked to Keith. He was a veteran of post-season play, an MVP. An outstanding player. But at this point in the season, even he applauded the Cubs.

"They are the best team in the league, by far. For us to win now it would take one of the greatest collapses in base-ball history."

"I'm running out of ways to describe Sutcliffe," Frey said. "He kept us in the game and then Jody got the big hit that finished it for us. But we've still got to keep this thing under control until somebody comes in here and tells us we've won it all."

Keeping an even keel, maintaining the club's perspective was one of Frey's strengths all season. Even in Arizona where outfielders were going after fly balls like they were live hand grenades, Frey's approach, at least outwardly, was one of a calm, calculated nature.

"I've been on all kinds of teams," he said. "Teams that got the big lead early and hung on, teams that got the lead early and finished way out of it. Teams that were mediocre until June or July and then played better than anyone and ended up winning it all. I know that there isn't anything to get excited about in this game until it's over. And this is far from over."

Before another sellout crowd, the Cubs moved another step closer to making sure it was over. They beat the Mets 5-4 behind Sanderson. Once again, the Cubs got in front early with a four-run first.

Johnson's rotation called for Sid Fernandez, a portly left-handed rookie that reminded people of Valenzuela. The kid walked Dernier and Sandberg to open the game and Matthews picked them up with a single for his 16th game-winner of the season.

Sanderson allowed two hits and two runs in the third and another hit in the fifth. Other than that the Mets were helpless against him until the eighth when they chased him with a walk and two straight hits. In came Smith and the Mets rally died.

The Cubs were 9½ games in front with 13 to play. The victory was their 90th.

In the ninth, the capacity crowd began waving the white scarfs that were given away that day. The umpires had to stop play. It was an awesome sight.

One of the great fans is a former Chicagoan now living in San Francisco. His name is Jerry Pritikin. He does work for a sporting goods store in downtown San Francisco. The front store window is loaded with Cubs memorabilia.

Pritikin has returned to Chicago for the last month of the season. He attempted to bring into the park a voodoo doll dressed in a Mets jersey that covered a Padres jersey. The guy is beautiful.

Ninety wins. Consider that the 1984 Cubs, 1969 Cubs (92 wins) and the 1945 team (98 wins) were the only three Cub teams to reach 90 victories in the last 46 years.

Sanderson pitched very well indeed. There is no telling how good he may have been this season if he could have pitched without worrying about his back going out. His ERA is barely above 3.00. His strikeout-to-walk ratio has been tremendous. He has pitched some great games.

"The guy is pitching in pain," Connors said. "A lot more pain than he'll ever admit to. I'm tired of hearing that he's just another pretty face. This is the guy who threw 152 pitches in Philadelphia the last time he pitched and he's a guy that will throw in on a hitter if he has to. Don't tell me Scott is just another pretty face.

"If we weren't in this race, he'd be finished for the season. But he wants no part of that."

"I thought we'd have a good team way back in spring training," Scott said. "I liked our offense right away. The pitching was going to be a question but I didn't think it was as bad as everyone made it out to be. I didn't think we'd have this big a lead at this point, but it's been a great year.

"Besides," he said with a smile," I've never pitched for a loser before and this was no time to start."

"At Long Last, Respect." The Cubs make *Newsweek*, the September 10th issue. The Cubs are not just a sports story, not just Chicago's story. No, they are a nation's story and a city's pride. Did the Tigers make *Newsweek*? Will the Padres? Will the Royals or the Twins or the Angels? Probably not.

Finally the Mets do what they haven't been able to do since the 1983 season—they beat the Cubs at Wrigley Field. Berenyi beats Trout 9-3.

The game bears a slight resemblance to the nonchalent days of the past when the Cubs and Mets were playing out the string trying to dump one another into last place.

"Both teams have improved so much," Jody says. "Just last year the big Met series meant who finished last."

The lead is 8½. The games remaining falls to 12. The Cubs bid farewell to the Mets.

"Gentlemen," Frey says, "I think we've got a chance."

On the day before the Mets series, President Reagan comes out and throws his support behind the Cubs. The President once did radio re-creations of Cubs games in the 1930s.

Frey reads of the President's loyalty and decides to send him an autographed picture. He signs it, "To the President. Thanks for rooting for us. We're rooting for you. Jim Frey."

On Monday, September 17th, the Cubs are idle as they await Pittsburgh's final Wrigley Field visit. The magic number is five.

The Mets are in Philly with Gooden pitching. He has been spectacular down the stretch. He is again superb on this evening. He fans 16 for the second straight game but balks home Shane Rawley with the winning run in a 2-1 Philadelphia victory. With Samuel hitting and Rawley on third, Terry Tata called Gooden for a balk.

"The replay showed it may have been and it may not have been," Frey said. "We'll take it just the same."

"Where did that theory go that the Mets kid pitchers would fold in the stretch," Vukovich says. "Striking out 16 isn't exactly folding."

It's eerie, the Mets losing 2-1 in Philly. In 1969, at the same point in time, Steve Carlton struck out 19 Mets on September 15th. Lefty was pitching for the Cardinals at the time. While Carlton fans 19 Mets, Ron Swoboda hits a pair of two-run homers and the Mets win. Here it is nearly 15 years to the date going back to the year that lives as a thorn in the heart of every Cub fan and a young phenom strikes out the masses and gets beat. Everything that goes around comes around. This one just took 15 years.

In the American League, Detroit clinches the A.L. East and the city goes berserk. The Tigers became the first team since the 1927 Yankees to win a title after leading from the first day of the season to the last. The Tigers are a great team. A Cub-Tiger World Series would be a classic: Morris vs. Sutcliffe. But first, the N.L. East has to be won and then the National League.

Sandberg has slowed slightly in his quest for 200 hits. With a dozen games remaining he has 185. He also needs one homer to become the second Cub since 1911 to have

20 or more homers and stolen bases. The only Cub since the 1911 left fielder Frank Schulte to accomplish it was Durham. The Bull did it two years ago.

The Met defeat puts them nine games back and reduces the magic number to 4. It remains a distinct possibility that the Cubs could clinch the division title at home. They have three games with Pittsburgh and the Mets have two more in Philly before the Cubs leave for St. Louis.

Tuesday, September 18 is a tribute day. How else to explain why 30,721 fans would pay their way in to see the Cubs play the last-place Pirates at Wrigley Field. The kids are in school. Vacations are summer memories. A Tuesday afternoon crowd this size is a tribute to two phenomena: 1) the Cubs' great season and 2) the Cubs' great fans.

It is mind-boggling to try and comprehend a crowd that size at this time of the season when other teams in contention, with the benefit of night baseball, don't draw as well with an even larger season ticket base. It is a tribute.

The Pirates and Mets ruin the faithful's chance to see the Cubs clinch at home barring a major collapse that would keep the race going into the final weekend when the Cubs host the Cardinals. Come to think of it, most Cub fans would rather watch it on television than be put through the trauma of waiting another 10 days and watching the Mets stampede back.

The Cubs are flat and commit two errors giving Pittsburgh a 6-2 win. The Cubs gather five hits, but never more than one in an inning. Later in the evening, the Mets pound Philadelphia. It's a small consolation for the Mets but they've stopped the Cubs from clinching at home. The number stays at 4.

On the other hand, the Wrigley Field security people, the

ground crew and city police are probably breathing easier. The chances of Wrigley Field being reduced to rubble in a few days are greatly reduced.

The next day, Sutcliffe gets bombed. There is just a hint of "what's going on here?" in the air. His 13-game winning streak remains intact, although it is no longer 13 straight winning starts. He allows nine hits and five runs, four earned, in 4.1 innings. The Cubs take him off the hook by grabbing a lead in the fifth, but Stoddard and Bordi can't keep the game in hand. Pittsburgh wins 11-6 due in great part to a six-run sixth.

For the first time, Sut doesn't look nearly as overpowering. One glance at his numbers shows only 137 innings before today's game. But that's only as a Cub. He threw just under 100 with the Indians also. The man is working toward 250 innings.

Everything considered, the ticket lottery is the fairest way to distribute the playoff tickets. The alternative plan of selling tickets at the ballpark could result in any number of unfavorable occurrences. The people in line are those people who can afford to either be unemployed or take off work and sleep outside for a couple of days. That doesn't necessarily qualify them as being a greater Cub fan than someone with a job and a family. The lottery gives everyone an equal chance.

How many people back in March dreamed the Cubs would be holding a post-season ticket lottery?

The Pirates continue to put a crimp in the celebration plans. They sweep the Cubs with a come-from-behind 7-6 win. The Cubs lead 6-2 after five innings and 6-4 after six. With leads after six innings the Cubs have won 90 percent of the games. This isn't one of them. The Pirates add one run in the seventh and two in the eighth off Smith and win 7-6.

If there is any doubt about why Frey wanted everyone to settle down and relax a little it's apparent now. The Mets are idle and can't gain any more ground. But the lead is down to 7½ with nine to play.

The Cubs are off to St. Louis. The crowds there will be just as wild as the ones at Wrigley Field. The St. Louis police and Busch Stadium security have the dubious problem of protecting their stadium not from a St. Louis celebration but from a transplanted Chicago celebration. Maybe.

Friday, September 20. It was 20 years ago today that Chico Ruiz of the Reds stole home and beat the Phillies 1-0 in extra innings. So who cares? It was the first of 10 straight losses for the Phils who lost a 6½ game lead with 10 to play.

"I remember it very well," says Ruben Amaro, a member of 1964 Phillies. "It was so strange. Every day something crazy would happen. We can't forget that it happened, but it was something that was out of all our hands.

"It won't happen here though. We're still playing good. We're going to be alright. One thing in our favor is nobody else is getting hot."

The Cubs batting average through the first 15 games of September was .219, the ERA was 4.90. The record was 10-5. The Cubs picked up three games on the Mets. So who cares about stats?

Is there interest in the Cubs in Chicago? Do the people want playoff tickets? There are 17,500 pairs of seats available through the lottery. The post office says it has received 1,850,000 cards. Not a promising ratio. Anyway, back to the task at hand—beating the Cardinals.

Oh brother. The Cards rip the Cubs 8-0. Kurt Kepshire,

a rookie, throws a seven-hit shutout. After watching the Cubs the last five games it's hard to believe that they lead the East. They have played uninspired and unaggressive baseball. The losing streak reaches five, the longest of the season. Nice time for a losing streak. The Mets keep their hopes alive by beating the Expos.

With the chance to catch history, NBC decided at the last minute to televise the Cubs-Cardinal Saturday game. Costas and Kubek are back again. After some deliberation, NBC decided to do the game. When it was all said and done, the game wouldn't have been the clincher even if it had been played. The rains came early and never let up. The NBC plans went up in smoke. Plans that included having Jack Brickhouse do some color work, as well as call the last out, had that last out been the one that clinched the title.

Jack, who has waited as long as anyone for the Cubs to win a title, took it philosophically. "I've waited this long," he said. "What's another few days."

The day off didn't bother the Cubs. In fact, it may have been the relaxer they needed.

"You watch what happens tomorrow," Vukovich said. "This will be to our benefit. We'll be back where we belong tomorrow."

"Nothing to worry about," Bowa added. "Worry only if you're a Met."

Sunday called for more showers. The rainout forced Sunday's game to two games. In the opener Frey went to Trout. "We've got to get a well-pitched game today," Frey said. "Maybe that will get our hitting back in line."

In what was the biggest start of his career, Trout was masterful. The Cards had a couple of early chances, but Trout shut them down going the distance in an 8-1 win.

Trout gave the Cubs a 1-0 lead with a sacrifice fly in the second, a rocket to right.

The Cards tied it in the third. In the fourth, the Cubs finally awoke offensively. With two outs and Bowa on second, Dernier held out for a walk against Rick Ownbey. Sandberg walked, loading the bases.

Herzog went to Jeff Lahti against Matthews. The Sarge came through as usual. He went with an outside pitch to right clearing the bases with a double. After a walk to Durham, Moreland singled home Matthews.

The Sarge came back to the dugout, a rejuvenated dugout. He must have set a record for most high fives delivered. Misadventures in left field or not, anyone who doesn't like watching Matthews play doesn't like baseball.

As he did when he first came to the Cubs, he had provided the lift, the spark.

Cey followed Matthews' cue with a double of his own scoring Bull and Moreland. Davis, who started the inning, went out short to first. But the damage had been done. The Cubs led 7-1. The game-winner went to Matthews, his 17th.

Trout got the Cardinals to ground into 23 outs. It was his sixth complete game. "How about Rainbow?" said Billy Connors. "He pitched great. He was tougher than ever and it was the biggest game of his life. The guy has grown up. He's been great."

In game two, Eck went against Andujar who was looking for his 20th win.

"Let's make sure this guy doesn't get it against us," Bowa said between games. "Let's bury these guys and make those Mets watch."

True to form, Dernier reached on an Ozzie Smith error leading off the game. After Sandberg fanned, Matthews took Joaquin deep to left center. Sarge did it again. His two-run homer gave the Cubs the lead, the momentum, the victory. Eck was tough as ever and won 4-2. Smitty came on and pitched two innings of hitless relief.

The Sarge had contributed his 18th game-winner. He was beautiful.

"I feel good. I'm confident," he said. "This is exactly where I want to be at this time of the season."

It took the Cubs a couple of years to win a doubleheader. But they are 5-0-2 in '84.

The champagne was still on ice, still packed away after its flight from Chicago. The win clinched at least a tie for the title. The Cubs were at the brink of washing it all away.

"It was a great day," Frey said. "And I don't say that very often. But I don't want to have anybody ask me about how I feel about winning it until we win it."

The Cubs flew off to Pittsburgh, off to history.

The Mets continued to hang tough. They beat Montreal for the third straight time behind Gooden's 17th win. They continued to scoreboard watch at Shea although they were watching a team other than the Cubs. They were watching the third-place Cardinals, who had come up hard on their heels.

The day dawns overcast. It could be any Monday in Pittsburgh. The good people of this region have been through tough times, desperate times. When the economy fell apart a few years ago, it collapsed on Pittsburgh. For generations the city worked and the steel mills coughed smoke to the heavens. While it was never pretty, it sure was prosperous. But those were the old days. Today the city struggles, with only hope to celebrate.

The Cubs spent the day as any other day. Frey and his coaches debated a post-season roster and then went to Three Rivers Stadium in the early afternoon. Most of the players were at the park hours before game time. Only a handful ever take the team bus that normally leaves two and a half hours before game time. Today it leaves three hours before because it is the opening game of a series. The extra half hour gives Vuk the chance to go over the opposing hitters with the Cubs.

The media converged on Pittsburgh. The press box was filled. Instead of the usual 30 or so media members there were perhaps 150 from all over the country. The same could be said for the fans. The Pirates were expecting 1,100. Instead the game drew 5,472; more than half of them rooted for the Cubs.

There were quite a few fans that came in from Chicago that day either flying or driving the distance. It was a festive gathering, a special night.

There was a job to be done. With a chance to put the finishing touches on a dream regular season, the Cubs struck early. After Dernier grounded out against Larry McWilliams, Sandberg doubled into the left field corner. Sarge was next. He promptly ripped a single to left center scoring Sandberg. It was 1-0.

With Sut pitching, the Pirates couldn't afford to fall too far behind. Pittsburgh went down in order in the first.

In the Cubs second, Sutcliffe drove in Bowa, who had singled and moved to second on Jim Morrison's throwing error. It was 2-0.

In the third, Sandberg led off with another double. Matthews walked for the 100th time this season. Moreland followed with a single to third. When Morrison again threw the ball away, Sandberg scored. It was 3-0.

The Cubs didn't score in the fourth, but Pittsburgh did. After Joe Orsulak broke up Sutcliffe's no-hitter with a triple, he scored on a ground out by Ray.

The Cubs got the run back in the fifth when Matthews

walked again and went to third on singles by Moreland and Cey. He scored on a double-play ball hit by Davis. It was 4-1.

From that point on every moment became one to cherish. The Pirates wouldn't threaten again. The only other base-runner for Pittsburgh was Orsulak who had an infield hit in the sixth. Sut took care of that by picking him off.

From the first pitch, the crowd's roar became stronger. It was a festive crowd that was incredibly loud for its size. With every pitch, history inched closer.

In the Cubs' clubhouse the preparations were being made for a celebration. Yosh Kawano, the longtime Cubs club-house man, and his assistant, Greg Nimietz, covered the lockers with plastic, put the champagne in ice buckets and sat back and waited.

In the eighth inning, Matthews, who had been replaced in the seventh, came into the clubhouse. He lit a cigarette and smiled. "So this is it," he said.

A sign unfurled down the left field line. It read "39 Years of Suffering Are Enough."
How true, how true.

As the game wound down, the Cubs went down as easily as the Pirates. Sut made the first out in the ninth for the Cubs. Dernier and Sandberg followed quickly with infield groundouts.

The crowd was standing, minus Dallas, his wife Sylvia and his assistant John Cox. They had left for the clubhouse a couple innings earlier. When Dallas left his seat behind the Cubs' dugout the crowd saluted him with applause, with respect, with warmth. There wasn't any doubt as to who had molded this club into a champion.

The Pirates opened the ninth inning with shortstop Ron Wotus. He took Sutcliffe to right field, to Moreland. That was one out.

The Cubs' bench was stone cold silent. Only Vuk yelled encouragement. Frey and Connors and Vuk sat side-by-side. With every pitch, Frey chewed his gum a little faster.

The second Pirate hitter was pinch batter Lee Mazzilli. He lofted a fly ball to left center where Dernier was waiting. That was two outs.

There was one out to go. One solitary out stood between the Cubs, their fans, the city and a championship.

The hitter was Orsulak. Lost in the drama of the evening was Sutcliffe's performance. As Orsulak came to the plate, Sut had allowed only two baserunners. Both times it was Orsulak who reached, once on a triple and another time on an infield hit. He had fanned eight to that point and hadn't walked a hitter. Orsulak was only the 28th batter he faced, one over the minimum.

The count ran to 1-2.

"I want the ball when this ends," Davis had told Sut. The words stuck with him. "I knew what Jody meant," Sutcliffe said.

He wound up and delivered. Delivered the Cubs from the past, all the failures, heartbreaks and ridicule. Delivered them to a championship. The pitch rode the outside corner, rode the black into Jody's glove. Orsulak began his swing, then stopped. Plate umpire Lee Weyer's right hand shot out. It was over.

Frozen forever will be the scene: Sut on the mound appearing as if the weight of the world had been lifted from him. Into his arms came Jody. Next was Cey.

The dugout emptied. Frey was running toward the scene, stuffing his hat into his jersey. The masses came spilling over the dugout roof.

Back in Chicago, the cork popped on the city. The emotions of nearly four decades and a few generations came pouring out. There was no holding back.

The clubhouse quickly became another precious scene unto itself. Dallas hugs Bowa. Dallas hugs Frey. Frey hugs Connors. Dallas hugs Oates, then Vuk, then Zimmer, then Connors, then Amaro. Leon hugs Smitty. Leon hugs Sut. Jody hugs Sut again. Cey hugs Sut. Sandberg hugs Sarge. Dernier hugs Moreland. Moreland hugs Jody. Dallas hugs Sarge.

All the world hugs.

This night was for Chicago, for Cubs fans, for baseball fans, for losers turned winners, for us all.

"I knew when the team came back from the first trip, the West Coast trip, and then played pretty well on the first homestand that we'd be competitive," Dallas said. "I thought we could be pretty tough. I also knew we had to do something about the pitching staff. Then when Sanderson and Ruthven went down it got a little touchy. But we were able to help ourselves with trades for Eckersley and Sutcliffe.

"We still have to win three more to get to the World Series, but I want our players and our fans to enjoy this, to savor this moment. It's a moment for all of us."

It was for all the players who wore Cub uniforms since World War II ended. This was for Ernie, for Hank Sauer, for "Moose" Moryn, for "Handsome" Ransom Jackson, for Don Elston and Roy Smalley, Sr. For the late Charlie Grimm, the last Cubs manager to win a pennant. It was for the 13 managers that followed Charlie as well as for the College of Coaches.

"We did it. We did it," Frey said. "It's beautiful. Finally it's over. I won't have to talk about the sun being too bright, about the temperature being too hot at Wrigley Field. We beat them all. I won't have to answer questions about the 1969 Cubs. We have become champions of the National League East. It is a night to remember."

It was for all the 1969 Cubs. For Kessinger, Beckert, Williams, Santo, Banks, Hickman, Hundley, Young. For Spangler and Smith and Nate and Gene Oliver and Popovich. For Fergie and Hands and Holtzman and Regan and Selma. For each and every one of them.

"I didn't throw well tonight," Sutcliffe said. "I must have thrown 50 off speed pitches. This night is very difficult for me to put into words. I owe so many people. I came here with this team in first place. It wasn't like I turned it around. I was lucky to be part of something so special, a group of people so special."

For Sutcliffe, the victory made him someone special. He became the fourth pitcher in baseball history to win 20 games in a season while pitching in both leagues.

An hour after the celebration had begun in Pittsburgh, the people of Chicago were still delirious. Cub players came out of the clubhouse, out of the third base dugout to watch the Three Rivers Stadium big screen in center field.

A hookup was secured to show the Chicago celebration back in Pittsburgh. As the camera panned around the outside of Wrigley Field, the players gasped. The intersection of Clark and Addison streets resembled Times Square on New Year's Eve.

It was the same on Rush Street, the heart of the nightclub district. It was the same in suburbia. The Cubs had lit up

many a life. It was a night to fill a glass, face the East and
Pittsburgh, and offer a toast to a team that won a title.

It was for all the old Bleacher Bums, for all the season
ticket holders who laid their hard-earned money down and
watched teams finish with 59-103 records. For the fans who
sat through frigid April openers and melancholy September
afternoons to watch the Cubs. It was for the apartment dwel-
lers across from the outfield walls, for the old men in the
grandstand who sat alone, for the kids whose reward for
perfect school attendance was a trip to the Cubs game. It
was for all those beautiful fans whose lives revolved around
ivy, hand-operated scoreboards and day baseball.

While the clubhouse had become one team's folly, the
trainer's room became another man's solitude. While the
everyday players, starters and year-long teammates, celebrated, others stood apart.

Davey Lopes, a Cub for only 25 days, left the partying
to the teammates he was just getting to know. Jay Johnstone stayed near the back of the room, no longer a part
of the active roster. Reuschel sat back and watched. It was
almost a bittersweet appearance he portrayed. He had accomplished one of his career goals—to be part of a Cub
championship team. On the other hand he wasn't pleased
with the way his own season had been handled.

Standing together were the players who had shuttled between Iowa and Chicago. Rohn, Owen, Meridith, Patterson and the new kid on the block, Billy Hatcher. "I'm just
happy to have been able to be here and be a small part of
this," Rohn said.

This night was for all the Cubs who played hurt and still
finished at the bottom, for all the pitchers who blew their
arms out trying to grasp that brass ring, that championship
season.

In the center of the room, Stanton Cook, Andrew Mc-Kenna and John Madigan of Tribune Company stood by and watched and smiled. Owners of the Cubs for little more than three seasons, Tribune Company had put together the management team first by hiring Dallas and then by adding Jim Finks. The combination made the whole thing work.

They smiled as their suits dripped Le Domaine. Class men who had put together a class organization.

This victory was for William Wrigley, Philip K. Wrigley and Bill Wrigley. For a family that had built one of the sturdiest sports franchises in history before finally yielding to the phase of baseball that demanded corporate ownership.

Stationed throughout the room were Jack Brickhouse, Vince Lloyd, Harry Caray and Steve Stone. In the radio booth, Milo Hamilton and Lou Boudreau were closing out the evening.

This was for Vince and Lou, who for more than half of their 20-plus years together had labored through teams that couldn't play .500 baseball. Yet, they rode it out and made it interesting. This was for Harry, who broadcast every game like it was the seventh game of the World Series. It was for Milo, who did his first Cub game in 1955, for Steve, who played in his first Cub game in 1974. But most of all, it was for Jack, who for more than 30 years brought life to a team that many days played lifeless.

The celebration in the visitors clubhouse in Pittsburgh lasted for two solid hours. Frey was here one moment, there the next. There were congratulatory messages, first one from his wife, Joan, and then one from Harold Washington, the mayor of a city up for grabs, a city about to go through a hangover of gigantic proportion.

"I said in spring training that my biggest job was to bring 25 guys together," Frey said. "If I could make them think like Cubs instead of ex-whatevers. . . . I had to make them believe they were Cubs and not ex-Phillies or ex-Dodgers. I also had to make them proud to be Cubs.

"It was like sending your daughter to college. One day, she's 18 and going away and she's still a little girl. Then the next day she comes home and she's a woman and she's gorgeous."

This was for a 7-20 spring training record. It was for all the players who fought through the frustrations of 1982 and 1983 and for the handful that had been through the 1981 Cubs season. For those who cried in defeat and swore they would never become accustomed to losing.

It was for Moreland, who changed positions as often as he changed clothes until he finally settled in right field and worked to become a solid everyday player.

It was for Cey, who played hurt and who played with his psyche constantly being battered about by the adjustments that go along with going from a contender to a second-division club. For Bowa, whose competitive nature helped the club through the first years and who had to hear the boos rolling out of the stands this year. For Leon, who moved to first and stayed healthy and poured his heart and soul into making every day a little better for everyone.

For Jody, who refined his catching mechanics in the big leagues, who struggled and never stopped trying to get better. This was for Sarge, the leader who took an active role on the club and gained the respect of his teammates and the love of a city in short order. For Bobby D., who took hold of perhaps his final big league opportunity and turned it into a season no one will ever forget.

And, of course, for Ryno—Kid Natural. A player to build a franchise around, a soft-spoken person, a heart of gold and a glove to match. A player who listened, who learned and who excelled beyond the wildest dreams.

This was for all the coaches, whose lifeblood is baseball.

"Give Dallas credit, a lot of credit," said Billy Connors, who along with Vuk were the only two coaches to survive the first three seasons. "He went out and put it together when few people thought it possible. We told him we needed pitching and when everyone said there was no pitching out there he found some anyway. The man deserves this moment. He has done the job."

It was for Dallas. For his trades, for his character. It was for Sandberg and Bowa for DeJesus. For Matthews and Dernier for Campbell. For Sutcliffe, Hassey and Frazier for Hall and Carter. For Trout and Brusstar for Fletcher, Tabler, Tidrow and Martz. For Eckersley for Buckner and Sanderson for Martinez, Lefferts and Connally.

For all the grief he took, for all the ill will he stomached. For all the time he gave to the Cubs, to the city, to dedication, time he took from his family. Yes, this night was for Dallas.

September 24, 1984. It was for everyone.

3 Extra Innings

The first step complete, it was time to look ahead.

There was one week before the National League Championship Series would open at Wrigley Field.

Padres manager Dick Williams flew to Chicago early. He decided to grab a first-hand scouting look at the Cubs. He took in the final three games of the regular season against St. Louis.

In the seven days before the NLCS, Frey and his staff had some major decisions to make. One was getting his pitching rotation in order. It would be Sutcliffe, Trout, Eckersley and Sanderson. Ruthven would be moved to the bullpen and would work long relief.

There was also the unpleasant duty of trimming the playoff roster to the 25-man limit. The Cubs decided to go with one less pitcher and one more lefthanded hitter coming off the bench. Rich Bordi was scratched from the roster as were Reuschel and Dan Rohn. Reuschel and Rohn could see the move coming. Bordi didn't.

Other than those two major decisions, Frey was left to keep the Cubs running smoothly, and injury free. For the first time all season, he could rest anyone he wanted without worrying about the charging Mets or Phillies.

In some cases, players had individual milestones to achieve. Sandberg, for example, was closing in on 200 hits and had the best chance in major league history to have

200 or more hits plus 20 or more doubles, triples, homers and stolen bases.

In the next-to-last regular season game, he collected his 200th hit. He started the regular season finale in search of a triple and a homer to complete the 200 20-20-20-20 quest. He went hitless in two at-bats before coming out of the game. Nevertheless, it was already an MVP season.

Frey gave his regulars a day off here and there, but didn't allow anyone to lose his edge.

There was also the preparation of Wrigley Field itself. It not only had been 39 years since the Cubs were in post-season play, it was also that long since Wrigley Field was used as the host facility for post-season baseball play.

Besides the bunting and manicuring, Wrigley Field was also being asked to accommodate more members of the media than ever before. It was indeed a monumental order.

On Tuesday, October 2, 1984 post-season play returned to Wrigley Field.

Dawn broke onto a clear horizon. Paint the prettiest picture of Wrigley Field, the grand old park. Strike the prettiest, most glorified and colorful pose you can imagine and that is what Wrigley Field looked like for the first two games of the National League Championship Series.

The people. The crowds. The masses clung from rooftops across Waveland and Sheffield. If it hadn't been an outpouring of love and adulation, there would have been concern. The situation just as easily could have turned into riotous chaos.

Among the Game 1 festivities was the return of Ernie Banks to throw the ceremonial first pitch. Ernie was brought back as an honorary coach.

"If you wait long enough good things will happen," he said in reference to the Cubs' championship season. "My ship has come in."

There were more than 650 media members on hand, the

vast majority stationed in a temporary press area in back of third base, under the upper deck and through the mid-section of the grandstand.

Through the print media and the electronic media, the world watched.

For the last two months, Chicago had one thought – the Cubs. For three days beginning with the Monday workout, the sporting world throughout North America had the same thought.

In the opener it was Sutcliffe against Eric Show. Both pitchers had a track record of terror against the opposition.

With the National League umpires beginning the first day of their short-lived strike, four amateur umpires were brought in to work the first two games in Chicago.

As Alan Wiggins stepped into the batters box to begin post-season play the wind was blowing straight out.

After the Padres went down in order in the first, the capacity crowd had become settled. Bobby Dernier led off the Cubs first.

On Show's second pitch, Wrigley Field gasped. Dernier caught a fast ball up and took it deep into the seats. The crowd was delirious. The Cubs were on their way.

Sandberg struck out. Matthews, the 1983 League Championship Series MVP, followed with a carbon copy of Dernier's blast giving the Cubs a 2-0 lead. The 13-0 rout was on.

Before it was over, before the Cubs would claim their first post-season win since Hank Borowy beat "Dizzy" Trout, Steve's father, on October 8, 1945 in Game 6 of the Series, the Cubs would delight the crowd with five homers and a new set of memories.

Matthews also hit a three-run homer, Cey hit a two-run homer and even Sut drilled one over the right-field wall practically all the way across Sheffield Avenue.

Besides the offensive showing the Cubs played solid

defense which included a great diving catch by Moreland in right on a liner hit by Carmelo Martinez in the fourth. If the Cubs 5-0 lead at that time didn't tell the Padres something, Moreland's catch told them they were out of business for this day.

Every Cub starter had at least one hit. Sutcliffe lasted through the seventh before Frey brought in Warren Brusstar to close.

If there was any reason for concern it was Sutcliffe not having exceptional stuff. In his previous two outings he had been hit hard by the Pirates and then came back and tossed a brilliant two-hitter the night the Cubs clinched. Through the happiness and hoopla, the question came through: "Was Sut feeling the wear and tear of the long season?"

"Today, I conceded I didn't have real good stuff," he said. "I had to change speeds a lot."

The Cubs' clubhouse was still a serious one. The music came from all directions and the laughter was no more, no less than after any of the previous 96 victories.

"You want to enjoy this," Dernier said. "So you don't want to get too low-key, but I don't know if it will make San Diego better prepared tomorrow. They didn't swing the bats bad today. They just hit everything at somebody. Plus when we gave Rick the lead early, I liked our chances."

If the early momentum had indeed been captured in a bottle by the Cubs, Frey denied being the one holding the bottle. His stance was no different than it had been at any time previous.

"I have refrained from talking about momentum because I don't believe in it," he said. "You can be strong with a bat one day, but if you face a strong pitcher the next day you lose that momentum. A strong pitcher can change that in a hurry.

"After a win like this," he continued, "it's easy to pop off and make all kinds of claims. I'm not like that. You can talk about the emotional and psychological impacts and stuff like that, but I'm not smart enough to figure all that out."

Matthews, who took the first steps toward repeating as the MVP, was seconding Frey's motion.

"I said to my teammates earlier 'don't be afraid to dethrone me.' If we win, it doesn't matter who wins the award. The most important thing is for the team to win. I'm glad we won the first game. It's important in any LCS to get that first one. San Diego has a lot of pride. You know they'll put their best foot forward tomorrow. What you have to do is not get too high when you win and too low when you lose. We've been trying to do that as a club since April and it's worked so far. There's nothing better than tasting champagne in September and October."

The weather, the atmosphere, and the outcome were all identical in Game 2 as in Game 1.

Steve Trout pitched one of the best games of his career shutting down San Diego on five hits, giving the Cubs a 4-2 win and a 2-0 lead.

Another crowd of 36,282 poured into Wrigley Field. Color the sky blue, the crowd a rainbow and the Cubs red hot.

While the Cubs used power in Game 1, a day later it was speed and defense.

Once again the Cubs scored in the first inning. Dernier opened the inning with a single off Mark Turmond. When Sandberg grounded out to third baseman Luis Salazar, Dernier kept running on Steve Garvey whose throw across the infield to third had no chance to catch Dernier. Matthews bounced a hopper to Templeton at short, scoring Dernier.

In the third, a Moreland single, a Cey double and a sacrifice fly by Davis gave the Cubs two more runs. Trout was breezing.

San Diego cut the lead to 2-1 in the fourth, but the Cubs came right back with more daring baserunning. After Dernier forced Trout on a fielder's choice, he stole second and scored on a double by Sandberg.

The Cubs were playing perfect baseball. Their execution was flawless.

The key defensive play for the Cubs came in the sixth when Durham made a leaping catch on batting champion Tony Gwynn in the sixth inning. It is likely that if Durham doesn't make that play, the Padres would have had runners on second and third with Garvey batting.

"If Bull doesn't make that play," Dernier said, "Gwynn has a double and they're in business."

"From the bench it looked as if it would have gone through," Padres manager Dick Williams said. Beside Durham's great play, the Cubs turned a pair of double plays to keep the Padres from breaking out of the frustrations. San Diego was 0-2 in games and had been outscored 17-2.

"Naturally, I'd like to be going back to San Diego 1-1 in games," Williams said. "But we have them in our park now. We'll be away from the Cub fans that have been a real advantage for them. It was their 10th man, no doubt about it. Hopefully, our home surroundings will benefit our club.

"I'm not counting us out. We've won three in a row before. If we don't, it's sayonara."

"I'm not counting us out either," Rich Gossage added. "I know from experience. Winning that last game is the toughest. I remember when I was with the Yankees in 1977 that the Dodgers won the first two games of the World Series before we came back to win the next four. Hey, it's a crazy game sometimes."

The Cubs left Chicago with a quiet confidence. Smiles said it all.

San Diego beckoned to many as a meeting in paradise. It wasn't to be. Pretty, blissful San Diego turned ugly and stormy.

Late into the day, the Cubs and later the Padres touched down in San Diego. A crowd of 60 Cubs fans met the Cubs bus at the Sheraton Harbor Island West Hotel.

The Padres rode a silent bus to Jack Murphy Stadium. To their surprise 2,000 fans were waiting for them.

It had been a long night's journey for the Padres.

It had been a long, long season for both clubs. It was time to get down to the finals and the toughest of times.

There had been talk that Jack Murphy Stadium would not be sold out, In fact, nearly 2,000 tickets were sold the day of Game 3.

But suddenly, San Diego was no longer the laid-back paradise it took pride in and advertised itself as being. The city was hyped into aiding its Padres in any way possible.

With Game 3 just moments away, Steve Garvey led a contingent of Padres through a few pre-game sprints starting at their first base dugout and ending in short right center field. It stirred the crowd the first time. It whipped them into a frenzy a second time and it was deafening a third time. Crowds can't hit and crowds can't field, but crowds can alter the psychological state.

The umpire strike continued. The crew working the first game in San Diego was from the Padres' spring training city of Yuma, Az.

Game 3 would match Eckersley and Ed Whitson. While people were captivated with Sutcliffe's unbeaten streak and his work in the clutch situations, it was Eckersley who actually had the better second half among Cub pitchers. Dennis was 8-3 with an ERA that was barely above 2.00.

The Cubs gave Eckersley a 1-0 lead in the second when Moreland opened the inning with a double and scored on a single by Cey. When Davis followed with another single the Padres were a hit or two away from throwing it all away.

But the rally ended there. Bowa lined out to Templeton, and Eckersley, trying to lay down a sacrifice bunt, popped back to Whitson. Dernier followed with another line out to Templeton.

Months later, while reflecting on 1984, Eckersley couldn't get his bunt attempt out of his mind.

"If I get the runners over who knows what happens?" he said. "We had Whitson on the ropes. But after that he was tough."

In the San Diego third, Wiggins was thrown out trying to steal. In the Padres' fourth, Gwynn led off with a single only to be doubled up on a ball hit by Garvey.

If only the Cubs had added to their lead in the second.

"Ultimately, getting only one run in that inning hurt us," Frey said. "Whitson wasn't going to give anything up after that."

"In our position you look for little bits of optimism," Garvey said. "We went from low tide to high tide after that inning."

It wasn't until the San Diego fifth that the Padres showed any life. San Diego scored three times, the key hit being a one-out, two-run double by Templeton giving the Padres their first lead of the playoffs.

One out later, Wiggins singled home Templeton. Just an inning later, Kevin McReynolds cranked a three-run homer off reliever George Frazier.

The Padres went on to win 7-1. There aren't many 7-1 games the losing team feels it should have won, but this may have been one of them.

"We should have never let them get back up off the floor," Dallas said. "That was our first mistake."

Moments after the game, San Diego was beginning to believe it could pull off the comeback.

"The Cubs weren't going to just come in here and take

this series from us," Templeton said. "And our fans really gave us a boost."

Perhaps the most surprising aspect of the final three games of the playoffs was the San Diego crowd. Jack Murphy Stadium was packed. The fans came in from the beach looking to do a little Cub Busting. They sang and they cheered. No San Diego baseball crowd had ever been louder. Californians may be stereotyped as being nothing but mellow and serene. But they also know an event when they see one and the National League Championship Series had suddenly become just that.

"We lost some momentum," Dernier said. "We had it and they took a little of it back. It still takes three to win this thing. We can come back in Game 4 and take it right back to them."

"It's still right there in front of us," Moreland said.

"Give San Diego credit," Frazier said. "You don't win a division by 12 games without bats. It's a fact that the toughest game to win in a championship series is the last one."

Meanwhile, Templeton continued to sing a different song.

"The pressure is beginning to come down on them," he said. "We've got a little momentum going."

An off day followed. The Cubs worked out. Frey would not stray from his rotation and neither would Dick Williams. It would be Tim Lollar for the Padres in Game 4 against Scott Sanderson.

When it was over, when Game 4 had ended with an explosion and a flash, it was chronicled as one of the greatest games ever played. In terms of drama it had to rank that high. In terms of Cub fans and heartbreak, it also sits at the top of the list.

The lead had gone back and forth all night long and with it the momentum. There was one fighting for life and another trying to deliver the final blow. In the end there was

Garvey, already three-for-three, hitting in the bottom of the ninth with Lee Smith pitching and the score tied at five. With one out, Gwynn singled to bring up Garvey, who was among the league leaders in grounding into double plays.

Smith missed with his first pitch. Then he tried to put a fastball past the 35-year-old Garvey. Garvey's bat came around and sent the ball on a high, deep arc toward right center. Cotto raced hard and scaled the right field fence going as high as he could possibly go. The ball landed out of his reach.

Garvey's homer tied the series at two and tied the Cub faithful's stomachs in knots.

"I hit it hard," Garvey said. "And everything froze. It's like a euphoria. The ball is up there, the fans are screaming. It's as if time stops and you realize you have completed a task."

The task would have been even tougher if the Cubs had taken advantage of their own ninth-inning rally that left the bases loaded without a run scoring.

The Cubs had fought back twice, once to take a 3-2 lead and another time to tie the game at five off Gossage in the eighth.

After San Diego grabbed a 2-0 lead, the Cubs scored three times in the fourth on a two-run homer by Davis and a homer by Durham. The Padres tied it in the fifth when Garvey knocked in his second run of the game with his second hit.

The drama continued as the Padre fans swirled their human wave round Jack Murphy Stadium.

In the Padres seventh, Garvey again singled, giving San Diego another lead. Before the inning ended, the Padres added another run to lead 5-3. Williams had his lead and it was late in the game. He brought in Gossage.

Sandberg led off the Cubs eighth with a single. Matthews

fanned. Ryno then stole second as the Cubs tried desperately to spark a rally. The move paid off instantly. Moreland singled and Sandberg scored to cut the lead to one run.

Frey put Cotto in to run for Moreland. That move also paid off. Davis doubled and Cotto scored from first tying the game with two outs. Durham was walked intentionally. Hebner pinch hit for Bowa and flew out to right.

There was one more Cub rally in the ninth, but it didn't produce the runs that would make Garvey's dramatic homer anticlimatic.

"Every time we needed a hit, Garvey got it," Graig Nettles said. "I got the same feeling tonight as I did in 1976 when Chris Chambliss homered for us and we beat the Royals in the playoffs."

As San Diego columnist Barry Lorge wrote, "This was Frank Merriwell out of Alfred Hitchock."

It was Garvey's first homer since August 15 and only his fourth since homering against the Cubs on July 17. Ironically, it was Garvey that Dallas had tried to sign to change the Cubs' fortunes around. The Padres signed Garvey for an estimated $6.5 million.

"I guess we saw tonight why they pay him all that money," Frey said.

The series was tied. It would not be tied again. Through 12 regular-season games and four playoff games the teams matched had each won eight. They were dead-even.

The Cubs took it in stride. It had been a long road to this day, this point in time. There were only three baseball teams still in the hunt for baseball's biggest prize. Frey, who wasn't big on pep talks, spoke briefly with the team before letting the media inside the Cubs' clubhouse.

"Several months ago if someone would have told us all we had to do was win one game to go to the World Series,

we would have taken it. No one said they would hand it
to us.

"We've got a chance to play for the National League
Championship tomorrow. There's a helluva lot of people
in baseball who would like to be in our spot. We've got the
best ballclub."

That said, the media entered. There wasn't much more
to be said. The two best teams in the National League had
come down to one game to determine a league champion.
It was Sutcliffe vs. Show, the two best pitchers on the best
teams.

There were many questions to be asked that Saturday
night. What impact would Garvey's heroics have on the
Padres? Would it leave them drained? Only time would tell.

"It's a one-game sudden death," Bowa said. "It's a shame
it's got to be this way. But whoever wrote the script for this
wrote a great one."

"They've got an opportunity to win one game for the pennant, same as us," Moreland said.

"Tomorrow is Christmas," Dernier said. "Get up early.
It's all down to one. We've got the big guy going and that's
just fine."

Sut hadn't lost in three months. He had also been vic-
torious following a Cub defeat seven times.

"It seems like I say this all the time," Sutcliffe was saying. "I've said the biggest game of my career was my first
game with the Cubs. I've said it a couple times before pitching against the Mets and I said it again before the first game
of the playoffs. And now this one."

There was an undeniable air of confidence in the man.
Someone said, it was as if losing Game 4 didn't put any
more pressure on him. It was almost as if he wanted to finish the Padres off himself. He is that type of battler.

The Cubs and the Padres were both but one win away.

It was early morning in San Diego. Sutcliffe left the team's Harbor Island hotel early.

The sun beat down on the already oven-baked Jack Murphy Stadium turf. The crowd came early for the tail-gating. Slowly, the crowd trickled into Jack Murphy Stadium.

In the afterglow of Garvey's incredible evening, the tension was still airtight.

Moments before the game, the umpire strike ended. For the first time in the post-season, the strike zones would remain constant. It had to be a break for both clubs.

There was no masquerading the emotion of this day, a season wrapped up in one nine-inning game. The Cubs and the Padres, who first met in 1984 on March 14, 209 days earlier, were charging down to the wire.

Show's first inning was troublesome to say the least. With one out, Sandberg hit a rocket down the third-base line. Nettles, who couldn't have possibly seen it, instinctively put his glove above his head and caught the wicked shot. It took him an instant even to realize he had made the play.

Matthews followed. After Show threw close to Gary three times, Matthews drew a walk. Durham followed with a homer. The Cubs had struck first and led 2-0. It was Leon's second homer in as many games. The Nettles play loomed big already.

In the Cubs second, Jody led off with another homer, giving Sut a 3-0 lead. Two batters later, Williams had seen enough of Show. He went to the bullpen, the most reliable group he had. Andy Hawkins came in.

For the next three-and-a-half innings, the score remained 3-0. The crowd could only cheer the retiring of Cub batters. Sut had silenced the waves. But all the while, Hawkins, followed by Lefferts and Dravecky, stopped the Cubs' offense completely.

It wasn't until the bottom of the sixth that the Padres made a comeback. With nothing but two hits to show for their efforts, the Padres tried to start a rally with their speed. Wiggins led off with a bunt single down the first base line.

Gwynn followed with a single to left, Wiggins stopping at second. Garvey was next. Sutcliffe, who had come to the mound without his usual overpowering stuff, walked Garvey on four pitches. He was quickly fading.

With the bases loaded, Nettles and Kennedy followed with hard-hit sacrifice flies. By the time the sixth inning ended, San Diego had cut the lead to 3-2 and had ignited the restless fans who filled Jack Murphy one more time.

The crowd couldn't wait for the bottom of the seventh. The Cubs went down quietly. The Padres came right out after Sut.

Martinez walked to lead off the inning. Williams was looking to tie the game at home. He had Templeton bunt Martinez to second. Williams called on Tim Flannery to hit for Dravecky.

Flannery hit a bouncer to first. Durham dropped to one knee. The ball, somehow, someway, continued through his legs. Martinez scored the tying run.

"It was a routine grounder," Durham said. "I thought that it was going to come up. I could see it fine. I'm sorry it happened. I'm sorry it started something for them."

The sound was echoing through the stadium. It was like standing on a runway in the midst of a dozen 747s with their engines roaring.

Wiggins kept it coming. He singled softly to left field. With Gwynn coming to the plate and Garvey on deck, Frey had lefty Steve Trout throwing in the bullpen. He decided to stay with the guy who had carried the club this far, Sutcliffe.

"This man has been one of the reasons we got here," Frey said.

Gwynn hit a smash at Sandberg. The ball exploded off the rock-hard infield at the feet of baseball's best-fielding second baseman. The ball went over Sandberg's shoulder. It was hit so hard that Moreland had to run it down in the right center field gap. Flannery and Wiggins scored.

The crowd sensed it. It was over.

The celebration began. The Padres scored once more in the seventh and held a 6-3 lead. Williams went back to Gossage.

The Cubs tried mightily to come back.

On the heels of the Padres seventh, Hebner reached with one out after being hit by a Gossage pitch. One out later, Sandberg singled Hebner to third. As he had done a night earlier, Sandberg stole second on a disinterested Gossage. With Matthews batting, the Cubs had runners in scoring position with two out.

Sarge represented the tying run. Gossage was on the spot.

He survived. The Sarge struck out.

In the Cubs ninth, Moreland was on first with two outs when Jody hit a grounder to Nettles at third. He took the short throw to second to force Moreland.

The Cubs' season was over.

San Diego was bedlam. Moreland sat at second base until Davis came his way. As if time would take the sting from defeat, the Cubs moved slowly from their dugout into the clubhouse.

The hurt and the pain were everywhere on a club that only dreamed of being this far into a season when it all began.

Frey, for the first time all season, showed the wear and anguish brought on by a season of day-to-day, non-stop deliberations and decisions.

One year and one day earlier, he had stood at a podium at Wrigley Field only promising that he wasn't afraid to work hard and do all he could to get the job done. He never made any predictions. To a person in that room, that day in 1983,

the idea of winning 81 games and breaking even for the first
time in five years and the second time in 11 years, seemed
like a nice goal to achieve. After 21 games of spring training and a 3-18 record, even an 81-81 season seemed like a
million miles away. The thought of winning 96 regular
season games and two more in the playoffs was beyond
comprehension on October 6, 1983.

The journey had been incredible. It had been filled with
victories written in Hollywood. It had been filled with
dramatic endings that brought life back to Wrigley Field
every day. It had been beautiful. But on October 7, 1984,
the hurt and the pain and memories of San Diego were
piercing.

The sights and sounds of the clubhouse were tied together
with the string of defeat. Dallas sat on an equipment trunk
staring at the floor.

Leon sat at his locker, head in his hands. Sut stood in
the opposite corner of the room speaking of the hurt. Frey
sat in his office answering question after question as he had
done after every game since March 7.

"It is an empty feeling," he said. "We got so close and
got a taste of what it could be, but we never swallowed.

"Who knows? If one ball comes up and another stays
down . . . I feel for the guys in the other room. I feel for
the people of Chicago, the Cub fans, the people in the
organization."

"We had them by the throat," Dallas said. "And we let
them get back up. I feel bad for our guys and for our fans.
It all came down to one ball game and we didn't get the
job done."

To the pure-breed baseball man there is no solace in coming close. There is little peace to be granted when a team,
even a team that came from the depths of defeat, comes
to the brink of winning a pennant and is beaten at the very
end. Even through a season of multiple success stories, win-

ning the pennant and the World Series are the only true bottom lines in baseball.

Sut tried to take the blame for the loss. But try as he might there was no way one man was to blame.

"They are going to the World Series and we are going home," he said barely above a whisper. "It is very hard to deal with. This will hurt for a long, long time.

"I take responsibility for this loss. I shouldn't have walked Martinez (leading off the seventh). It's my loss. Tomorrow in the box score there will be an 'L' next to my name."

Slowly, the players showered and packed and made their way through the maze of tunnels underneath Jack Murphy Stadium to the buses waiting to take them to the airport.

Meanwhile, back in Chicago a city felt its pain, a land dotted with Cub faithful let the tears fall.

Night was falling on a quiet Rush Street. A gathering of fans embraced at the intersection of Clark & Addison. In the quiet of the evening, the Western Union machine in the Cubs' front office began clicking off the first of many tributes from fans throughout America. Tributes to a team that had brushed away years of losing and agony and had given a city and a legion of tremendous fans a year to remember, to celebrate and to cherish.

4 Epilogue

There was little time to rest on the laurels of the 1984 season. While the Cubs did make a giant move toward a World Series appearance, Dallas Green's work was far from finished.

He had in theory put together a very good pitching staff on credit with three of his first four starters all eligible for free agency once the season ended.

Few people thought Dallas could pull off another coup by signing all three, Sutcliffe, Eckersley and Trout. If he was able to sign two of the three, people reasoned, it would be enough to keep the staff respectable.

Dallas wasn't buying any two-of-three theory. True to his word he had all three signed by Christmas.

First came Eckersley, then Trout and finally Sutcliffe. The free agent scenario that followed Sutcliffe was as heated as any since free agency became a part of the game. The Kansas City Royals, Atlanta Braves and Padres came on hard. All three organizations had something to offer. Kansas City is where the Sutcliffes call home. San Diego had the beautiful Southern California lifestyle to offer and Atlanta had a bundle of money. All were tempting, but in the end, after hours of negotiating and days of contemplating, Rick came back to Chicago.

"It was a sense of loyalty or whatever you want to call it," he said. "But something happened in the 3½ months

253

I was here. Dallas took a person who had been spinning his wheels for a long time and got him on the track.

"It was the fans, the players, everyone who turned it around for the Cubs. I had feelings playing here that I've never had before."

Once again, Dallas was active at the Winter Meetings. In 1984, he acquired another lefthanded pitcher, Ray Fontenot, along with a power-hitting outfielder named Brian Dayett from the Yankees in exchange for four players, Bordi, Hassey (who had demanded to be traded and would have become a free agent in March), Cotto and Porfi Altamirano.

One week before Christmas, Jim Finks resigned as President of the Cubs. Tribune Company acted quickly and named Dallas as President and General Manager. In three years, he had risen from a field manager to President and General Manager of one of America's great sports franchises.

"Titles never have meant much to me," he said. "But I am honored. I'll still yell and scream as much as I ever did and I'll still get involved as much as ever. Our job here isn't finished yet."